The Story of a Survivor

A MEMOIR FROM THE BALKAN

Surviving the Holocaust in Croatia
and Growing up in Communist Yugoslavia

Isac Meier

Names of persons in this memoir have been changed so as to protect their privacy. Known names of public record have been left unchanged. If any living or dead person bears the same name as one in this memoir, it is a coincidence.

© 2010 Isac Meier

All rights reserved. No part of this publication may be reproduced or transmitted in any form or by any means electronic or mechanical, including photocopy, recording, or any information storage and retrieval system, without permission in writing from the copyright owner.

ISBN: 978-1-62550-496-8

This memoir was initially intended only for my children and grandchildren. However, because denials of the Holocaust persist in twenty-first century, I felt the need to bring my story to a larger audience. This memoir should serve as one more testimony to the Holocaust. It also offers recognition to those exceptional people who dared to defy the Ustaše government by saving the lives of innocent people.

I am thankful to my dear wife Dobrana for patiently reading the draft stages of the manuscript, and particularly for the many invaluable suggestions she gave, to shape the script into its final concise form. I am also grateful to my daughter Lucinda for her advice to the introductory part of the script.

Dedicated to my dear parents, whose image remains clear in my memory, to Uncle Stanislav and Aunt Ester, who gave me a second home, to the Professor, who saved my life, and to all those who put their lives in peril by sheltering me, particularly Bishop Janko Šimrak and Msgr. Spiridon Petranović

FOREWORD TO SECOND EDITION

The front cover of this book shows in its left lower corner three little symbols which require an explanation. At the bottom is a swastika, the well-known sign adopted by the Nazis, and just above it is a capital letter U, a symbol used by the ill-reputed Ustaše, the Croat nationalist military under their leader Pavelić who ruled Croatia during the Second World War. The third little symbol is a five-pointed red star used by the Soviet communists and later adopted by most communist regimes. The first two symbols are there to indicate that this memoir describes a life cruelly altered by the Ustaše who were put in power by the Nazis. The red star points to the life under a communist dictatorship. The large symbol with a torch on the front cover needs no explanation.

During eight years since the first edition of this memoir, the multiple (eight) small countries and entities that now occupy the territory of former Yugoslavia underwent many changes. They first repaired and rebuilt what was destroyed during their wars of separation, and then started to develop some tourism. However, nothing much has changed in the Balkan concerning the beliefs and the attitude of the local population. Most people there still exude hostility towards "others". If one hears them talk and if one understands the Serbo-Croatian language, there is a prevalent hatred and intolerance directed at people of other ethnicity, or religion, skin color, or sex preference. Sadly, in their attitudes, the local people have remained just as they were 80 years ago. Their hostility is directed not only at their close neighbors in the Balkan, but also at most other people. This enmity is inspired by a fervent nationalism which is nurtured by their spiritual and political leaders, and is happily accepted by the people.

In Serbia, the largest country of former Yugoslavia, the people still celebrate as their hero Mladić, a person who 20 years ago massacred eight thousand people in the worst act of genocide after the Second World War. In Croatia they continue to celebrate as their hero Pavelić, the leader of Ustaše, who 75 years ago presided over the massacre of 250 thousand people belonging to other minorities. The local ethnic, tribal and religious hatred is so profound, that Serbs, Croats, Bosnians and Montenegrins, who all speak one and the same Slavic language, now steadfastly claim to speak four different languages. Indeed, their common language has been defined by linguists and is well known as "Serbo-Croatian".

The two symbols, the U and the swastika are very much alive and active in today's Croatia. In the past two years there have been open gatherings and parades of men dressed in uniforms with black shirts and carrying insignia worn by Ustaše, marching and giving a Nazi salute right on the main square of the capital city Zagreb. Open commemoration of Ustaše and their leader Pavelić is practiced without any interference by the government which has been elected by a solid majority of people. One of the supporting reference books about the holocaust in Croatia has a very appropriate title: "1941, a Year that is Returning".(25) It is hoped that those who read this memoir will see beyond the political myths with which they have been living, and will embrace friendship rather than hate.

Contents

PROLOGUE	ix
MY ANCESTRY AND BACKGROUND	1
"THE GOOD TIMES"	7
THE "HARD TIMES": THE WAR	17
THE ALTAR BOY	37
WITH PARTISANS	53
A LITTLE FARM HAND IN THE BISHOPRY	65
END OF WAR: THE LONG SUMMER OF 1945	75
THE FIRST YEAR IN SCHOOL AND LIFE IN MY NEW HOME	89
JUNIOR HIGH: LITTLE PRANKS AND NEW AWARENESS	103
SENIOR HIGH SCHOOL – FURTHER AWAKENING	119
THE GLORY OF COMMUNISM: UNDER THE TABLE AND THE HOME MANUFACTURE	131
NATIONALITY: THE CONFLICT OF BEING	147
LITTLE MEMORIES FROM THE FIFTIES	151
AT THE UNIVERSITY	157
A PRIZE	175
THE FAMILY ONE MAY NOT CHOOSE	185
THE GERMANS	199
TOGETHER	207
"WE ARE FREE"	217
OUR NEW HOME	229
CONCLUSION	237
EPILOGUE	243
BIBLIOGRAPHY	245
INDEX	247

Prologue

The memories written on these pages are the thoughts and feelings from my childhood, before and during the Second World War in Europe, and from my adolescence in postwar communist Yugoslavia, with some references to historic events that define the turbulent past and haunt the present.

All through my adolescence, I carried and nurtured two secret wishes. My foremost wish was to have my own family. My parents were denied seeing me grow up. I wanted the joy of having children and being present while they grew up. My second great desire was to live in the land my parents wistfully spoke of during my early childhood: "Amerika."

Only by the grace of a few exceptionally good and brave individuals did I survive the Second World War. At times, my life hung by a thin thread. During that war, my parents and most of my family were robbed of their property, mistreated and abused as slave labor, and finally killed. The cause of my parents' death was their Jewish origin coupled with pervasive anti-Semitism. In 1939, having heard of the persecution and horrors that Jews were subjected to in Nazi Germany, my parents converted to the Catholic religion. As baptized Catholics, they hoped to be protected from persecution. It didn't matter. Despite their conversion, they were killed for their Jewish origin.

This story shows how the persecution of Jews in the twentieth century affected my life. Already, as a small child, I was aware that my parents, all of our family, and I were different from most people around us. We were Jews; some people called us "čifuti" (kikes), but I did not know what that meant. We became Catholics, and again, I did not know what it meant except that my parents said it was good to be Catholic. My parents loved me, I loved them, and that is all that mattered.

Around the age of four or five, I began to sense from my parents' conversations that there was a menace somewhere outside our home, a danger I could not comprehend. Even before I knew the name of the land I lived in, I learned that the danger came from the word "war" and the people called "Ustaše." First, my father was taken away, then my mother was taken away, and finally, at the age of five and a half years I, too, was arrested in the middle of the night and taken to a prison. By the valiant effort of a friend of the family, I was released from that prison before being sent to an extermination camp. Between the summers of 1941 and 1942, the whirlwind of war tossed me from a sweet, gentle, and beautiful childhood into premature adolescence. With no warning and little preparation, I was forced to make rapid adjustment and move from a much loved and somewhat spoiled single child to a boy without parental protection or guidance. I was left to fend for myself in an environment replete with hard rules, tricks, and deception. I became a "child adolescent," and in this forced, accelerated adolescence, I discovered all the negatives of human character: the lies and dishonesty, the greed and selfishness, anger and hostility, meanness and cruelty, power and abuse, robbery and murder, injustice and the law of might, and all "facts of life" I had never seen or experienced in my parents' home. I learned to trust no one. Yet, between all the bad experiences, even in the darkest moments, some of the people around me showed traces of care and friendship and let me have hope, taste moments of happiness, and sometimes let me enjoy the feeling of being loved.

PART I

The War Comes Home

MY ANCESTRY AND BACKGROUND

What I know of my ancestors does not go very far back. My few remaining relatives and the friends of my parents who survived the Second World War in my native city of Zagreb told it to me. Zagreb, the capital of Croatia, used to be in Yugoslavia, a country that no longer exists. For seventy-two years, Yugoslavia was a mostly mountainous land on the Balkan peninsula of Europe, a land approximately the size of the UK or Italy. In 1940, Yugoslavia had a population of about twenty million, many illiterate peasants, and a minority of educated people living in a few larger cities that offered the amenities of Central European culture.

My parents were Jews born in the Austrian-Hungarian Empire, another country that no longer exists. They were secular Jews, meaning they attended public schools and went to the Jewish temple only once or twice a year on high holidays, mostly out of respect for their parents' tradition. They belonged to a generation of modern, emancipated Jews. They were also among the first generations of Jews in Europe who received the rights of citizenship, which made them, at least on the paper, equal to the rest of the population. Prior to that, Jews in Europe were, for nearly two thousand years, aliens without citizens' rights.

The Austrian-Hungarian Empire at the time of my parents' childhood and adolescence encompassed a large part of Central and Eastern Europe, extending from the Adriatic Sea in the south to Poland in the north, and from Ukraine and Romania in the east to Italy in the west. Aside from Austria and Hungary, this multi-ethnic and multilingual empire contained Galicia (southern part of Poland), Czech, and Slovak lands with Moravia, Bukovina (western part of Ukraine and northeastern part of Romania), Croatia, Slovenia, Bosnia, the northwestern part of Serbia (Vojvodina), and the northeastern part of Italy, with the city of Trieste.

My parents grew up and were educated in this multinational empire amidst Central European tradition and culture. Despite its imminent economic and political decline, Austria, and especially Vienna, at the beginning of the twentieth century was one of the most advanced world centers for art and science, offering the modern trends in architecture, design, painting, music, and literature, and new discoveries in medical science. My parents witnessed the First World War and saw the Austrian-Hungarian Empire fall apart. In their youth, they strived to adjust to a new life in the twentieth century and the aftermath of the First World War, when the map of Europe was radically redrawn. Life in the western part of the newly formed Yugoslavia did not differ much from life in the former Austrian-Hungarian Empire. Thus, the background and milieu of my early childhood was nothing but an extension of the Austrian-Hungarian background of my parents.

The Allies created Yugoslavia in 1918, right after the end of the First World War. The country was cobbled together by joining former Austrian-Hungarian provinces of Croatia, Slovenia, and Bosnia with the existing independent countries of Serbia and Montenegro, and by adding part of the province of Macedonia, which had been administered by the Turkish (Ottoman) Empire. The new country was at first called "Kingdom of the Serbs, Croats, and Slovenes," and was governed by the Serbian king. In 1929, the country's name was changed to Yugoslavia, meaning literally, "the land of southern Slavs." The rationale for the creation of Yugoslavia was that most of the people living in that part of the Balkan were of Slavic origin, and the Serbs, Croats, and Montenegrins all spoke the same Serbo-Croatian language. Two of the smaller Slavic nations, the Macedonians and the Slovenes, numbered only about one million each, and each spoke a different, though similar Slavic language. The country also had a number of minorities of non-Slavic origin: Albanians, Austrians, Germans, Greeks, Hungarians, Italians, and Romanians, mostly living along the borders of the new country, and in Bosnia, there were still a few Turks who settled there during the 450 years of Turkish rule. At that time, the majority of people in Bosnia were Serbs, with a sizable minority of Croats, including those who, during Turkish rule, converted to the Muslim religion. The Serbs, Macedonians, and Montenegrins were of Greek-Orthodox religion, whereas the Croats and Slovenes were Catholic. The country had about one million Muslims, many of Albanian origin. There were about seventy thousand Jews in Yugoslavia, and most lived within larger cities formerly administered by the Austrian-Hungarian Empire, and some were in Serbia.

Zagreb, in prewar Yugoslavia, was a clean, pleasant city with a population of about 300,000. It had a long history, beginning as a small Roman colony in the ancient province of Illyria, centuries before the Croats, Serbs, Slovenians, and other Slavic tribes migrated from Eastern Europe and settled in the Balkan. Under the Austrian-Hungarian Empire, Zagreb was the capital of the province of Croatia, and it blossomed into a small center of culture, including a university. The city had beautiful, nineteenth-century buildings, parks, plazas, and an opera house that was a replica of the one in Vienna, built by the same architect. Much of cultural life was fashioned and influenced by Vienna, and most prominent people sent their children to Vienna for higher education.

From the outset, the Serbs politically dominated the other, smaller nations of Yugoslavia. The Croats, though, yearned to have their own independent country. The Croats had, nearly one thousand years earlier, voluntarily placed themselves under the protection of the Hungarian king, and had since remained under Hungarian and Austrian domination. The policy of the Serbian king was to expand Serbian power and suppress the Croats' aspiration for independence. Soon after the formation of Yugoslavia, a serious political rift appeared between the Croats and Serbs. In 1928, Serbian ultra-nationalists assassinated several prominent Croat leaders, and the most ardent Croat nationalists went into exile in Italy and formed an ultra-nationalist group called Ustaše (Insurrectionists), choosing a lawyer, Dr. Ante Pavelić, as their leader. In Italy, the fascist government of Mussolini protected them. In 1933, this group organized the assassination of the Serbian king Alexander during his state visit to France. The group's motto was to use any means: violence, terror, "knives, guns, and machine guns" to achieve their goal of making Croatia an independent state.

In April 1941, Nazi Germany attacked Yugoslavia and created an opportunity for Ustaše and their leader, Pavelić, to return to Croatia. The Independent State of Croatia, with its capital in Zagreb, was established with full approval and support from Hitler. As Nazi Germany defeated and occupied Yugoslavia, it relinquished the provinces of Slovenia (Dravska Banovina), Montenegro, and one third of Croatia (the coastal Adriatic region) to its ally, Italy. As compensation to Croatia, Hitler gave it the province of Bosnia and Hercegovina. The representatives of the Muslim minority in Bosnia in 1941 declared their loyalty to Ustaše. In turn, the Ustaše proclaimed Muslims Croats and called them "the flower of the Croat people."

This was the political background of the Independent State of Croatia, in which my parents and my entire family found themselves at the onset of the Second World War.

My father was born in 1898 in Hungary, the second of four brothers in a well-off family that originally had its roots in the Czech capital of Prague. My paternal grandfather, Adam Meier, lived most of his life in Hungary, where during the Austrian-Hungarian Empire he manufactured metal stoves for heating and cooking. He lived in a small town, where the four Meier children were born. The oldest child was Felix, my father Leonard was second, and then came Louis and Ernest. At the turn of the twentieth century, my grandfather moved his family to a large, comfortable house in Zagreb, sold his business in Hungary, and retired. My paternal grandmother, Greta Eisner, came from a Viennese business family. Her brother stayed in Vienna, but his son, Stefan Eisner, after seeing the spread of Nazism and anti-Semitism in Austria in the early thirties, moved to Zurich, Switzerland.

Three of the Meier brothers followed the business tradition of their father. The fourth brother, Louis, went to Vienna to study at the university and became an engineer. He died around 1927 of congenital heart disease. My father, Leonard, had a small retail store in Zagreb. His older brother Felix worked as a sales representative for a factory, and his business required frequent travel around the country and often abroad. The third brother, Ernest, had a small business in Peteranec, a town near the Hungarian border. In 1932, Ernest's first wife died and left him with a small daughter, my cousin Luisa. A few years later, Ernest met Mrs. Kalina, a widow who lived with her two young sons in the town of Varaždin. He married Mrs. Kalina, but before marriage, he and his daughter Luisa converted to Catholic religion. With marriage, Ernest also adopted the two Kalina sons and took his wife's name, Kalina, as his own. At the same time, he moved to Varaždin, where he managed his wife's hardware store and added to it a small forge. The family attended church on Sundays, and their business prospered. Several years later, Mrs. Kalina took ill and died. Ernest thus survived the Second World War in Varaždin, where people knew him only as "Mr. Kalina," and did not know that he was of Jewish descent.

My mother, Hanna Silber was born in 1904 in Verkhovina, in the east end of Austrian-Hungarian Empire, that is today Ukraine. She was the youngest of ten children. The five older Silber siblings immigrated to America around the turn of the twentieth century. The five younger siblings stayed in Europe, and after the First World War ended, they did not wish to remain in Galicia, which had become a part of Poland. All five—Herbert, Isac, Jonas, Ester, and my mother Hanna—moved to the newly-formed country of Yugoslavia, where the lifestyle was not much different from that in the old Austrian empire. The oldest brother, Herbert, settled in Zavidovic´i, Bosnia; Isac and my mother Hanna settled in Zagreb, the capital of Croatia; and Jonas settled in Dubrovnik. Finally, their sister Ester and her husband Moritz Jablonski moved from Czernowitz, Romania, to Zagreb. Ester and Moritz had two children, Michael and Bluma, and my maternal grandmother lived with them. My maternal grandfather died during the First World War, and I never knew him. Meanwhile, the five older Silber siblings in the U.S. had prospered, and after the First World War, they financially supported their mother in Europe and invited the younger brothers and sisters to join them in the U.S. However, their siblings in Yugoslavia did not wish to move. My mother was at the time still single, and she did obtain the required affidavit for immigration, but she never used it. She had a career and a profession. My mother went to work at a time when respectable middle-class girls were supposed to sit at home and wait to get married. She worked with her older brother Isac, who learned his trade in Vienna, and then opened the first hat manufacturing company in Zagreb. In the twenties, everyone wore a hat, and hat making was a good business. Isac invested their earnings into real estate in Zagreb, mostly a group of factory buildings with a large parcel of adjacent land and a few low-rise apartments facing the street. The property carried considerable rental income, while the land behind the factories was a meadow with an orchard around it, all of it located in the central part of Zagreb. In the late twenties, my mother met and started dating a young man who would become her husband and my father, and her immigration to the U.S. was put off indefinitely.

My parents dated for several years, and then they were engaged and were married in 1933. They had a large, catered wedding reception, and as was the custom at the time, right after supper they quietly left, changed clothes, and boarded an overnight train for a three-week honeymoon on the Italian Riviera and in Monte Carlo. Aunt Ester, my mother's sister, meanwhile, supervised the furnishing of their new apartment in Zagreb. When the young couple came back, my father, with my mother's financial backing, opened a much larger store in the center of the city. The store carried fine china, crystal, and objects of art.

In 1935, my mother's older brother and senior partner, Isac, suddenly became very ill. Dr. Epstein, a renowned internist from Vienna, was called in, and he declared that Isac had only a few more days to live. His diagnosis was severe acute inflammation of the pancreas, a rare condition that in those days invariably had a fatal outcome. I was born in December 1935, several months after Uncle Isac's death, and in honor of my recently deceased uncle, I was named Isac. Because I was born by cesarean section, I would remain a single child. At that time, women delivered by cesarean section were advised not to have another pregnancy. Since both of my parents worked (my mother still kept a small retail hat store), they took a maid to clean and cook and a nanny to take care of me. My parents lived comfortably and had many friends in the business community and among the professionals in Zagreb. In 1936, soon after I was born, my parents moved to a larger apartment in a residential area not far from the downtown business center of the city. That apartment remains the first place I became aware of my parents and my surroundings.

The wedding photo of my parents, 1933

"THE GOOD TIMES"

My earliest memories go back to 1938, just before I was three years old. Those early memories were renewed and re-enforced by the many family photographs saved by my Aunt Ester. I wish to recount some tidbits from my early childhood, not necessarily in chronological order. Until I was five years old, the language spoken in our home was German, though my parents lived and I was born in Yugoslavia, where most people spoke Serbo-Croatian, a language that, though well defined by scholars and linguists, is no longer recognized by the very people who still speak it. My parents actually spoke Serbo-Croatian only in business or with their friends, or if they did not want me to understand, which worked only for a short while.

One of the first and earliest remembrances is the comfort my parents gave me when they were around. I felt their tenderness and care, I felt their love, and I felt their joy. I dearly loved my parents. My mother I called "Mena" (pronounced like in "me"), which was easier to say than "Mama," and my father I called "Tatek" or "Taty." I often overheard my parents' quiet conversations, from which I realized just how much they loved me and enjoyed every move or sound I made. They called me "Izzyly," a diminutive form of Isac. No matter what naughty thing I did, they just smiled and melted with joy. When I was naughty, they tried to conceal their joy. I also noticed that they loved when I pouted. So I often pouted and offered them happy diversion in every way I could, and I reveled in all the attention I got. Mena and Tatek often looked at me and said "süss" (sweetie). They knew I sometimes deliberately showed off for them, and my mother would quietly say to father, "Er produziert sich schon wieder." (He is again performing for us.) I overheard and understood.

From other people, I learned that I was "slatki" (cute) before I even knew what the word meant. My parents' friends used to say "cute" when they saw me. I disliked that word, because along with "cute," the people usually proceeded to grab my cheek and squeeze it between two fingers, and then they would give me a smelly, slobbering kiss. "So cute," I would hear while ripping myself away from their embrace and rubbing off the awful wet kisses. As soon as I heard or saw my parents' friends' approach, I ran away and hid in the farthest corner of the apartment. My grandparents, aunts, and uncles used to kiss me on the head or the temple, and they never pinched my cheeks. Only Mena and Tatek kissed me on the cheek, but their kisses smelled good and were dry and gentle, and I liked them.

When I was really exuberant and naughty, my parents threatened to put me into a little wooden chicken coop, a small cage that stood in a corner of our kitchen balcony. I soon realized that they never really meant to put me in there, so I continued with my shenanigans. The chicken coop was used for the live chickens that were brought home from the market with their legs tied by a strip of old cloth. In the cage, their legs were untied, and I was allowed to feed them with dry corn, while our maid Attita put in a little bowl of water. I never saw or understood how Attita transformed the live chickens into a delicious Sunday lunch. I liked the juicy drumstick and did not worry about the miracle of chicken metamorphosis. As I grew bigger, my naughtiness increased, and one day Tatek brought home a short crop made of thin, braided willow branches. He kept it high up on an armoire, and when I was naughty, he would take it down and swing it through the air. The crop made a swishy noise, and Tatek would ask if I wanted him to try it out on my behind. That sounded scary enough to make me stop whatever mischief I was doing, and I always begged him to put the crop back in its place on top of the armoire, as far as possible from me.

In the "Kinderbet" (crib), I always had my "Rosena." I gave this name to my pale pink security blanket. It was an old, retired silk scarf of my father's, and it had very fine fronds at each end. I loved to hold it against my face and brush my cheeks with the tips of the silk threads. When it was time for my afternoon nap or my evening sleep, Mena would give me the Rosena. Holding it tight and close to my face and nose, I was content and fell asleep. When I woke in the morning, I used to get on all fours (knees and arms) and rhythmically rock my body back and forth. With every move forward, I yelled "ghim," and with every move back, I yelled "bham," and so I went rocking "Ghim-bham, ghim-bham, ghim-bham" until the crib moved from the corner to the middle of the room. My parents would thus know that I was awake and ready for their attention. The maid Katica (Kathy), who I called "Attita," also loved me, and she tried to spoil me on every occasion. When I pursed my lips and blew my lunch spinach onto the kitchen wall, she would let out a long whistle and then laugh with joy. She happily wiped the green mess off the wall tiles. I wanted badly to learn to whistle, and Attita patiently taught me to make a whistling sound with my lips and tongue.

The reason my parents spoke German at home was that my mother could not understand Hungarian, and my father did not speak Polish or Yiddish. Both spoke German in the Austrian public schools they attended. German was also convenient, for it afforded them privacy from the maid. Attita spoke to me only Serbo-Croatian, and at that, a cozy dialect spoken in Zagreb and its surrounding hinterland. So I learned the Serbo-Croatian language first from our maid, and then by playing in the courtyard with children from neighboring apartment buildings. Of any of my nannies I have only a vague recollection, for none lasted long enough for me to remember. The nannies were frequently changed, either because they were unsatisfactory to my parents, or because they could not bear the competition from "Attita," and perhaps they quit because I was a spoiled brat. I clearly showed preference for "Attita," whom I was used to, and who was always there to protect me, even from my parents.

My parents often visited Aunt Ester and Uncle Moritz, who lived in an apartment not too far away. There I got to know my maternal grandmother, "die Omama." She was very short, had completely white hair and sea blue eyes, and she spoke what I thought was a different kind of German that I could not always fully understand. (It was Yiddish.) Each time we visited, Omama gave me a coin worth a quarter of a dinar (Yugoslav currency). I especially liked the coins with the hole in the middle, so I could put them on a string. Sometime in 1939, Omama died, and my mother for a long time after wore black clothing. On Sundays, we also often visited my father's parents at their house, which was a little further in the peripheral zone of the city. Those occasions were festive, with a big, formally served, three-course lunch and a leisurely afternoon spent with the family. My paternal grandma, Omama Greta, always appeared very dignified and spoke either German or Hungarian. The Hungarian language sounded as if somebody was poking fun; at best, I thought it was gibberish. When Omama tried to teach me Hungarian, I repeated the words in a funny, exaggerated manner, which made my mother laugh. It had the desired effect: Omama soon gave up teaching me. My grandpa, Opapa Adam, appeared very old, and he talked slowly and softly. In his presence, I had to be very quiet, so that everyone could hear him speak. Uncle Felix, my father's older brother, sometimes came to visit us, or we met him at the grandparents' house. I remember being warned to be especially well behaved and quiet in his presence, for he had "ein schwaches Herz" (a weak heart), and should not get upset. So, in the presence of Uncle Felix, I always made an effort to be on my best behavior. Sometimes Aunt Bella (Silber) and her son, my first cousin Oliver, would visit us. His father, Uncle Jonas, died in 1937 from a ruptured appendix. They used to live in the beautiful city of Dubrovnik, but after Uncle Jonas's death, they moved to Zagreb. There, Aunt Bella sometimes helped my mother manage our retail hat store, which was on a main street near the center of town.

With my parents at grandpa's home, Dec. 1936

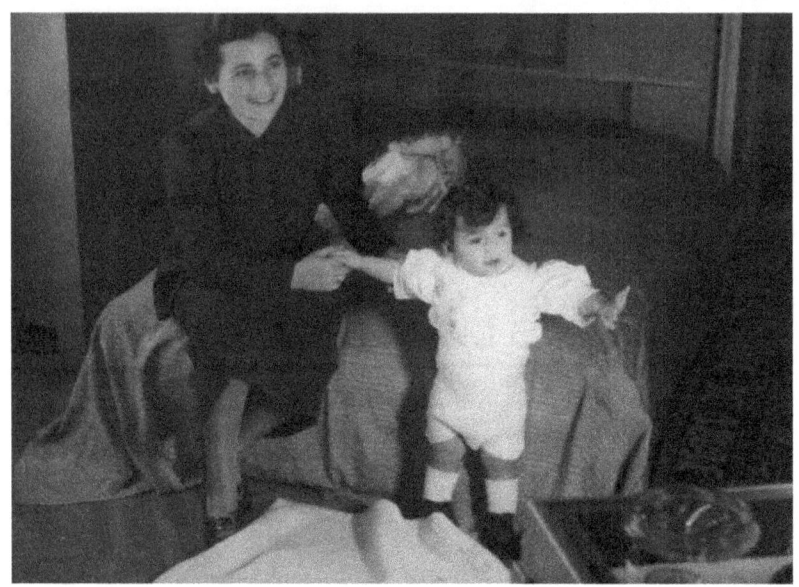

With my mother at home, Dec. 1936

With my father, Dec. 1938

With my parents by grandpa's house, Dec. 1938

In the fall of 1938, when I was nearly three years old, I was taken to a strange place full of children I had never met before and several "nannies" or teachers. It was called "the French kindergarten." I was given a blue apron with little yellow chicks on it. All the children wore little aprons—girls red and boys blue. There were many toys to play with, crayons to draw with, and even wet paint to use with hands and fingers. Despite all the toys and games, I was not happy, and I cried every time Mena left me there. I disliked that kindergarten. Unlike at home, where everything and everyone was familiar, that new place was strange and different, with too many children milling about, pushing me, occasionally pulling on my clothes, and not always being nice and friendly. No one ever pushed me at home.

The teachers spoke French, a weird language that sounded like their noses were forever stuffed, and they tried to teach it to us. I found some nice toys, but I never felt comfortable. I was very shy, and often I would suddenly start crying for no reason, but then I would ask for my Mena. Mena was at work, and crying did me no good.

The kindergarten regularly organized visits to parks or a playground, and I dreaded those outings. I was terrified of dogs, especially big ones. Each time I saw a dog approach, his red tongue hanging out and teeth showing, I screamed in fear. I wanted to be lifted high into the teacher's arms, or at least, be surrounded by the rest of the children. When I was walking on the street with my parents, they would, of course, lift me high on their shoulders, far out of the dog's reach, and I felt safe. There was no such protection with the kindergarten teachers. As if my unhappiness in that kindergarten was not enough, I once wet my pants. To train me to behave, the teacher shamed me in front of the children. I thought I was the only "popišanac" (pants-peeing child) there. Another time, when I needed to pee, but was too shy to ask to go out, I made it quietly into the corner behind a tall, wide credenza, where I thought no one would notice. Unfortunately, a puddle soon appeared in front of the credenza, and after a thorough investigation, the teachers had no doubt who it came from. When Mena came to get me that day, I was still sobbing from shame and misery, but that time, at least, I could show Mena that my pants were dry. After several months in that school, my parents had me transferred to a different kindergarten, and there I was happy. It was a smaller place, less crowded, and I understood the language spoken there. As I was brought in, I heard a familiar little song:

"Der Fuchs hat die Gans gestollen!
Gib' sie wieder her! Gib' sie wieder her,
sonst wird dich der Jäger holen
mit dem Schüssgewehr, mit dem Schüssgewehr!"
(The fox caught a goose and stole it!
Give it quickly back; return it with no harm,
or else will the hunter get you,
with his firearm, with his firearm!)

In that happy little German kindergarten, I remained several mornings a week till the onset of war in Yugoslavia.

On Sundays, when the weather was nice, my parents used to take me for afternoon walks in an uptown area of the city with quiet walkways in a park-like setting and homes and villas of the well-to-do. In a garden adjacent to one villa was a big green and red parrot, Laura. Sitting on the perch by her cage, Laura greeted any passer-by, and she answered greetings from people. I loved to watch the parrot and tease her by making her repeatedly answer my greeting. After several greetings, the parrot would sometimes say things I did not understand (and apparently was not supposed to understand), and my parents would start laughing. Laura was very popular. Everyone in town knew her. I heard my parents saying that even the local newspapers carried a funny gossip column titled, "What Laura Says."

The area at the foot of the mountain, Medvjednica (Sljeme), had lots of undeveloped land with meadows where we picnicked in summer or rode sleds in winter. I loved those outings, especially when my parents pulled me up on a little sled and let me go down-hill by myself. In summer, at one point on the road, there used to be a man with a little monkey who turned the handle of a "Wergel" (organ grinder) and produced funny tunes. I loved to watch the monkey, which would every now and then stop turning the handle, grab the man's hat, and bring it towards the surrounding group of people to throw coins into it. The monkey was much smaller than I was, and I was not afraid of him. Tatek always gave me a coin to toss into the monkey's hat.

Many years later, the memory of that "Wergel" inspired me to help one of our daughters with her music homework. She was supposed to write down the seven instruments of jazz, but she was able to figure out only six. When she came to me for help, I told her that the seventh instrument of jazz was the organ grinder. The following evening, she informed me that she got an A for the music homework. When the teacher handed her the graded paper, she told me he gave her a nice, big smile, too.

Going to the zoo was the dearest of all outings. I loved to see the animals, and I loved to watch the monkeys. I wanted to stay there forever. I cried when my parents wanted to move on. A monkey called Štefek was very popular, for he played all sorts of strange tricks that made people laugh. My second favorite area in the zoo was the one with large cages holding the birds, especially the parrots. I did not like the area with the large animals, the lions, wolves and tigers, because they all smelled bad. The elephant was okay, and the otters were fun, too. The final prize of the zoo visit was always a ride on a small donkey, which I was a little afraid of, but wanted to try. Tatek had to walk along and hold my hand.

My parents' best friends were Mr. and Mrs. Cacciatore. They had two daughters. The older one, Ero, was nine years older than I was, but the younger one, Edda, was just a few months younger. Mr. Cacciatore was the regional director of a large European shipping firm (somewhat like UPS today), and he had a business relationship with my father. The Cacciatore family lived with their "nonna" (grandmother) in a big, modern villa, on a hill in the upper town. At home, they spoke Italian, and were originally from the northern Adriatic coastal area called Primorje, part of which had been under the rule of the Venetian Republic for centuries and at the time was still part of Italy. My parents and the Cacciatore family saw each other many weekends and often in the evenings during the week. Mr. Cacciatore loved music and played the piano, and Mrs. Cacciatore, who had a trained voice, sometimes sang arias from operas. My parents also loved music, especially the opera. I fondly remember in our family room a large, box-like piece of furniture that contained the turntable, called a "gramophone." It was made of dark polished oak and had a shiny metal crank on the right side. Inside the heavy wooden cover was a picture of a dog listening to a tuba-like instrument with a sign saying, "His master's voice." My parents often wound it up in the evenings and listened to records of their favorite operas: *Tosca*, *La Boheme*, *La Traviata*, *Rigoletto*, and *Madam Butterfly*. To their delight, I learned to sing along with many of the songs, though I did not understand the words.

My parents often went with the Cacciatore family on short outings into the countryside, attended the opera and concerts, or simply visited one another at home. Sometimes, on Sundays, we all climbed to the top of Sljeme. We first went up the foothills by streetcar to its last stop in a little village. From there we started slowly climbing the well-worn path through the woods. When I could no longer walk, my father carried me on his back. Mr. Cacciatore was an avid photographer, and thanks to him, many pictures of my parents and me were saved and left to me after the war. On one occasion, my parents received from them as a gift a beautiful album that had been miraculously saved during the war, and it is this album, and a box full of old photographs, that helped me preserve much of my earliest childhood memories, especially those with my parents. The photographs were meticulously dated, and if from outdoors, the place was written on the back. I frequently looked at those pictures throughout my adolescence, brooded a little, and understood what my parents meant when they spoke of "the good times."

Mr. Cacciatore had a big American-made motorcycle, an Indian with an attached sidecar. There was a small metal head of a Native American chief with feathered headgear on the front fender. He used to put his little daughter Edda and me in the sidecar, bundle us together with a blanket, and give us a ride, and we would squeal with joy. The Cacciatore family had a telephone. Not many people in those days had a telephone. There was one in my grandfather's house and one in the Professor's (our friend) apartment. Uncle Moritz did not have a telephone, nor did we, nor did most of my parents' other friends. People used to communicate by walking to a friend's house and ringing the doorbell, or by making the next appointment for meeting just before parting. Cars were then even less common than telephones. People walked or bicycled. The city had more horse-drawn carts than automobiles. The ice slabs for the ice chest and the heavy, wire-glass seltzer bottles were all brought to the house on horse-drawn wagons. There was no television. People read books. Radio receivers were also not very common; we did not have one. One could read the daily newspaper. A record player was sufficient. In retrospect, it seemed that my parents would rather not hear the radio news, which was in the late thirties more and more depressing and "degoutante," for it was the era of the Nazi rampage in Europe.

In our apartment courtyard, when I was four years old, I occasionally played with a little girl approximately my age, Renata, who lived in the next apartment building. I noticed that she was different from me: she seemed to be missing body parts that I had. On one occasion, she and I went into a corner of the courtyard, took off our pants, and began to explore our differences. A neighbor observed the scene from her balcony and told the girl's mother, who told my mother. The two mothers interrupted our play and decided that Renata and I would no longer be allowed to play together without supervision. Anyway, I discovered that girls were made without the "pimpeck" (penis), a little part I had to pee with. Instead, the girls only had a little slit, and they had no way to swing their pee from side to side, and therefore could not make nice yellow circles and lines in the snow. This was my first experience with girls.

The Good Times

My parents' friends, Dr. and Mrs. Bresslauer had a car, and a few times they took us on short weekend trips to the mountains. This is when I discovered that car rides made me sick. I had to be kept in my father's lap in the front seat so I could see out, and then I felt better. Most roads outside the city were not paved, the speed was at most fifteen miles per hour, and seat belts and children's seats did not exist. On one of those trips, when I was about five years old, I said something that caused our friends real consternation. They asked what I would like to do when I grew up, and I said I wanted to have a car of my own and drive it around. They were taken aback that such a small child should have such "grandiose ideas." After we came home, my parents were upset, and they kept talking about it. They finally concluded that since our friends had no children, they could not understand a child's fancy.

One day, when Mena was taking me home from kindergarten, she met a friend, a gentleman she knew from Tatek's business. They got into an important and long conversation on the wide sidewalk of a quiet street. I badly needed to pee, and several times I tugged at Mena's hand and skirt, but each time, Mena signaled me to be quiet till she finished talking. I had to pee so badly that I was dancing on my feet. Mena, though, was absorbed in the conversation. I did not want to wet my pants, so I pulled my "pimpeck" through the slit in my pants and started peeing. My pee somehow arched a little too far, and it caught the leg of the gentleman's pants. When he noticed, the gentleman was really nice and told Mena not to scold me. He said he noticed that I was asking for attention a little while before. At lunch, Tatek was not happy when Mena told him about my accident, and he scolded me very hard, but after lunch, I overheard both of them quietly laughing about it. Tatek said something like, "Das ist ein feines Kind, dass wir haben!" (This is some fine child we have!)

THE "HARD TIMES": THE WAR

From the earliest days of my childhood, I remember my parents as happy people who liked to laugh and make jokes. Then something changed, and they laughed less and became more thoughtful and concerned. When my parents spoke of life before the war in Yugoslavia, they referred to it as "die goldene Zeiten" (the good times), and in my memory, "the good times" came to an abrupt end when we had to move out of our apartment.

In 1938, when Nazi Germany annexed Austria, stories about the persecution of Jews, "Kristallnacht," and other bad news became more frequent and scary. The source of the news was much closer to home, right on the northern Yugoslav border. That same year, Nazis in Germany enacted the Nuremberg laws, by which the Jews were segregated, thrown out of public jobs, banned from being teachers (except in Jewish schools), and banned from practicing law. Jewish doctors could not treat Gentile patients. Jews could not have any relationship with Gentiles, so as not to spoil the purity of the "superior" Aryan race. Jewish businesses were first boycotted, then vandalized, looted, and destroyed. The owners were beaten and often dragged away to concentration camps. Jews could only live in designated areas. Some of the horror stories were so fantastic that many people did not believe them, or did not want to believe. [21] And yet, it was all happening, but it was somewhere else, and it appeared unreal.

"Das kann doch nicht wahr sein!" they said. (But it cannot be true!) "Das sind doch nur alarmante Neuheiten!" (These are just false news of alarm!)

Denial was a powerful means of keeping one's mind in a state of balance, especially when denial was coupled with hope. Most people did not read, or did not want to read the book that had it all spelled out, Hitler's *Mein Kampf*. In addition to the bad news from Germany and annexed Austria, there was plenty of bad news right at home in Zagreb. A chronicle about Jews in Zagreb, published in 2004 in Croatia, states that in the nineteen-thirties, there were several sharply anti-Semitic publications in Zagreb, as well as occasional outbursts and incidents against Jews, organized by groups of local ultra-nationalists. [14]

Among our family's many friends was an intellectual nicknamed "the Professor," because he taught at the University of Zagreb. He lived alone in a residential apartment run by the nuns, wrote books, and was semi-retired. Sometime in 1938, he suggested my parents and Uncle Jablonski's family convert to the Catholic religion. Based on incidents rumored to be happening in Nazi Germany, this was a good and practical advice. Our families had been secular Jews, and the change in religion was considered a convenient formality that might have an advantage. Uncle Moritz Jablonski at the same time changed not only his name, but also his address. His new first name was Stanislav, and his new last name was Rubin, which was his mother's maiden name. Uncle Moritz moved to a newly built apartment house where no one knew him. Since Uncle Moritz had his business in a village outside of Zagreb in the neighboring province of Slovenia (then Dravska Banovina), not many people in the city knew him by his original last name. Years later, I learned that thousands of Jews all around the world had made a habit of changing their names and religion, of course, only for practical reasons. I learned that some people dislike foreign names, which they call "funny names." Now I know Jewish people whose names are Scott Sherman and Alan Warren, and most everyone has heard of Kirk Douglas, Elizabeth Taylor, and Madeline Albright. The latter underwent such a thorough change of name and religion that when the news of her Jewish origin broke out, she was reported to have been completely unaware of it, and she could no longer remember the Jewish first cousins she played with in her native Czech Republic.

Our conversion to the Catholic religion took place in 1939. I clearly remember the day my parents dressed up in fine dark suits and took me to a small church on the outskirts of the city, where a priest intoned all sorts of prayers in a strange language (Latin) and poured a few drops of cold water over my parents' and my heads. We were baptized. On the way home, my parents said, "Now this is done. We are Catholics, and nobody will bother us."

My parents had many good friends in the city, and they felt safe remaining at the same address and keeping their name unchanged. Anyway, too many people in the city knew my father by the name "Majer," and changing his name would only make sense if he also left town and settled in some other city. My father had lived in Croatia since early childhood, and he felt that he was a Croat. In his youth, to affirm his feeling of being a Croat, he changed his German first name "Leonard" to the Croatian "Lavoslav," and the German spelling of his last name "Meier" he changed to the Croatian "Majer."

Life continued to run its course. Mena sometimes took me to Tatek's store, where I was allowed to play with the little figurines in the storage area. I particularly liked the small porcelain animals, and at home I had a whole collection of them. Once, on the way home from the store, I asked for a banana, which I dearly loved. My mother said no, for it was nearly lunchtime. As we approached the grocery store Sumatra, on a busy corner in the middle of the city, I asked again for a banana, and when I did not get it, I ran into the street and sat between the streetcar rails near a tram stop. My mother ran after me, grabbed me by the hand, and pulled me through a door into the hallway of the nearest apartment building, and there I got the first real hot spanking that I can remember. I wailed, whined, and sobbed all the way home.

From that event, I learned that protesting by sitting in front of a streetcar yields no bananas, and more importantly, that there was an invisible barrier beyond which the mere threats of spanking become a reality. I had to find out just where that barrier was. In the coming years, I became quite an artist in recognizing the point of danger, where it was best to quit my shenanigans.

My parents used to take annual summer vacations on the Adriatic Sea coast, and one of my earliest memories from that time is the vacation in 1938. I remember my first encounter with the sea; I did not like it at all. I did not appreciate being put into a huge, frightening amount of water. It was much colder than the warm tub at home, and it tasted awful. I did not like to play in the sand because it somehow found its way into my mouth or eyes, and washing it off was most unpleasant. Walking barefoot on the beach was difficult, too. The sharp pebbles in the sand pricked my feet.

In 1939 we had a great summer vacation in Novi Vinodol on the Adriatic Sea, and my parents also took along my cousin Bluma, Aunt Ester's daughter. I was allowed to ride a little cart pulled by a donkey, and we picked and ate fresh figs from the trees, which gave me the most dreadful diarrhea. Otherwise, life was wonderful. Bluma made sand castles and whole towns of sand on the beach. She watched over me while I played in the shallow water and made sure no water got into my eyes or mouth when she carried me deeper into the sea. The only thing I did not like was that I had to wear a hat. I hated having it on when it was not cold. I kept pulling my hat off, and they kept putting it on.

In Novi Vinodol, summer 1939

With my mother in Novi Vinodol, 1939

That same year, in 1939, I learned a new word: "der Krieg" (the war), a word that was constantly repeated by my parents. I did not understand what it meant. Mena explained that it was dangerous, like a hot stove. I was much more afraid of dogs than of a hot stove. It was 1939, and the Second World War had begun in Europe, but Yugoslavia stayed neutral. In the days following the outbreak of war, my parents became more apprehensive, and their moments of joy and laughter were less frequent. I heard them almost every evening, holding long, serious conversations, in which they repeatedly said more strange new words, like "Amerika" or "Palestina." I learned that those words referred to far-away places where my parents would perhaps like to go, but they would not or could not go. My parents' discussions about leaving never ended.

They kept asking the same questions. "Was sollen wir tun? Weg gehen oder da bleiben?" (What should we do? Should we go away or stay here?)

Tatek would say, "Wir müssen uns noch überlegen." (We need to think about it some more.)

How could he leave the old parents alone, when their two other sons, Felix and Ernest, lived so far from the city? Then suddenly, all those discussions and questions stopped. After the Second World War started, the countries where my parents wanted to emigrate closed their borders and would no longer accept foreigners.

In the summer of 1940, to relax from the pressures of bad news, my parents took their usual vacation to the Adriatic Sea, this time to Malinska on the island of Krk. I finally began to enjoy the beach and the sea and learned to play in the sand without getting it into my mouth or eyes. I had a great time spending all day with Mena and Tatek. Toward the end of that year, I was five years old, and my birthday gift was a great surprise. Tatek gave me a pair of shiny new ice skates with adjustable latches and a key, so that the skates could be attached to the thick soles of my heavy winter shoes.

Caught by a street photographer, walking with my father, 1940

Ice skating became very popular in the thirties. Adults, even my parents, learned to skate. They used to go to evening skating sessions, which were accompanied by light dance music. I was taken to the skating rink on some afternoons to join a small group of children who received lessons. At first, I was a little scared of the slippery ice, but then they let me hold on to a wooden stand that I could push around on the ice. After several sessions with the trainer, I got the hang of it and found that I could keep a good balance. Eventually, I even learned a few steps of figure skating, and by the end of the winter season of 1940-41, I was quite comfortable on the ice.

One early morning the following spring, I was awakened by loud thunder that continued for quite a while. I was scared, but my parents were home and Mena reassured me. I saw Tatek in his nightshirt running through the apartment and rolling down all the shutters. The thunder continued, but it became less frequent.

Now I know that the "thunder" happened on Sunday, April 6, 1941; it was the first day of war for Yugoslavia. The thunderous noise was made by the Yugoslav anti-aircraft guns, and it was aimed at the German attack planes, which were merely flying over. Zagreb was not bombed, but Belgrade, the capital of Yugoslavia and Serbia, received a heavy bombardment that killed thousands of civilians. The Serbs were thus punished for breaking the pact with Nazi Germany and not letting Nazi armies pass freely through the country to help their Italian allies in the war against Greece. The Serbs' stubborn resistance to allowing Nazis free passage through Yugoslavia ("better war than pact," they chanted in the streets) forced Germany to declare war on Yugoslavia. Consequently, Hitler's planned surprise attack on Soviet Union was postponed from early spring (April 1) to mid-summer (June 21) of 1941. That nearly three-month delay played a critical role in stalling the Nazi army in the bitter Russian winter, so that it was unable to win the war with a quick "blitz" (lightning strike), as planned. The core of the Soviet Russian army was thus preserved and it gained time to regroup; eventually aided by massive U.S. supplies the Russians won the battle of Stalingrad. From there on the tide of the war in Eastern Europe changed in favor of the Allies. A few days after the invasion of Yugoslavia, Hitler approved the creation of the Independent State of Croatia, with Dr. Ante Pavelić at the helm. The new Croat government soon printed numerous proclamations and posters, which were glued on every corner of the city. A Jew could no longer keep a maid or any Gentile in his or her employ. It was against the law that a Gentile serve a Jew; both could be punished. Jews had to live under the Nuremberg laws. They could not associate with Gentiles, were not allowed to have a telephone, and so on. [13]

Within the first days of the new Independent State of Croatia, our friend the Professor offered to arrange for documents granting our families the Aryan Right, which would protect us from being treated as Jews. My father felt he was a good Croat and had many good friends who were considered influential with top members of the new government, and anyway, our family was Catholic, so he felt sufficiently protected. Uncle Stanislav did not know many people in Zagreb, was an immigrant who spoke with a foreign accent, and he felt any protective document could be useful. He immediately applied to the authorities for the Aryan Right, and with the Professor's intervention, he promptly received it. The Rubin family thus survived the war without a major incident. Nevertheless, they lived for four years in great fear, with daily worries and anxiety that turned Aunt Ester and Uncle Stanislav's hair prematurely white. All that stood between them and the Ustaše authorities was a piece of paper stating that they had the Aryan Right, and the hope that no one would treat them as Jews.

Within weeks after the new Independent State of Croatia was established, my parents became extremely upset and worried. They no longer felt so safe. With great concern, they noticed that many of their trusted, good, old friends crossed the street and looked the other way to avoid meeting and talking to them in public. Most of my parents' friends abandoned them and betrayed their friendship. Being seen with Jews would be compromising. A few friends remained steadfast and loyal, and those sounded hopeful, saying that the situation was not as bad as it seemed. My parents applied for the Aryan Right document, but the authorities would no longer issue any. Even our friend the Professor was no longer able to intervene. My parents always referred to him as "the Professor" so that no one would hear them mention his real name. At that time, any name mentioned by a Jew might compromise that person. To be a "Jew-lover" was just as dangerous as being a communist.

According to the new laws, I had to be taken out of the kindergarten. I was happy. Staying home every day with Mena was much nicer than going to any kindergarten. We could no longer have a maid, and I was sorry to lose our dear Attita, whom I loved, and who loved me very much. She often used to intercede on my behalf with my parents. She even protected me when I stole the bag of raisins from the pantry cabinet just before lunch and ate nearly half of them. I liked those sweet golden raisins more than any other food. In my defense, I said I ate the raisins slowly, one by one.

In those days, I would get exuberant and run as fast as I could through the length of our apartment, only to stop myself with both hands against the glass pane door of the kitchen balcony. I grew bigger and heavier, and one day, running through our apartment my right hand went through both panes of glass. Blood started squirting from the underside of my wrist. I was scared of the blood, and I felt sick to my stomach. I screamed, coughed, and retched. Mena heard my screams, ran into the kitchen, squeezed my bleeding arm with her hand, and brought me into the bathroom, where she firmly bandaged my wrist and washed off the blood. She asked a neighbor to call a taxi, and I was taken to my doctor's office. Dr. K., my pediatrician, first sent Mena out of the room. Then, assisted by his wife, he held my arm firmly and slowly opened the bandages. He put some white numbing liquid (cocaine) on the wound, and I felt no pain. Then he tied up a small, squirting blood vessel with a thread and slowly and patiently, with a pair of tweezers, picked out of my wrist many tiny splinters of glass. When he was satisfied that the wound was clean and free of glass and that all the bleeding had stopped, he put white stinging powder everywhere. He finally used little metal clips to hold the skin together, covered everything with gauze, and over that he put a big bandage. I had to keep my right forearm in a sling that hung from my shoulder for several weeks. It took some weeks before the bandages and metal clips were removed.

Back then, a medical doctor, even a pediatrician, could do everything that was necessary, treat nearly any problem, including surgical repair, treat a skin rash, and handle eye injury, earache, and joint pain. Now I know that the white stinging powder the doctor used on my wound was sulfonamide, used to prevent infection. Penicillin was not yet discovered. The use of a clean aseptic method and sulfonamide after removal of the glass splinters served to achieve a faster healing.

Then came the day we had to move out of our apartment in a hurry. Jews were not supposed to live in the central part of the city. The movers came, carried our furniture onto a truck, and we walked away, leaving behind Tatek's beloved oleander tree in a container on the large family room balcony. We moved in with my paternal grandparents in their big house, which was further from the city center. Omama and Opapa also no longer had a maid. Now only my father still went to work, but even he had lost interest in his business. The store had a government-imposed "trustee," who sat at the cash register and controlled everything because, according to the new authorities, Jews could not be trusted to run an honest business without Gentile supervision. Our hat store also got a trustee, and Mena hardly went there. Mena made for each member of the family a nice big yellow Star of David to be attached to our clothing when we needed to go out on the street, and we had a wide yellow band to wear on the sleeves of our shirts or jackets. The new laws required this. Opapa and Omama preferred not to go out of the house at all. The telephone was taken from Opapa's house. The new regulations said that Jews must not have a telephone.

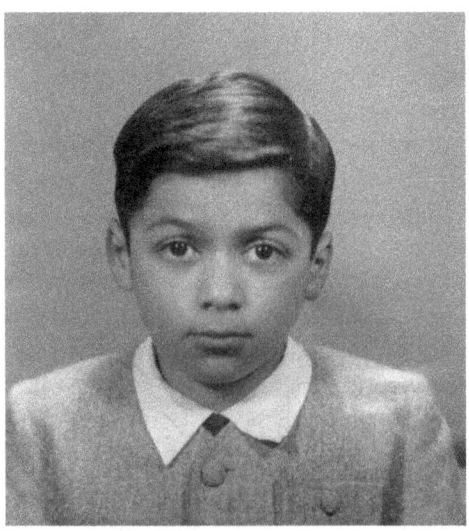

Photo made for ID registration of Jews in 1941

The "Hard Times": The War

Every now and then, Tatek would pack a day bag and go away for several days to stay at a country inn in Samobor, a small resort town outside the city. It was deemed safer to sleep over in an out-of-town resort, for there were increasing rumors that at night men of Jewish descent were being taken from their homes, and it was not certain where they were being sent. I still have a postcard that my father sent us, with shaky, upset handwriting from one of his stays in Samobor. People kept wondering where the Jewish men were taken. Soon enough, it was whispered that they were being sent to a "Koncentracionslager" (concentration camp), somewhere in or near a town called Jasenovac, where they had to do manual labor. After the Second World War, Concentration Camp Jasenovac became known as a notorious death camp, an extermination camp. It has been referred to as "the Auschwitz of Croatia." [16]

In the late summer of 1941, the three generations of Meiers were gathered for lunch, the main meal of the day. I remember that for dessert we had grapes, which Opapa liked very much, although he could not swallow the skins. I did not like to watch him taking the grape skins from his mouth and putting them back on his plate. Suddenly, just after dessert, while everyone was still sitting around the table and talking, Opapa started gasping. Mena whisked me out of the room and told me to go play outside in the courtyard. After a while, Mena called me into the house and told me that Opapa had passed away, and that he was safe and content.

That same evening, I overheard Mena speaking to Tatek about Opapa and saying, "Gut hat er gemacht!" (He did the right thing!) This was odd, and it bothered me. How could she say that? As if she was glad that Opapa died. This strange pronouncement was burnt into my memory forever, and several years passed before it dawned on me why Mena was happy that he died.

Opapa's house was divided into four small apartments with separate doors, and two other families moved in upstairs. We kept the first floor, and the janitor remained in a small apartment on the ground floor. My parents sighed a lot, and they kept saying that these were "die lila zeiten" (hard or bad times). The color "lila" (purple) had a stigma of bad taste. Then they would recall the times before the war and call them "die goldene Zeiten" (the good times). I also learned a new word: Ustaše. That word was always spoken very softly and with great fear. When my parents spoke about Ustaše, it was clear that they were scared of them. Usually, they did not even pronounce their full name. Instead, they just said "the U's" using the plural of the first letter of their name. Similarly, when they spoke of the Nazis, they referred to them as "the D's" also using the plural of the first letter for "die Deutschen" (Germans).

More and more often, my parents whispered rather than talked. They said, "...weil die Wände Ohren haben" (...because the walls have ears). Our curtains and drapes were now drawn even during the day. Perhaps it was because we were in mourning for Opapa. Our apartment was quiet, and it stayed in constant twilight. Opapa's big, old grandfather clock broke the silence on every quarter and every half hour, beating the time with a pleasant sound, and on the hour it played a whole little tune that we all liked, maybe because it was a Westminster. The shiny brass weight hanging on the rod behind the clock's glass door was continuously swinging back and forth. For a long time, there would be silence in the house, and I would play, pushing my little toy cars along the imaginary "roads," following the design of the ornate Persian carpets. Now and then, some whispering would be heard from the next room. There was fear, an almost palpable anguish that felt like an invisible evil spirit floating in the air. I did not understand what was wrong, but something was clearly amiss. I understood that "out there" was something terrible and frightening, and I gathered that it had to do with the "U's" and the "D's." There was a mood, as if a frightful dragon was lurking around. I would move the curtain and peek through the window to the street, but I could not see anything unusual. Was there a huge dog or a wolf somewhere? I always instinctively feared dogs. I could not see it, but it felt as though a giant hound was running through the city. Maybe he was just around the corner. Any minute, the vicious beast might come into the house, break down our door, and take a big bite from one of us. Nearly every day, some friend would visit briefly and in whispering tones tell about someone who had been taken from his or her house the previous night.

At night, I had dreams that were strange and scary. Of all those childhood dreams, the one I remember as most frequent was the frightful dream of flying through the air and then suddenly starting to fall down from a great height. As I was falling, sometimes from the height of the third-floor balcony in our old apartment, I felt I was with increasing speed approaching the hard ground in the courtyard. I would wake up just before smashing into the pavement and realize that I was in my warm, soft bed, safe. I would find my silky Rosena, press it against my face, and again fall asleep.

On some nights, I still occasionally wet my bed, and those rare accidents were usually connected to a dream. I was on an outing with Mena and Tatek, walking on a path in the woods, and I had to pee. I saw a big tree and peed against the tree trunk. Then I would wake up, the woods and the tree trunk would disappear, and I felt just warm wetness around my butt.

As a child, I was extremely curious. From as early as I can remember, I had a habit of silently standing in a corner of the room and observing the people around me, attentively listening and absorbing every word they said. I wanted to see and hear what people were doing and saying, and I thought and tried to understand. Later at night, in the dark, before falling asleep, I would remember events and words from the past day and think about them. Sorting things out sometimes brought me relief or happiness and sometimes it caused fear, anguish, or anxiety, and then I could not fall asleep for a long time. This pattern has followed me into adulthood, and many problems in my later life I learned to resolve in the quiet of the night. Only then, could I finally find peace and fall asleep.

Then it happened. One night, just when Tatek chose to stay and sleep at home, the doorbell rang several times, very loud. I do not know who opened the door. Two men entered and asked Tatek to come with them. He had to dress. I heard Mena ask them to please come later in the morning, but they would not. Mena had Tatek's little suitcase ready. Tatek wanted to wake me up, but I had already been awake for a long time. He lifted me from my "Kinderbet" (crib) into his arms and hugged me very hard. He kissed me and said he was sorry for the day before. I thought he was crying. He put me back down, and then for a long time, he hugged and kissed Mena. One of the two men called for him to hurry. Tatek slowly let go of Mena then turned around very fast and went out with the men. I heard the door slam. Mena was sobbing, and she slowly put me back to bed.

"Gute Nacht, mein lieber Izzy!" (Good night, my dear Izzy.) I could not fall asleep for quite a while. It was the early fall of 1941.

Just the day before, Tatek had given me my first and only hard spanking, which I well deserved. For the first time, he used the short braided willow crop, which till then was waved at me to scare me with its noise. I had figured that the crop served only to frighten me, and that it was an empty threat, never to be used. Afterwards, my butt so burned that I could not sit on it. Mena tried to stop Tatek and calm him down, but he did not listen. Tatek said it was high time to teach me a lesson, how to behave. All together, he seemed to have been very upset over something for a long time. While I was feeling my hot and painful behind and still letting out sporadic sobs, I overheard my parents talking. After Tatek gave me the spanking, he became even more aggravated and miserable. That was my last evening with Tatek.

The cause for spanking was a new "Stück" (prank) I pulled that day. In the afternoon, I was let out to play in the courtyard of the house so that Mena and Omama could "have a little peace" to talk to one another. There were no other children in our courtyard to play with. I felt like showing off all the letters and words Mena had taught me to write, but there was no chalk or crayon. Instead, I found a big fresh pile of dog's poop by the side of the house, and with a long wooden stick, I wrote big brown letters over the white stucco of Opapa's house. When Tatek came home, he first thought someone else had done it, but on closer look, he decided to question me. When I admitted the misdeed, I finally got the beating—for that, and for all my previous naughty pranks.

Soon after Opapa's death in the fall of 1941, despite the danger and despite her age, Omama Greta decided to escape to Italy. While preparing for the trip, she kept reciting from Goethe, "Ich möchte dort hin wo die Zitronen blühen!" (I would like to go where the lemons blossom!) During the first few months of the new, Independent State of Croatia, many Jews tried to escape over the border into Slovenia, which was then part of Italy. The border was very close to Zagreb, and there were some mountainous areas suitable for hiking into Italy. Some people succeeded, but most did not. Slowly, the news came back that most hired guides were unreliable. The guides often led people into an ambush manned by the Ustaše border patrol, robbed them, divided the loot, and sent the arrested people to a concentration camp. Occasionally, an arrested person managed to send a message to his or her family and warn the others. We never heard from Omama Greta again. Mena and I were left in the big apartment at Opapa's house all alone. It was dark, eerily quiet, and a little scary, and only the big, relentless clock regularly reminded us that the time was slowly passing.

Mena decided to visit Uncle Ernest in Varaždin, to see if it might be safer for us to stay with him in that small town. I was happy to travel on a train and look at the countryside through the window of the train compartment. Uncle Ernest's second wife had recently died, and he was living in a big house alone with his two teenage stepsons and his daughter Luisa. I met my step-cousins Boris and Željko for the first time, and they were nice to me. So was Luisa, whom I had known from before. I was again my naughty self and did to Luisa the same prank I did to Bluma. Little as I was, I grabbed the edge of her skirt with both hands and lifted it high up. I enjoyed the shrieks of embarrassment that came from Bluma and Luisa on such occasions. They learned to keep their hands on their skirts to guard themselves from my mischief.

Mena thought she could stay in Varaždin and help keep Uncle Ernest's house. Uncle Ernest was at work all day in his hardware store and the forge, and late in the evening, after I was put to sleep, I heard him and Mena carry on long conversations. It turned out that it was impossible for us to stay permanently without being registered with the police, which would expose us to the same danger we faced in Zagreb. On the other hand, if we stayed without registering with the police and were discovered, Uncle Ernest and his whole family would be in great trouble. Sheltering Jews was punishable by law. After several days, Mena and I said good-bye, and kissed and hugged everyone, and we left for Zagreb. Uncle Ernest seemed relieved, and Mena was disappointed. She kept saying, "Man muss alles probieren." (One has to try everything possible.)

Shortly after that, Mena took me on another trip to visit her brother Uncle Herbert and Aunt Rebeca Silber, who lived in Zavidovići, in the province of Bosnia, then part of the Independent State of Croatia. We had not seen them in a very long time. Aunt Rebeca was originally from Trieste, Italy, but she spoke fluent German. Uncle Herbert had a general store in town, and his only son Siegfried studied at the University of Vienna and had become an engineer. He had remained in Austria, now part of Germany. The train ride was slow and long, and I wanted to look through the open window. Each time I leaned out to see the locomotive ahead, a small bit of soot from the chimney of the steam engine blew into my eye. Mena thought it was time I "grow up a little," and she told me I had to give up my security blanket. My Rosena had become anyway quite dirty and tattered from heavy use. At one point, she waved it through the window of the train, the wind caught it, and my Rosena was gone, taken by the wind. I cried a little, but Mena said I was a big boy, nearly six years old, and I should manage without it. She was right. I soon forgot the Rosena. Instead, I found my fingernails and started biting them, and that felt good.

Uncle Herbert also had a trustee in his store, but life in the small Bosnian town seemed quite relaxed. Uncle Herbert and Aunt Rebeca lived in a big house with many rooms, both upstairs and downstairs, and underneath there was a deep, damp cellar. Our second-floor bedroom had window screens, and when I asked what they were for, I was told that they were to keep the mosquitoes out of the rooms. Soon I found out what mosquitoes were. The insects buzzed around my ears, bit me, and left itchy red bumps on my skin. At the end of the upstairs hallway was a funny toilet, the likes of which I had never seen before. It had a wooden bench with a round hole and a wooden cover, and it needed no flushing. To sit on it, I needed to climb on a little stool. No matter how hard I looked into that hole, there was just a deep dark void below, and everything I threw down quietly fell somewhere three stories deep into an invisible pit in the ground. I wanted to see how deep the hole was, so I threw a few things down and waited to see how long it took before I heard a "plop." In our room was a rough, very scratchy brown blanket that I hated. One day, I rolled it up to fit the opening of the toilet hole and stuffed it through. It went down without making even a sound.

On a nice sunny day, Uncle Herbert took us to the nearby riverbank. The water was too cold to bathe, but it was a beautiful warm day. Uncle Herbert took off his shoes and sat on the riverbank with Mena, and they talked and talked. While they talked, I made paper boats from old newspapers, the way Tatek had taught me. I floated them in the shallows of the river edge, where they were soon soaked with water and sank. I needed a sturdier, bigger ship, and for that, I took one of Uncle Herbert's shoes. It floated much better than my small paper boats. The big ship was a delight; it would not sink, and it could even withstand little waves. While I made more paper boats, the big ship got away, into deeper water, and it went faster and faster down the stream. I thought, should I interrupt Uncle Herbert and Mena in their lively conversation? Interrupting grown-ups was not polite. While I tried to decide what to do, the rushing water made the decision for me; my big ship sailed downstream, around the bend of the river, and disappeared from sight. So Uncle Herbert had a good long talk with Mena.

When it was time to go home, Uncle Herbert could not find his other shoe, and I started crying. When Mena found out about the "boat," she was upset, but Uncle Herbert laughed and said he wished that this were his worst problem. I thought he was happy because he still had both of his socks. He limped home with only one shoe, and Mena was embarrassed and scolded me. I was truly sorry, too. I had such bad luck; I was a real "Pechvogel" (bad-luck person). Oh, why did such things happen to me?

Staying with Uncle Herbert and Aunt Rebeca was just as dangerous as staying with Uncle Ernest. Some Jews from the little town had already disappeared. We might as well return to Zagreb. After about a week, Mena and I hugged and kissed Aunt Rebeca and Uncle Herbert, and they saw us off to the train station. A few weeks later, Mena received a postcard from Aunt Rebeca with the sad news that Uncle Herbert had died. It happened very suddenly. When he was informed that the Nazis killed their only son, Siegfried, he suffered a heart attack and died the next day. Not long after that, we lost contact with Aunt Rebeca. After much inquiry, Mena finally learned that Aunt Rebeca had "disappeared" without a trace. Mena wondered if it had anything to do with the trustee in Uncle Herbert's store. He probably wanted to take over Uncle Herbert's house, too.

Uncle Moritz Jablonski, we now better call him by his new name, Stanislav Rubin had graduated from the school of forestry in Romania, and he ran a lumber and heating wood business. His business and source of lumber was in a small village in the neighboring province of Slovenia, now a part of Italy, but not too far from Zagreb. By working in the border region, Uncle Stanislav had the documents needed to cross the border any time, even on a daily basis. Since Italy was known to be safe for Jews, it was decided that Uncle Stanislav, with the aid of a trusted man who worked for him at his lumber business, would take Mena and me over the border to Italy. There we would be safe. We could stay in the village on the other side of the border. For the trip, Uncle Stanislav took Aunt Ester's documents with him, and if caught by a patrol, he would pretend that Mena was his wife and I was his son. Small children at that time did not need a travel document.

In the morning, we went by train from Zagreb to Jastrebarsko, and then for a while by a horse-drawn wagon to a small village at the foot of a mountain. I learned later that the region was called Žumberak. There we met Uncle Stanislav's employee, took our rucksacks and bundles off the wagon, and started slowly walking up a narrow mountain trail towards the border. It was early December 1941, and it started to snow. The wind blew and it was bitterly cold, but we were well bundled in our warmest clothes. We all wore heavy hiking shoes. As we climbed higher up the mountain, the trail got narrower and steeper, and the snow became more and more slippery. I could no longer walk, and Uncle Stanislav, rather than dragging me by the arm, carried me on his back. The snow got deeper, and with the wind, some of the drifts were up to his waist. Mena followed the leader, who knew the path, and Uncle Stanislav went last. At least it was safe. In such weather, there would be no border patrol. Before the evening, wet and tired, we crossed the mountain pass into Slovenia. We were in Italy and out of danger. Going downhill was even more slippery than climbing. I could walk, but Uncle Stanislav had to hold my hand to keep me from falling. We arrived at the small village of Dragoševci in the darkness of the late afternoon.

Mena and I were given a small room in a farmer's house, adjacent to Uncle Stanislav's office. There was a nice fire in the stove, and we ate and drank something as we warmed up, and then Mena made the bed and I fell asleep. Uncle Stanislav stayed in his office, where he had a couch to sleep on. As soon as the weather cleared, Uncle Stanislav went home to Zagreb, and several days later, he came back with Uncle Felix, who got a room in another farmer's house in the village. We were waiting for Tatek to be released and join us. The Professor had learned that Tatek was in Jasenovac, and he intervened through his connection to have Tatek released. Together with Tatek and Uncle Felix, we planned to move further away from the border into Italy.

The "Hard Times": The War

Although Italy was a German ally and under Mussolini's fascist rule, the authorities there did not persecute the Jews in the same manner as the Nazis and Ustaše did. This changed in 1943, after Italy capitulated. Then the Nazis took over and started rounding up Jews to send them to death camps in other Nazi-occupied territories. Remember the movie La Vita e Bella or the stories of Primo Levi, the writer who survived Auschwitz and later described his ordeal, but then committed suicide. [7]

On the farm, I saw for the first time a barn with a sty and real farm animals: cows, oxen, horses, donkeys, goats, and sheep. I learned not to stand behind the donkey, for the naughty beast nearly kicked me in the head. I also learned not to stand in front, for donkeys sometimes wanted to bite. I learned that water does not come only from a faucet in the kitchen or bathroom, but also from a well, a deep, round hole in the ground, with a wall around it. The water was pulled up with a winch and a long rope with a pail at the end, and it was carried to the house in large earthen crocks loaded on each side of the donkey. I also learned other new and interesting things. Unlike what I had thought, the cow was not the "wife" of the horse. There was the bull, and there was the mare. Not all small horses were ponies, and there were calves. Now the toilet was not only a wooden box, like in Uncle Herbert's house, but it was also in a tiny, separate hut completely outside the house. All through the winter, to go to the toilet in that outhouse meant to freeze one's butt. I expected my pee to turn into a yellow icicle. Mena got me a chamber pot with a cover, so I would not have to go out at night.

One day, I noticed that my dear Mena's pretty face had changed. Her forehead was wrinkled with three deep grooves just above the nose, and each cheek had a groove. These were not the fine wrinkles she used to have around her eyes and cheeks when she laughed. These sharp grooves seemed to be there all the time. She looked grim and appeared older. I felt sad. Mena kept saying that Tatek would soon come to join us, and together we would all be happy again.

Uncle Stanislav sent us from Zagreb more of our clothing and other items Mena needed, and for me books and a few toys. Mena read me the books and every day taught me to read and write. She always put the pencil in my right hand, though I preferred to write or draw with my left. On a small wooden abacus with beads she taught me to add and subtract numbers. During the cold days of winter, time passed slowly, and we stayed mostly in our room. Mena said it was not good to be seen outside. We saw Uncle Felix only rarely. We kept waiting for Tatek.

Spring arrived, the weather was nice, snow on the roofs melted, and long icicles hung and glittered in the sun. It got warmer, and we began to spend a little time outdoors. There was still no news from Tatek. One day, while Uncle Stanislav was back at his home in Zagreb, people in uniforms came and asked Mena to pack up and come with them. They were Italian border police, *carabinieri* (Italian militia), and they were very polite. Mena begged them to let us stay a few more days; she would send a message to Uncle Stanislav to come and show them our documents. That they could not do, and they patiently waited a long time till Mena finished packing. Then they put our suitcases onto a carriage with two horses, and accompanied us on horseback to the nearest train station in Metlika. There they gave us free train tickets and a special *lascio passare* (temporary pass) document from Metlika to Karlovac in Croatia.

During the Second World War, the village of Dragoševci belonged to Italy because in prewar Yugoslavia, it was part of Slovenia (Dravska Banovina). In 1945, after the war ended, that Croat village was annexed to Croatia. After the war, Uncle Stanislav told me that somebody in the village of Dragoševci had denounced us. Only after the war did we receive news from Uncle Felix. He wrote to us that when he noticed the arrival of the carabinieri in the village, he hid in a hayloft and was not discovered. The following night, Uncle Felix moved out of the village and went through Slovenia as fast as he could to get deep into Italian territory. He went to the region of Como Lake, near the Swiss border. He had money saved in a Swiss bank and hoped that his first cousin, Stefan Eisner in Zurich, might help him enter and stay in Switzerland. Neither one of his hopes was fulfilled. The Swiss would not let Jews enter their country "because of the war," and so Uncle Felix remained in Como. When Italy capitulated in 1943, Uncle Felix was compelled to escape from the Nazis in Italy. He hiked over the mountain and entered Switzerland illegally. Then he found out that by Swiss regulation, all foreigners' savings accounts were blocked. The bank refused to release his money till after the war ended. Meanwhile, Uncle Felix had to stay in a Swiss detention camp for illegal aliens. He was allowed to do occasional odd jobs, sometimes tending people's gardens. At least he survived the war. Uncle Felix did not stay in Switzerland and after the war he returned to northern Italy, where he felt well received. He wrote that he would remain in Italy and never come back to Yugoslavia.

Expelled from Italy, Mena and I arrived in Zagreb and went from the train station straight to Uncle Stanislav's apartment. When Aunt Ester opened the door and saw us standing there, her face looked as if she had seen a ghost and was going to faint. We entered the apartment, and Mena hugged aunt Ester. It was the spring of 1942. According to the law, everyone had to be registered with the police at their permanent residence, and so we dutifully registered. We could no longer go to Opapa's house because it had been confiscated and occupied by people placed there by the Ustaše government.

While staying at Uncle Stanislav's apartment, I was sometimes allowed into the courtyard to play with other boys. On one occasion, a boy I was playing with threw a handful of sand in my face, and I yelled at him in a scornful tone, "You Ustaša!" Aunt Ester, who was watching from the kitchen balcony like a hawk, yelled at me to come immediately up to the apartment. I was never again let out to play with the other children. Luckily, no adult in the neighborhood heard me say the ominous word. Afterwards, I heard Aunt Ester say to Mena, "dieses Kind könte uns alle ruinieren," (this child could ruin us all) and I was very sad, especially because I later found Mena quietly crying, and that time she sobbed very hard and for a long time.

The "Hard Times": The War

Tatek was still away, Mena's eyes were red, and she looked sad all the time. Several weeks later, in the middle of the night, the apartment bell rang loudly and Uncle Stanislav went to open the door. Two men were at the door, and they demanded that Mena come with them. She dressed, took me out of my bed, and carried me quickly into the pantry room behind the kitchen. She closed the door, hugged me hard, and kissed me. Mena then told me to stay in the pantry and be quiet, and always to be very good and obey Aunt Ester and Uncle Stanislav, and to be patient until she came back. Then she went out into the kitchen and locked the pantry door. Through the door, I heard her say to Aunt Ester, "Ich bitte dich, tue alles was du kannst. Zumindest das Kind soll leben!" (I beg of you, do all you can so that at least the child should stay alive!) Those were the last words I heard Mena say. I heard them kissing, and I knew that they were hugging. After a short while, I heard steps in the kitchen, and then I heard the apartment door slam. My Mena was taken away. I heard Aunt Ester crying and sobbing in the kitchen, and I knocked on the door. Uncle Stanislav unlocked the door and let me out of the pantry. Aunt Ester took me in her arms, hugged me, and put me back to bed. After a while, I fell asleep.

That morning, without Mena, the apartment felt strange, and all day I kept thinking of what happened during the night. Mena was not there to cuddle, but she said she would be back, only she forgot to say when. I had to wait. Aunt Ester and Uncle Stanislav said they did not know when Mena would be back, nor did they know when Tatek would return… I decided to try very hard to be a good boy and be on my best behavior. In the afternoon of the same day, someone visited and told us that Aunt Bella, cousin Oliver's mother, was also taken away that same night. Oliver was left all alone, but the Professor would take care of him. Within a week, Aunt Ester received a postcard signed by both Mena and Aunt Bella, saying that they were together and well and that they were on their way to be "resettled" at a "work camp." The card had very few words, was stamped "censored," and had a stamp from somewhere in the German Reich. We never had any other message from either one of them, and we never found out to which camp they were taken. It could have been in Austria, which was at the time part of Germany, or in Germany proper, or in neighboring lands occupied by Germany. It was the summer of 1942.

What is now known from documentation about the Holocaust is that most of those Jews who were transported from Croatia to Germany in 1942 ended up in Nazi-occupied Poland, where the closest camp was Auschwitz. [1, 4]

I stayed in Uncle Stanislav's and Aunt Ester's apartment. I was never allowed to go out. With the war going on, food was getting hard to find. The shelves in the stores were empty. To get milk, Uncle Stanislav went once a week in the early morning to a village outside the city and carried back two large cans of fresh milk, which Aunt Ester boiled before it could be stored and used. Part of the milk was made into yogurt. I begged Uncle Stanislav to take me with him on the milk run, and one time he gave in. We first went to the last tram station past the city zoo, and then we had a half an hour walk to a village. On the way there, Uncle Stanislav took a shortcut over a creek that had to be crossed using a thick log. The log had a thin wooden rail mounted on one side for a handhold. I was scared of crossing so high above the water. Right nearby, I noticed the creek was very shallow, though somewhat wider. I also noticed tracks of wagons and horses crossing through the mud and shallow water. Uncle Stanislav crossed over the log with empty cans in his hands, without even holding on to the rail—to show me how easy it was to cross. While he encouraged me to start crossing, I took a run through the shallow water, which felt a lot safer. I got all wet and muddy. While Uncle Stanislav had the milk cans filled, the peasant let me go into the house to warm up and partly dry my clothes by sitting on a step of his wide, tiled stove. On the way back, Uncle Stanislav took another, longer path with a decent little bridge over the creek. I came home wet and dirty, and that was my first and last milk run.

One night in late summer, our doorbell rang several times, and Uncle Stanislav went to see who it was. Two men stood in front of the door and asked for me. They told Uncle Stanislav to get me ready to go with them. As I was waking up, Aunt Ester put a wet compress on my forehead and told the men, "The child is ill; he has fever and has to stay in bed," but to no avail. Fever or no fever, I had to be dressed and let go. Aunt Ester gave me a tiny suitcase with a change of clothing and things I may need, including a small bottle of my favorite refreshment, homemade *Himbersaft* (raspberry syrup). She hugged and kissed me, and off I went. Through the dark and deserted streets, I walked between the two men to the nearest police station, located a few blocks away in Vlaška Ulica. In the police courtyard stood a great number of people, mostly men, and only a few children, most of them older than I. The men were all standing and whispering or talking in hushed tones. I was sleepy and could not understand anything. A tall wall with barbed wire on top surrounded the yard. Soon, it was dawn. In the morning, everyone was told to board two trucks. Somebody lifted me and my suitcase onto the truck. We went for a long ride through the city, all the way to the main police station and prison compound on Savska Cesta *(the address of the notorious prison that was, after the war, also used by the communist secret service)*.

The prison compound had a very large courtyard, and there was an enormous crowd of people huddling in the yard and in a few rooms in the surrounding ground-floor buildings. Everyone looked worried. I heard people say that this was just a transit station before we were transported further, most likely by train, to a concentration camp. I sipped some of my raspberry syrup and wandered with my tiny suitcase from room to room and back into the courtyard, without finding anyone I knew. The rooms were stuffy and crowded, and I could not see anything, for I reached only up to the waist of most people. The morning lasted for an eternity. I was tired. There was no place to sit except on the floor, and the floor was dirty. In the rooms, it was warmer, but the dense crowd was suffocating. No one paid any attention to me. I ate a part of a sandwich Aunt Ester had put in the suitcase. I felt lost.

Sometime in the afternoon, I heard someone yelling my name, and that made me happy. A man asked me my name and told me to follow him into an office in a taller building. A lady in that office told me to sit down on a chair and again asked me my name and some other questions. Another lady in the office gave me a hard candy. After a short while, I was led out of the office, and a man showed me out through a large door. Suddenly, I was standing on the sidewalk outside the building, on a small side street. For a long time, I used to think it was just my good luck that made me walk out of the prison office right onto a street, that it was just "my fate," and that it somehow happened fortuitously.

As I write this down, my memory is quite clear. I was shown to the door that led to the street. Obviously, someone had told those people to let me out. Otherwise, I would have ended up like thousands of other Jewish children, in a concentration camp. Standing in the bright light on the sidewalk in front of the prison door, I heard someone calling me by my nickname.

"Izzy, Izzyly!"

I looked around, and I saw past the corner of the little street and across the major road. Two familiar figures were waving to me—Mr. and Mrs. Cacciatore. Mr. Cacciatore ran across the road and down the little street, took my little suitcase in one hand and my hand in the other, and led me back across the road to a tram stop. Mrs. Cacciatore hugged and kissed me, and we boarded the streetcar and went straight to Uncle Stanislav's and Aunt Ester's apartment. Aunt Ester hugged me for a long time, and all the while thanked Mr. and Mrs. Cacciatore for bringing me back.

As I found out after the war, on the morning I was arrested, Uncle Stanislav went to the Professor's home and asked him to intervene. The Professor called on his connections at the authorities and argued that as a baptized Catholic child, I should be released. My release was approved, and the Professor called Uncle Stanislav and advised him to wait for me in front of the prison on Savska Cesta. Uncle Stanislav was too scared to go anywhere near that prison, and he instead went to my parents' old friends, the family Cacciatore, and they were glad to go and wait for my release.

As soon as I arrived home, Uncle Stanislav went to inform the Professor that I was free. The question then was what to do with me. The Professor had a good friend, Bishop Janko Šimrak, the head of the Greek-Catholic bishopry and boys' school in the town of Križevci. Even though I was too young to be accepted into the boys' school, the Professor would try to have me placed there. He had arranged the placement of my cousin Oliver into the boys' school the day after Aunt Bella and Mena were arrested. Oliver, however, was almost thirteen years old, whereas I was only six and a half, much below the minimum age of ten that was required for acceptance. I did have a small advantage. I could read and write, and I knew how to add and subtract as if I were older. Mena had taught me all that during the long winter days in Dragoševci.

The bishop agreed to send a trusted priest to visit Uncle Rubin and see if, despite my young age, I might be fit for acceptance. All this took several days to arrange, and by then it was the late summer of 1942. In the meantime, Aunt Ester and Uncle Stanislav told me that a priest would come to our house, and ask me to read and write some words and add some numbers, and he would ask other questions to see whether I was ready to go to a special boys' school. From the many conversations I overheard in our house, I knew that there were in town many dangerous people, the "U's," who wanted to take us all away from home. Uncle Stanislav told me that in the boys' school, I would be safe from the "U's," but I had better be on my best behavior and obey the priests and all other adults.

THE ALTAR BOY

The priest, Monsignor Spiridon Petranović, arrived one morning and for a while he spoke only with Uncle Stanislav and Aunt Ester. I was in the room, and all the while, he was looking at me. Finally, he asked Uncle and Aunt to leave the room, and he turned to me.

He said, "Now listen carefully," and he intoned a strange prayer in a language I did not understand (it was Old Slavic). He said a few words at a time, and he asked me to repeat the prayer after him. The prayer was short, "Our Father", and he slowly and patiently made me repeat it and helped me along until I could do it by heart. He seemed satisfied, and then he taught me a second prayer, "Hail Mary". Soon I was able to recite both prayers without interruption. I did not understand what the prayers meant, but I was able to parrot them quite well from beginning to the end. Then I had to read to the priest from one of my books, and I had to write a few words that he dictated to me, and I added and subtracted a few numbers. Then the priest wrote the name "Petar Bastašić," and I read it back to him with correct pronunciation. This was easy. Serbo-Croatian is a completely phonetic language: each letter always denotes only one sound, no exception, no change, no doubt. If one knows all the letters of the alphabet and their corresponding sounds, one should be able to read and correctly pronounce any word, and soon one would be able to write, as well. What you hear is what you write.

The priest then called Uncle Stanislav into the room and said to him that I was apparently ready to be accepted into the boys' school. Next, he told me that I must forget my name, and from then on, I would have a new name: Petar Bastašić (Petar was my baptismal name, anyway). I should never tell anyone my old name or anything about my past or my parents; I was to say that I was born in the village of Dragoševci in the Žumberak region of Italy, which I was familiar with from my stay with Mena the winter before. If asked about my parents, I was to say that they died of an illness when I was a baby. I was made to understand that this was very serious and important, and that I must absolutely follow and obey what I was told. I also must never let on that I could speak or understand German—just forget that! All this seemed serious and exciting, and fun, and while it might be a little difficult, I felt I could handle it. I promised to follow all instructions and obey all orders given to me by the priests and everyone else in the boys' school.

Some discussion about the payment for my "tuition and board" at the school was held with Uncle Stanislav, and this was quickly settled. Aunt Ester served us all lunch, and before lunch, the priest taught me one more thing: to cross myself. Again using the same strange language as in the prayers, he intoned, and I repeated after him, "In the name of the Father, and the Son, and the Holy Spirit, Amen!" While I repeated the words, he took my right hand, folded my fourth and fifth fingers and left the first three fingers straight (in the Greek-Catholic fashion), and put my hand to my forehead, then down to my stomach, and then up to each side of my chest, making the sign of the cross. I had to cross myself, he said, before eating in the morning, at lunch, in the evening, and after evening prayer, before going to bed. Well, this did not seem at all so difficult. The crossing became a habit very soon after my arrival at the boys' school. I eventually also learned to stand up and cross myself each time the church bells rang in a certain way, signifying a holy event, baptism, marriage, or someone's death.

After lunch, I said good-bye to Aunt Ester and Uncle Stanislav, and Monsignor Petranović took my little suitcase and me to the railroad station. On the way to the train, he told me that my cousin Oliver was already at the boys' school, and that he also had a new name. He was now Pavle (Paul) Bastašić, and I should never call him Oliver. His parents also "died of an illness," and being my cousin, he came from the same Žumberak region. I was happy to know that wherever I was going, there would be at least one person I had known from before. I would gladly obey him, too, and I promised to call him Pavle, always and forever. All this sounded mysterious, like in one of those good stories that Mena used to read to me. Soon we were sitting on the train to Križevci, a town of about 30,000 people in northern Croatia. More of my belongings were to be sent after me later.

Greek-Catholics practice religion much like the Greek or Eastern Orthodox; their priests are allowed to marry and have families, and their liturgy was written in the ancient script called Glagolica, which I could not read, and it was sung in the Old Slavonic language, which preceded modern Serbo-Croatian by more than one thousand years. The Greek-Catholic sect came into existence through politics. In some regions, the Greek or Eastern Orthodox people found it convenient to recognize the Pope in Rome as their primate, rather than the Orthodox patriarch. As compensation, the Pope allowed them to keep their original Old Slavonic liturgy (instead of the customary Latin) and let them retain most of their customs. Most of the Greek-Catholics lived in Ukraine, but many were also present throughout other Slavic regions, and later they spread to other countries. The Eparchy of Križevci was the Greek-Catholics' center for all provinces of the prewar Yugoslavia of 1929-1941. Many of the Greek-Catholics in Croatia, particularly the ones in the Žumberak region, were originally Serbs of Greek-Orthodox religion, people called "Uskoci," meaning "people who jumped in," that is, migrated to escape the oppression of the Turkish Empire. Austrian authorities allowed them to settle in the border region, with the provision that they serve in the military and protect the area from Turkish attacks. Around 1611, many of those Serbs became Greek-Catholics, and in the course of centuries, they became assimilated into the Croat nation.

The bishopry and boys' school in Križevci lay on the main street, several blocks from the center of town. After a good half an hour walk from the train station, we approached a fortress-like, three-story building. The building was square, with the church forming the left side of the square and the other three sides housing the offices, apartments, school dorms, and classrooms. The building was much taller than anything around it was; its height was the same as a five-story apartment building. A black wrought iron fence separated the whole compound from the street. On the left side of the church was an orchard with a large gate for horses and carts. The church had a grand entrance door with broad steps to the street, but we entered the square main building through a small wooden door in its center. Msgr. Petranović first took me to meet Bishop Šimrak, who I was instructed to address as "Preuzvišeni" (Your Highness), and not by his name or title. I was also instructed to kiss the large ring on the middle finger of his right hand when he offered it to me. I was a bit scared of the bishop and of the encounter itself. When we entered the bishop's room, he was sitting on a large armchair, his big hands resting on the side arms. In his black, purple-trimmed robe, the bishop appeared huge, and I immediately saw the ring with the large red stone on his right middle finger.

The bishop looked at me for a long moment and then asked me my name and a few simple questions that were easy to answer. Apparently, I did well kissing his ring and following the rest of the required protocol. The bishop turned to Msgr. Petranović, briefly spoke with him, and then just said, "Go, go; go with God at your side." As I soon learned, this was what the bishop usually said when the audience was over and he wanted to signal that you were excused and should leave.

After greeting the bishop, Msgr. Petranović took me to meet several other priests, who were in their rooms, and then the nuns, who were doing chores in the large kitchen facing the courtyard, and finally all the boys, who were in the dorms and classrooms on the third floor. We quickly walked through the long corridors of the main building, in which I was to spend most of the next three years. The boys' ages ranged from ten to eighteen, and I was by far the youngest and the smallest. Here, also, was my cousin Oliver and I constantly had to remind myself to call him Pavle. On seeing me, he was at first a bit apprehensive because of my youth, fearing that I might mistakenly blurt his real name or something else that would reveal our identity. Within several days he gained confidence because I called him Pavle, did not hang around him too much, and most of the time simply kept my mouth shut. With his blond hair and blue eyes, Pavle blended well with the other boys, whereas I with my black hair, well, I looked a little different.

In my first days at the boys' school, I was withdrawn and content to just look around, observe everything and everyone, and listen attentively to all conversation. I spoke only if I was asked a question. It was a new environment, and I did not feel comfortable in my new role. I was shy, and to protect myself from making mistakes, I wanted to remain that way.

In the next several days, I became well oriented in the main bishopry building, and soon became familiar with the adjacent buildings and farm fields that lay behind them. The main floor of the bishopry contained a large kitchen facing the courtyard in the back of the building, the nuns' apartments overlooking a shady park with pine trees and landscaped pathways on one side of the building, and various bishopry offices facing the street. The second floor housed the bishop's apartment, rooms for single priests, and several guest rooms. The third floor, facing the back courtyard, had two dorm rooms and several classrooms for boys. Each floor had a very high ceiling. In the basement was a vast, dark cellar used as a storage area for food and wine. When I first went to the cellar to help bring out some potatoes, the darkness, thick walls, heavy pillars, and cold damp air made it feel like a dungeon from a fairy tale. The door to the cellar was always locked, and the key was in the nuns' quarters.

The backside of the courtyard was delineated by an L-shaped barn, and behind it was a gentle downhill slope with a farmhouse that was surrounded by an orchard and vegetable garden. At the bottom of the slope was a tall hedge separating the orchard and vegetable garden from the large, flat meadow behind it. A creek lined with weeping willows ran across the meadow from left to right. Beyond the creek were additional meadows and pastures, and further yet were fields of wheat, corn, and other crops, extending for about a mile up a gentle slope. All that land belonged to the bishopry, and it ended at the edge of a dense forest. In the distance, at the end of the fields, as if leaning against the dark wall of the forest, was a small white farmhouse visible from the dorm windows. I was told that one should not venture beyond the edge of that forest. The steep, desolate, and rocky gray mountain, Kalnik was visible to the north of the town, and its top was usually crowned by a white cloud.

On one side of the bishopry was the house that belonged to the family of Msgr. Petranović, and next to it was the house that belonged to the family of another senior priest, Msgr. Bukatko. On the other side, adjacent to the bishopry, was the girls' school, completely fenced in by a two-story high brick and stucco wall. In nearly three years, I never saw any of the girl school's inhabitants, neither the girls, nor the nuns who took care of them. They had their own chapel for prayers, and apparently never came out of their compound. We looked for them on Sundays in the church, but they never showed up.

The courtyard barn was very large, and it housed eight cows and four horses, a garage for the old cabriolets and carriages, a room with rabbit hutches, a room with chicken and turkey coops, and storage areas for plows, other farm implements, and agricultural tools. Some of the implements I was familiar with from my stay on the farm in Dragoševci, but the bishopry farm was very large, and there were many things I had never seen before. On top of the barn was a huge loft for the hay and straw, and it could be reached by a tall ladder leaning against an open window in the roof. Several openings in the ceiling of the sty allowed hay and straw to be dropped directly into the feeding troughs. The straw was used only to keep the area under the cows and horses clean, and during clean up, it was mixed with the excrement and it all ended up tossed through a small side-door onto a huge pile of manure, which, as I later learned, was regularly carried into the fields for natural fertilization.

In the courtyard was a large stone trough, and next to it an iron hand pump. The trough was used to water the cattle. One side of the courtyard had separate smaller barn buildings, the pigsty with an adjacent pigpen, and the coops for geese and ducks. Adjacent to these two buildings was a shallow, muddy pond that took the run-off water from the pump and trough and served as the playground for the ducks and geese, and occasionally, for the pigs. The entire area, including the courtyard, had a tall wooden fence to keep in the fowl and other animals.

In the garden farm house behind the barn lived a large peasant family that helped with the gardening and farm work, and tended the animals. Part of that house contained a carpentry workshop, a smith's shop, and a small forge used to maintain the farm tools. Along the side of that house was a row of wooden boxes on little stands; those were the beehives. A narrow footpath led from the main courtyard through a small gate, downhill through the orchard, over the pastures, and into the fields on the other side of the creek. Low green hedges delineated the individual crop fields. The creek cut deeply through the pasture, and to cross it, there was a wide log cut flat on the upper side. This log bridge was only a foot wide and good twelve feet long, and it had no rail to hold. I learned to walk over it, but at first, out of fear of falling, I crossed it only by crouching down on all fours and crawling. The creek was shady, but at one point downstream, it opened into a wide shallow pond called "the hole." There one could bathe in the summer in the cool and quiet shallow water. Farther downstream, the creek was again narrow, deep, and fast, until it came to the mill house where, next to a little waterfall, it turned a giant wooden wheel. Coursing through the fields on the far side of the creek was a major dirt road that went over a bridge, past the mill house, and wound through the center of the town.

In the middle of the pasture on the near side of the creek was a small, dark, deep pond, only about twenty feet wide, and it was surrounded by thick reeds growing out of muddy clay. This area was full of noises from frogs and birds, and from it would sometimes emerge a frightful green water snake. The whole area presented a tranquil rural landscape that I enjoyed for three summers. On closer look, however, a rough brown furrow running from left to right and cutting across the pastures and meadows on the near side of the creek for as far as the eye could see disturbed the peaceful pastoral picture. This furrow was made of fresh earth piled along a newly dug trench that was about five feet deep and three feet wide, with little concrete "pill box" bunkers at every three to four hundred feet. The dirt from the trench formed a mound on the side facing the creek and outer fields, as if a dirty wound had been cut into the green grass, exposing the bowels of the earth. The boys in the bishopry said that the trench was dug recently around the entire town. It was done for defense from guerrilla fighters called "Partisans." The bunkers would soon be manned night and day by the "Domobrani" (home militia), an army of conscripts that acted as a home guard and were not as fearsome as the all volunteer army of the Ustaše. The Partisans had apparently been seen in the area and were said to be roaming through the forests and the nearby mountain Kalnik.

When I arrived, the boys' school had seventeen boys; I was the eighteenth. The school had a hierarchy of seniority by age. Each year, the priests named a leader from among the oldest boys. The leader was called "ductor" (leader), and he reported to the overseeing priest. The ductor was responsible for keeping order among the boys, and he saw to it that we all followed the rules. We slept in two dorm rooms on the third floor. One room was larger and housed twelve boys; the smaller room housed six. The rooms had double windows, and the walls of the building were so thick that an adult could comfortably sit sideways on a windowsill when the outer window was shut and the inner one was open into the room. An old-fashioned, tall, tiled stove provided the heat, with step-like ledges protruding from the wall into the room. On a cold day in winter, one could sit on those ledges and warm up. The stove had two heavy metal doors near the bottom, the upper, larger one for putting in logs of firewood or lumps of coal, and the smaller bottom door for air circulation and cleaning out the ashes. In winter, the fire was lit only once in the morning, usually on top of the embers from the previous day's fire, and then the upper door was shut tight, and the lower one left only a little ajar, so that the fire would smolder slowly, and the heat would last long into the night. The chimney was inside the wall between adjoining rooms, so that the same stove could be serviced from either of the two rooms, and would heat both rooms at the same time.

The water in the bathrooms was provided by an electric pump installed in a deep well in the small, central, inner court of the main building. The pump pushed the water into a reservoir in the attic of the building, and from there the water flowed to the kitchen and the bathrooms on all floors. As electric outages during the war became more frequent, the water for our daily washing and toilet flushing had to be manually pumped from the main courtyard well and carried in metal pails up to the third floor. The pails were so heavy that I could not lift them when they were full. The manual pump had to be primed by sixteen fast, hard strokes before the water even began to flow, and then one had to continue pumping fast and hard to keep the water going. Only after two years was I strong enough to get the water up and keep it going for a while. Only big boys could do that job. The water for the morning washing was kept in individual washbasins, and each boy had one stored under his bed, with water ready for the morning washing of face, hands, and body. The boys at that time were brought up to be very private when washing or going to the bathroom, so I could easily follow the stern warning given to me by Uncle Stanislav never to let anyone see my penis. Dirty water from the morning washing was carried to the bathroom and used to flush the toilets. Sometimes, because it was hard to carry a full basin through a long corridor without spilling some water, we tossed the dirty water through the window—if there was no one in the courtyard to see. This was, of course, against the rules, but I soon learned that it was all right to break a rule as long as one was not caught. First, I had to learn the rules. During my first few weeks at the boys' school, the ductor and priests were lenient when I made a mistake, but I soon learned to follow the rules like all the older boys.

Beside the rules, there were responsibilities: every boy had a job to do. My first job was to collect the eggs from the hens, ducks, turkeys, and geese. This was relatively easy, but the sloppy birds sometimes made a nest and deposited their eggs in an odd place. The hens liked to nest and spend the night among the cows, horses, or pigs; I would find their eggs in the corner of the pigsty, in the sty corners near cows and horses, in the cows' feeding trough, in the seat of an old carriage, and any other imaginable place within the barn. It was also my job to see to it that all poultry were in their coops at sundown, with the doors closed and latched. There were only a dozen turkeys and geese and two dozen ducks, and those were easy to count, but there were over two hundred chickens with a few roosters, too many to keep count in the evening. The nuns, however, counted the eggs I collected every day. They praised me, for I seemed to find more eggs than they expected. I did not know that, previously, some eggs ended up in the boys' stomachs. I caught on before long.

The food was rationed. Eggs and milk were almost the only source of protein. Beef was available if a cow was close to dying of old age, and by then it was all gristle, hard like shoe leather, and impossible to chew. Veal was sometimes available from the bullocks, but it was never sufficient. From the original eight cows when I arrived, only four remained by the end of the war. There were four horses, two broad shouldered Belgians for plowing the fields and pulling the hay wagons, and two slender, full-blooded Arabians for pulling the carriage and for travel. At times of urgency, even the Arabians, Sultan and Frieda, were used to pull the plows. In the following years, I would watch over and gather the cows from the pasture in the afternoons, and tie them up at their places in the stalls. Each cow and horse had a name, and they all turned their heads when called. The cows and horses always walked to their proper places in the sty and waited to be tied up. It seemed as if they did not even have to be tied up. The cows and horses were brushed daily and kept clean. The pigs had no names, were dirty, and often wallowed in the mud around the pond. I understood why a sloppy boy was called a pig and not a horse.

Every evening around nine o'clock, a priest would come to lead the prayer before bedtime and take a head count. He would then lock the dorm room from the outside and leave the key in the lock. How could anyone escape for an evening date? It was almost impossible. More and more often, there was no electricity in the evenings, and we had to use carbide lamps, similar to those used by the miners. Kerosene was hard to come by, candles were too dangerous, and anyway, they had to be saved for the mass or an emergency. "Carbide" is a salt which, when mixed with water, creates a gas that burns through a fine nozzle on the side of the lamp. In the morning after each night's use, we had to clean out the messy residue inside the lamp, dry it, and fill it with carbide powder and water to be ready for the next evening. This was quite a nasty job, but when there was no electricity, it had to be done daily, and we had a rotation of two boys each day.

From the first day, I felt that the boys liked me, and each day I felt more comfortable and secure. The ductor said I was under his protection. They marveled at how small I looked among them, and they immediately gave me a nickname: Peritsa, a diminutive form of Peter.

The biggest of the boys was Stevo Savić. He was tall, dark, handsome, and strong. On the very first day, he looked at me, saw how tiny I was, and then told me I could hit him in the nose as hard as I wanted. I did not dare do that. Then he challenged me to do it in front of the others, and said I'd better obey. Then the ductor told me to go ahead. The whole group of boys observed the scene with amusement.

Reluctantly, I folded my little fingers into a fist, aimed, and took a good swing at his nose tip. It was my first time seeing blood running out of someone's nose. It would not be the last time, including some time later from my own nose. Seeing the blood, I was both scared and sickened, but there was the sound of approval and admiration coming from the boys, and Stevo gamely declared that he "now really liked" me, and went to the bathroom to wash off the blood.

One boy observed, "Little one, but he has a punch!"

Despite my tiny size, I felt accepted into the group. As I would soon learn, acceptance carried a price. I, too, became a subject of the boys' pranks and jokes and teasing, just like any boy. To my delight, I witnessed some neat pranks played by the boys on one another. One day, while a boy was sitting on the windowsill reading a book, two others jumped up in unison and shut the inner pair of windows so that the fellow was left sitting in a glass box between the inner and outer windows. With his legs folded up to his chin, he looked like a big, funny, squawking bird in a glass cage. They left him there for an hour despite his pleas to be let out. He was finally freed when the ductor walked in. Not to fall behind in amusing the others, I began to devise little pranks of my own, but when the older boys started playing jokes at my expense, I did not like it so much.

In all this, there was a strict code of silence. No matter what was done to anyone, no one ever whined to the priests. The effect was that everyone was eventually the butt of a joke, except for the ductor. He was the only one spared, for we all needed a referee who would be fair and without grudges. The ductor, Stevo Milivojević, was one of the older boys. He was thin and small, with a big head; he wore thick glasses, coughed a lot, and appeared sickly (he had a touch of consumption, a common illness in the Balkan), but he was smart, wise, and well respected.

In the evening before the prayer and lock-up, everyone went to the bathroom. The bathrooms were in a cluster at the middle of a second hallway, way around the corner from the dorm rooms. The hallways were not lit, and on dark, moonless, winter evenings, they were quite scary to pass through. From some older boys I heard that ghosts roamed the building, sometimes suddenly appearing and running down the dark corridors. Everyone was quite scared of them. One dark winter evening when I was going to the bathroom, just as I turned the corner of the long corridor, I saw at the other end two white apparitions, each with wide spread wings. The ghosts! There was a faint glow of light coming from behind their wings, and they slowly advanced towards me. I froze in place. I wanted to yell for help, but my throat felt tight and dry, and my voice failed me. No sound would come out. They came closer and closer, and with its wing tip, one of the ghosts tugged at my arm. I was petrified. Finally, my voice returned, and I let out a scream that must have reverberated through the whole building. One ghost dropped his white wing, and I saw a folded arm holding a lit candle. I realized that the "ghosts" were two boys wrapped in bed sheets trying to scare me. Just in case, I continued screaming till more boys ran out of the dorms, and they all started laughing. I did not think it was funny.

After that, for quite a while I went to the bathroom only way before darkness. The trouble was that I would wake up at night and need to do number one, but the door was locked. There were no chamber pots in the dorms. A few times, I had an accident in my bed. To hide it I would pretend to sleep late, till hopefully, from my own body heat, the sheets would dry, but with a huge yellow stain in the middle, while most of the liquid was lost somewhere in the thirsty mattress, which was stuffed with dry grass. I soon found a different way to deal with this problem. While all were asleep, I would quietly pull a basin from under a bed and pee into someone's water for the morning wash. For the longest time, no one noticed anything wrong with the water. The white basins were old and had acquired a yellow stain. On nights when I desperately needed to go, to be fair, I always changed my target. Of course, a night came when another boy was awake, and I was caught doing it. They thought it was just a prank, and they would think of some new prank to pay me back.

At first, I was "too young" for school, though in reality it would not have been safe to let me go to the city school, where my identity might be uncovered. Msgr. Petranović taught me informally mostly the catechism. I learned to be an altar boy. Each time, after helping with the mass, the priest gave me a different holy picture. The pictures were all in beautiful color, and I collected them and spent time looking at them. I liked the pictures of the saints, especially Mary, the Holy Mother of God. She was really pretty. In addition to "Our Father" and "Hail Mary," there was another prayer I needed to learn: "the Creed." Each strophe started, "I believe," and each time I said, "I believe," my belief became deeper and stronger. The monks knew it centuries ago, and they probably learned it from ancient Greek philosophers, who said, "Repetition is the mother of learning." So, with a good dose of the Creed, soon after arriving into the boys' school, I began to feel quite religious. With my whole heart, I believed in all the stories that the priest quoted from the Holy Scriptures.

Aside from the stories about Jesus, the saints, and the Holy Mother of God, the older boys took time to explain to me other, more earthly happenings, which, they said, were evident in daily life. The story about the stork bringing new babies into the world, they said, was a tall tale made for little children. Babies came from inside the mother's womb, but first there had to be a lot of fun going on between the mother and the father. They taught me all kinds of new words that went along with it. To prove it, they pointed to a very fat, slow-moving cow in the yard. Soon, they said, she would have a calf. Within a few weeks time, I saw that they were not joking: the story about the womb was true! They also pointed to the funny goings-on between the rooster and the hens in the courtyard, the pigeons, dogs, and other animals. The dogs I observed carefully and noticed that they jumped on one another regardless of their sex, even a male with a male. The boys explained that the dogs had learned it from men who were called "fags," and I learned yet another new word.

The cows, I learned, had no such fun. All oxen were "fixed" to make it easier to handle them, and there was only one bull left in town. The cows had those melancholy eyes, the boys said, because they were taken to the bull only once a year and the cows hoped he would be in a good mood that day. Soon, I was able to witness such an event. On the day a cow had to be taken to the bull, they let me come along. They took three cows, because, I was told, a single cow would refuse to go very far on a road. A cow had to see at least one or two other cows from the herd coming along, or she would refuse to budge. When we arrived at the bull's farm, the lucky selected cow was let through the gate, the gate was closed, and the two accompanying cows were left standing with us in the outer courtyard. Through a slit in the fence, I observed the bull and the cow, but nothing was happening. It took nearly half of the morning before the bull became interested in our cow and came closer. He suddenly reared and jumped with his big chest on the cow's rump. The cow stood firm and lifted her tail up and sideways. The trouble was that the bull was taking very poor aim, and he finally jumped off the cow. This was repeated a few times. Then the bull's handler entered the corral, and on the next try, he helped the bull reach his target. Only then did I see what hard work it was to make a calf. This was no fun! There was a lot of huffing and puffing, and the poor bull was sweating and foaming around the mouth before he called it quits and jumped off the cow. The bull's job was done, I was told. The whole scene was not pretty, and it was a little scary. I wondered how this type of work could be as pleasurable as the boys described it. At least, the rooster and the hen did it fast and easy, without foaming around the beak. On the way home, I was told that there was no guarantee the cow would get a calf from this one try, and that sometimes, "the copulation" had to be repeated several times. I also learned that most male horses and pigs were fixed to make them easier to handle. Fancy words, like "biology" or "animal husbandry," were not known to me at the time, but my knowledge in those areas was rapidly expanding.

While I was advancing in the farm sciences, the boys in the dorm made sure that my knowledge of human biology was not left too far behind. I was told that the slit the girls had was not meant just for peeing; it had hidden behind it a real "pleasure vat," and if the man did it right, the woman would meow like a cat, and that's how babies were made! They said that my dick was not meant just for peeing, either, but also for having fun with the girls—but only later on, when I grew a little older. My education was progressing at an accelerated pace, and without knowing it, in a relatively short time I became a lot more grown-up than my age or size led one to believe. As I heard Aunt Ester say a few years later, I was being "geschmiert mit allen Salben!" ("Anointed with every cream").

The older boys attended regular classes in the city school, and then returned to the bishopry classrooms to do their homework and attend religious lectures given by the priests. Aside from the bishop, the school had five priests. Two of them, Msgrs. Petranović and Bukatko were senior, had families with children, and lived in their own houses next door to the bishopry. The other three priests were young and single, and they lived in individual rooms inside the compound. I only remember one of them well. He was called only by his nickname, "the American." He was tall, slim, and funny, and he came from the U.S. to Yugoslavia on a two-year exchange fellowship from a parish in Michigan. The war caught him in "The Independent State of Croatia," and there he was, serving a fellowship much longer than he could have foreseen. He had his own radio receiver, and we all knew that he surreptitiously listened to the "enemy" news from London and knew what was going on with the war. The Ustaše government forbade listening to enemy radio broadcasts, and nobody dared to talk about it. However, among the older boys there was occasional whispering, and some of it I overheard. About one year before the end of the war, the American was unfortunately sent to take over a small, remote parish, and the older boys' source of news dried out.

The priests had to say the mass once each day, usually in a small, heated chapel inside the compound, adjacent to the church. On Sundays, two masses for the local believers were served in the church: one of the younger priests gave a shorter early mass at eight a.m., and the longer main Sunday mass was usually served by a senior priest, or sometimes even by the bishop himself, at ten in the morning. The longer mass lasted about one and a half hours. The mass in the chapel was done on the average in thirty to forty minutes, depending on how fast the priest could recite the required prayers. For each mass, the priests needed an altar boy, and the youngest boys in the school had to serve on a rotating schedule. As an altar boy, I learned quickly what I had to do, and it was not difficult. All priests had a strict schedule of masses, sharing the chapel between them, and since each priest had to give one mass a day, they generally started at six in the morning; by nine, they were all done. In the winter, the church was freezing cold, and it was a pleasure to serve in the chapel, which was separated from the church by the sacristy, a large storage room with many cabinets of all sizes containing the various elaborate priests' service garments and a multitude of chalices and other objects needed for the mass. The sacristy had a small door that led into the church, opening just behind the main altar. The wine for the mass was stored in bottles in a sacristy cabinet under lock and key. The nuns baked the host. It looked like a round white bun, and the nuns sliced it into small, wafer-like squares, and finally cut into each square two grooves in the shape of the cross. In time, I was allowed to help cut the host, which was placed in a beautiful, small, golden, covered bowl kept in a cabinet in the room behind the chapel.

Each priest had his favorite altar boy, though from time to time, we rotated. The priests' schedule was also changed every few weeks. If a priest needed to give mass outside of his allotted time schedule, he had to do it in the cold church, and we always dreaded such schedule changes. The priests had different dispositions; one of them was quite rigid and known to mete out cruel punishment for small mistakes. Another one was unpredictable and moody. We all hoped to be assigned to the three other priests, who were kind and easy going. The American was most beloved by all of us, for he was not only the most forgiving, but he also liked to joke and be funny. He normally spoke very fast, and he said the prayers so fast that he sounded like someone conducting a country auction. His mass was over in a record twenty-five minutes. It was a special honor to be allowed to serve with the bishop, though he was slow, and the mass went on forever. After mass, I cleaned up: I rinsed and dried the chalice, emptied the remaining host from the gold cup into the bowl, and returned everything to the cabinet. A few times, out of curiosity, I tasted the remaining wine before rinsing the chalice after mass, and it tasted just like any wine, which I did not like. The wine was supposed to have been transformed during the mass into the blood of Christ. It did not smell of blood, either. I tasted the host, also, before and after the mass, and it had no taste of flesh at all. It tasted like a really good white bread roll. I did not dare to ask about those things because I knew I was too young to understand them, and I did not want anyone to know that I tasted the wine. During the mass, people receiving the host were supposed to swallow it without chewing, like a small pill, so there was no way to feel the taste. The quantity of wine consumed by each priest during the mass was different—some needed more and others drank less, and we all knew their habits.

There also was the job of helping to chime the church bells, and that, too, had a schedule. The chiming was done on special occasions. Different religious events had a special way of chiming, and each bell or combination of bells had its meaning. Soon, I learned to recognize specific events or announcements by the sound of the bells. When I first tried to help with chiming, I was too light to move the bell, and I was exempt from the schedule. I hung on the rope and swung around, and nothing happened. One day, I climbed the stairs and ladders all the way to the top of the bell tower and looked at the four bells. One of them was much smaller, and I was told that the little bell was used only on special occasions. Finally, the time arrived I was allowed to help and I was able to chime the smallest bell. The bell tower had another interesting feature: pigeons roosted everywhere, so the area was well fertilized.

The nuns wore stiff white headgear that completely hid their hair, necks, and parts of their shoulders. It had a round frame to show a moon-like face. A long, dark blue habit covered their whole bodies from their shoulders to their feet. Their apartments were taboo: the doors were always locked, and no one had the key but the nuns themselves. Being a small child, shortly after my arrival, I was allowed a few times to enter their apartment, which appeared very simple, but warm and cozy. They had a small side room serving as a pantry, where large sacks of flour, sugar, and similar precious food supplies were kept under special lock and key. I do not remember all the nuns' names, except Sister Polycarpa, Sister Marta, and a novice, Slavica. Among themselves, the nuns spoke a different language that I was told was Ukrainian. On the rare occasions I was allowed into their apartments,

I got a glimpse of the nuns in a more relaxed state, without the starched headgear, and I saw the color of their hair. The head nun, the Honorable Mother, was all gray, others were brown, and Sister Polycarpa had orange-red hair. Sister Marta was very ill, and it was rumored she would not live very long. When I first met her, she coughed a lot, kept a bloody handkerchief in front of her mouth, and spoke very softly. She had consumption and lived in two separate rooms where she slept and prayed. When I arrived, Marta could no longer work, and she spent most of her time in a chair next to her bed. She was the bishop's niece, and I was told that she used to be quite mean when she still worked with the others. The meanness, they said, was due to her illness. Sister Marta died during my second year at the boys' school. One of the two novices, Slavica, had a very pretty face, and all the boys, especially the older ones, were delighted to meet her in the corridor and exchange a few words, all the while looking at her face. I had to admit that Slavica's face was prettier even than the nicest one among my holy pictures. One of the older boys said it was a pity Slavica wanted to become a nun—he would much rather marry her. The nuns regularly allowed me to enter the large kitchen where they prepared the meals. There I either observed and enjoyed the warmth of the stove, or helped with small chores. Just like the priests, the nuns differed in their dispositions. Most were kind, but two were occasionally mean, and everyone knew which ones had to be avoided.

Not long after arriving at the boys' school, I got some itchy little red dots on my skin and had to scratch a lot. The boys explained that all of us had "tenants" in our beds: the fleas. I had never heard of fleas before. These tenants got into our clothing and bit our skin. I was shown how to look for them, catch, and kill them. The fleas were hard to catch, for they jumped in all directions. When caught, they had to be rolled between my fingers to stun them, and then quickly put on the thumbnail to be squeezed with the opposite thumbnail until they popped, and a droplet of blood came out. They were apparently everywhere in the country, and it was impossible to get rid of them. I soon discovered other tenants that liked to reside in my hair. These were called lice. Still others were invisible and resided in the thin skin between the fingers of hands, where they caused a terrible itch (scabies). Lice could be destroyed with a good kerosene rub, but that was a nuisance, for one had to sit for at least two hours with one's head wrapped in a smelly, kerosene-doused rag. The procedure killed the lice, but it also gave a little burn to the scalp. To avoid trouble with lice, soon after I arrived at the boys' school, my head was shaven and thereafter the hair was allowed to grow no more than half an inch long. That made it easier to keep the lice away by regular combing with a fine-toothed comb and washing the head with soap. With their freshly shaven or very short hair, the boys in the school looked like military conscripts. The older ones cheated and let their hair grow a little longer, keeping it down with some sort of ointment, but the priests caught on to them, and every now and then, one would get a fresh head shave. The others then made fun of him and called him a "naked-ass moon-head."

My first fall and winter in the boys' school passed relatively quickly. I had a lot of learning to do. I got used to the food and ate it because I was hungry. My hunger was somewhat alleviated because the nuns let me do little chores in the kitchen while the older boys were in school. While in the kitchen, I was occasionally able to catch a few bites of "something special" being prepared for the bishop or priests. I was also allowed to bring things from the basement storage, where, if no one saw me, I would steal an apple and eat it later. The apples were arranged in neat rows on the shelves, and I had to carefully rearrange them so that no one noticed an empty space. From the boys, I also learned to put a pinhole into a warm, freshly laid hen's egg and suck it out. The trouble with the eggs was that they were counted, and the nuns expected a certain number each day, though in winter for some reason, the hens laid half as many eggs as in the summer. Around Christmas time, there was a little more food, because at that time, the pigs were slaughtered to prepare provisions for the winter.

For the first time, I saw the slaughtering of a pig. Four pigs destined for slaughter were driven into a small corral. The largest pig was about three years old and weighed about five hundred pounds. To make him fatter, he had been fixed. Four men lured the pig into a small pen, knocked him off his feet, and while he was on his side, quickly grabbed his legs, turned him on his back, and kneeled on him to hold him still. It all happened in a flash. The pig did not like it and started squealing very loudly. One of the men pulled a long knife from a sheath in his belt and stabbed the pig through the neck, deep into his chest. The pig's squealing became horrible. The man kept moving the knife up and down. The blood started squirting, and someone caught it in a basin. I don't know how long it lasted before the pig's squeals became weaker and he started grunting and croaking, and then just lay still. The men jumped off him. Suddenly, he started moving and twitching his legs in the air, as if he were trying to walk. When he stopped moving, the men tied a rope around his hind legs and pulled him up to hoist him on two hooks on the pen wall, his head down, and the blood still dripping onto the ground. I felt numb and sick, and I just stood there, behind the fence. Did the other three pigs understand the big pig's squealing? I wondered if they sensed it was coming to them, too. The men poured several pails of scalding hot water over the pig and started shaving his body hair. The pig's skin was pink and clean. As the butcher cut open the pig's belly and pulled down his bowels, liver, lungs, heart, and innards, I again felt sick, turned around, and walked away. I had seen enough. Oh, and the smell!

Later on, while I was in the kitchen, the butchers brought in huge basins full of lard, pieces of meat, hams, livers, lungs, hearts, brains, the heads, and all the various little pieces, down to the feet. Nothing was wasted. The blood was partly used for making special blood sausages, and part of it was fried like an omelet. Blood was very healthy, they said. Except for the hams and larger cuts that were to be smoked, the meat and gristle was put through a large grinder, and the ground meat was salted and peppered to be made into sausages. The sausages were made by a machine that stuffed the ground meat into a length of the pig's gut, and this was twisted every six inches to separate each sausage. I learned that the gut had been first thoroughly washed through with a hose. Then I saw the lard cut into one-inch cubes and cooked in a cauldron till it melted. The shriveled, solid leftovers of lard, the cracklings, were poured off and saved to be salted and eaten later. When the molten lard cooled, it turned into soft, smooth, white cooking fat. In winter, we often got for supper a slice of bread smeared with fat and sprinkled with salt, or just bread with cracklings.

The hams, most of the good cuts of meat, and sausages were reserved for the bishop, the priests and their families, and the nuns. It was for such occasions that the boys taught me a folk saying: "God first made his own beard." Some of the good food trickled down to us, and especially for Christmas lunch, we got a good piece of sausage cooked with beans, and for Easter a nice slice of ham with a cooked whole potato. At the end of winter, just before Easter, the food was really lacking. On top of it, before Easter, one was supposed to fast, as if the entire winter menu had not been one long binge of fasting. Occasionally, a boy got a food package from home, and they sometimes shared a little. Pavle and I never got any packages because both of our parents "had died long time ago." In the spring, the hens laid more eggs, fresh fruit and vegetables appeared, and the food got more plentiful.

The first fruit in the spring were the cherries. They ripened slowly and in batches on various parts of the trees, so one could never have too many. They all had one or two thick, short, white worms in them. This was true organic fruit. I first discovered it when I felt something moving around my mouth. To deal with it one had to open each cherry, remove the pit and the worms, and then eat the cherry. Many boys did not bother—they said the worms were healthy—and some of the boys swallowed even the pits. Štefek, the monkey in the zoo in Zagreb, ate the whole banana with the peel, but I knew it was best to keep quiet about that. I had quickly learned that before saying something, I first had to think very hard. Would it be the right thing to say? Frequently, while I was thinking, the conversation went to another subject, and I was spared from saying something really dumb. Often I realized how much better it was for me to have kept my mouth shut. Words could get one into real trouble. It was better to listen a lot and say very little, for that way one could learn a great deal without getting into trouble. And learning I was.

During the day, I liked to play in the barn, especially in the carriage room. The carriages were beautiful, particularly the cabriolet, which was completely enclosed with a roof and two doors. Its cab had glass windows on all sides and plush upholstery lined with blue velvet, and I loved to sit in it with the doors closed. I would imagine all sorts of adventures from the stories Mena used to read to me. The cab also had a small glass box attached on each side up front for light. The boxes had a little door that could be opened, and inside each box was a thick, short candle. I used to take a box of matches from the kitchen, and while playing in the cab I would light the candles. With the candle light flickering, my imagination took me on all kinds of fancy trips to the lands of the fantastic tales I heard before. One day, however, a farm hand came into the carriage room, and he started screaming, "Fire, fire!"

He blew out the candles in the light boxes. Then I was discovered in the cab and taken to the priest. First, I was lectured by the priest and later by the ductor, and both said that I could have set the whole barn, the hayloft, and all the animals on fire. Then followed the punishment. I had to kneel for the whole afternoon on dry corn, facing the corner of the dorm room, and later, for penance and forgiveness, I had to say ten "Our Fathers" and six "Hail Mary's," and I was never to touch any matches again and never to go near those carriages. Of course, the whole bishopry knew what horrible calamity I nearly caused. That terrible deed put the worst shame on me. I thought it served me right, for I disobeyed the little song that I heard from Mena so many times:

"Messer, Gabel, Schere, Licht
sind für kleine Kinder nicht!"
(Knives, forks, scissors, light,
are for children not all right!)

It was not just the matches that were not for me to play with. It was all in line with other things I was asking about, only to be told, "You have to wait until you grow up." It seemed like there were a thousand things a grown-up could do, but I could only do a lot of waiting and hope that I would someday grow up.

WITH PARTISANS

In summer of 1943, I had spent about a year in the boys' school, and when I looked in the mirror, I was skinny like a stick, with a big head, two dark, bulging eyes, and very little flesh covering my bones. The mirror was not lying. I had frequent colds and a cough I could not get rid of. The priests noticed that I looked sickly, and the bishop decided I would do well if they sent me for a few months to a remote farmstead out in the country. The farm was called Lepavina, and it belonged to the bishopry. It was remote from any town or village, and it lay about twelve miles from Križevci. There would be plenty of food there, and I would be taken care of by the priest's sister, who kept the household. She was unmarried and had no children. So one day, I and a few of my belongings were put on a wagon, and one of the trusted bishopry workers hitched up two horses and drove me to Lepavina. The farm looked like a tiny hamlet. There was a long, ranch-style house, and across from it was the church. Further along was a very large yard with several barn buildings and many more cows and horses than in the town compound. Further on were several small houses for the farm workers and their families. There was much more land and many more farm workers than at the bishopry. The food on the farm was good and plentiful, the kitchen was neat and cozy, and it reminded me of our home in Zagreb, before we had to move away. From the first day, the priest's sister was kind to me, and in her presence, I felt very comfortable. She prepared all the food for the priest, herself, and me. I was given a little room next door to hers, as cozy as if it were in a city apartment. The furniture was nice, the windows had curtains, and the bed was clean, soft, and without any tenants. There was no electricity, and in the evening, we used kerosene lamps. The toilet was at the end of a long hallway, attached to the outside of the house. It was wooden, with a cover over a round hole, very much like the one I saw in Uncle Herbert's house.

For the first time since I left Zagreb, I did not have to put up with so many other, bigger boys, priests, and nuns, and I felt free from pressure to be constantly on guard, lest I make some mistake. I was relieved to be out of the humdrum of the boys' school. Unless I wanted to help in the kitchen, I had no chores to do. I had peace and ample time to think, and I wondered where my Mena and Tatek were, what my Aunt Ester and Uncle Stanislav and cousins Bluma and Michael were doing. The priest's sister liked me, and soon she started knitting for me a pair of woolen socks. My knee socks had huge holes at the heels and toes, and the bottom parts that went inside the shoes were disappearing. The socks were beyond repair, but I would not throw away the upper parts, which were whole and warmed my calves and shins. Instead of socks, I was given new "foot wrappers," simple large square pieces of cotton cloth. I was shown how to wrap my feet with them and then put on the shoes. Most peasants and farm workers never wore socks; they used those rags, the foot wrappers, inside their shoes. I quickly learned the art of wrapping the foot without too many wrinkles so I would not be hurting inside the shoes. For my tall walking shoes, I received new laces made of leather. They were thick and hard to tie, but they held the shoes tight around the foot wrappers. In general, I was happy on that farm, as much as one in my position could be.

During the year in the boys' school, I began to like all food. I forgot to be picky about it, as I used to be in my parents' home. If before the war, I had been spoiled as a single child, it was long forgotten. Without being aware of it, I was growing up, more so on the inside than in my outer appearance. I was still very small for a boy of my age, and the grown-ups considered me younger than I was. When they heard me talk, they saw that I was not so young, and they sometimes said, "Listen to this midget talk."

My shoes were getting very tight, and it was clear that I needed new ones, but with the war on, leather was neither available nor affordable. My sweaters could stretch, and my jacket and shirts had been made larger so I could grow into them. My woolen hat fit well, and I had a good, thick woolen scarf to protect my neck. The main thing was that my stomach was full, and I was warm. The shoes and the socks could wait.

The farm lay at the foot of a steep, wooded hill that was the beginning of a long, ridge-like mountain called Bilogora. The mountain extended from that point on for miles in a southeasterly direction, and in some points, it rose up to 1800 feet. The nearest foothill was only about a thousand feet high, and it could be easily climbed using a steep winding footpath. From the top of that hill, one had a view in all directions except the one obscured by the wooded mountain ridge. I liked to climb up, stand on top, and look at the lay of the countryside. On a clear day, one could see the entire landscape. Close by were the fields belonging to Lepavina, and further out were pastures and fields that belonged to the neighboring villages. At a distance of several miles, villages looked like little winding lines of brown and red roofs. Every now and then, a dark stand of trees formed small wooded areas, and willow trees outlined the meandering line of a creek; here and there, a straight green line of tall poplar trees shielded the fields from the wind, and many sharp, dark lines of hedges separated the fields and pastures. In the hazy distance, I recognized the tall, gray, rocky mountain of Kalnik.

One day, at the beginning of autumn, I woke up to much noise and commotion coming from the yard. People in military uniforms and some in civilian clothes were milling about, and most had weapons at their sides. The yard was full of horses, with carts and wagons loaded with supplies in boxes. The people looked tired, and their commander and officers demanded the priest give them food and quarters. They had apparently marched all night. In time, they were accommodated, and they settled down. Their hats had three pointy horns in line from front to back, and I immediately knew that these were the Partisans. Rumors and tales about them were occasionally whispered at the boys' school. There were about four hundred soldiers, and some had to camp in the church, for all the barns and houses were not sufficient. Their commander's name was Štrok, and he was quartered, along with a few other officers, in the guest rooms of the priest's house. Within a day or two, the house acquired little tenants, just like at the boys' school.

Members of the Communist Party organized the Partisans in 1941, immediately after the onset of war in Yugoslavia. The communists were the first to escape from the cities into the countryside to avoid being arrested by Nazis or Ustaše. The Communist Party had been outlawed already in prewar Yugoslavia. Atrocities committed against the civilian population gave communists the opportunity to organize all those people who ran away from the Ustaše and the occupying Nazi army. The Partisans' leader, Tito, had been trained in Soviet Russia, and he gained experience in guerrilla warfare during the Spanish civil war. The core of the Partisans in the first two years of war was made of the Serbs, the Croat communists and the Jews. Partisans especially attracted Jewish physicians. The ragtag army of Partisans, spawned of desperation, without proper arms or training, but with enormous morale, had the support of only part of the Yugoslav population, but it grew in four years to an army one million strong. It defeated and drove out the Nazi army and the Ustaše, who possessed airplanes, tanks, cannons, and all possible technical advantages.

The Partisans stayed at Lepavina for four or five days. Commander Štrok was very friendly. He once lifted me on his horse and gave me a little ride as he inspected the area around the farm. He asked where I was from, and I stuck to my story: "Petar Bastašić, from the village of Dragoševci. My parents died of some illness, and I was at the boys' school in Križevci."

At one point, he asked me quite seriously whether I would like to join him and come along with the Partisans. They could use me as a courier. His question took me by surprise, and I did not know what to say. I said that I had to think it over. His offer seemed exciting, and I had to think real hard what to do. I had to promise that I would not talk about it with anyone. On the day the Partisans were leaving, everyone felt a relief. Having so many guests around the farm was not easy, and it caused a certain tension. It also presented a dangerous situation. The Ustaše would have taken it very badly if they thought the priest voluntarily gave shelter and support to the Partisans, although the priest was in no position to refuse.

When I approached Commander Štrok to say good-bye, he asked me one more time very quietly if I wouldn't rather come along with him and stay with the Partisans. The priest and his sister were standing not too far away, and I could not say much. I had not decided, and so I just quietly said "no". When all the Partisans left, I felt a heavy burden inside my chest. What was the right thing to do? I knew that Partisans were fighting "on my side" and that I really belonged with them, but I liked the priest and his sister and I did not want to disappoint them by leaving, and I also had an obligation to stick with the boys' school, where the bishop had accepted me. Talking to and getting advice from the priest or his sister was out of question.

For the next two days, as life in Lepavina returned to normal, I thought about the Partisans a lot. On Saturday, I made a decision: I would join them. From the talk in the house, I knew they were at a village called Mali Poganac, about ten kilometers (six miles) down the road to the north. I climbed the hill by the farm and saw the village in the distance. I knew that everyone slept in on Sunday, and the priest normally served the morning mass after breakfast, around half past nine or at ten in the morning. I could get up before dawn and quietly slip out of the house. I would dress in my best and warmest clothes and have the rest of my clothing rolled into a small bundle and hidden outside the house the night before. I would get under way while all were still asleep. I was excited and woke up several times during the night, not to miss the dawn. Finally, I saw the first, faint glint of light come through the window. I dressed and got out of the house a little before dawn without being noticed. It was a cool, dewy morning, but it was going to be a nice day. By the time that the morning fog cleared and the sun was shining warmly, I was already quite far away, walking in the proper direction and using footpaths through and between the fields rather than the road. The few people that traveled the road on an early Sunday morning were easy to spot with their noisy wagons and horses, and I crouched and hid in the brush until they passed. All was quiet, except that at one point, when I was quite near my destination, three German Stuka airplanes flew over, quite low, and after a while, I heard the distant thunder of explosions. It was wartime, and this was not unusual.

Before noon, I reached the village of Mali Poganac and found the house with the brigade headquarters and Commander Štrok. He was not surprised, he said. He felt that I might join him and the Partisans. The soldiers were again quartered as guests in most of the houses and barns in the village. The house with the headquarters was large, with many rooms. There was no toilet, not even an outhouse; instead, one was supposed to go behind the barn, between the bushes. Going out, one had to watch one's step. There was no toilet paper, either, and to clean myself I had to use large leaves from the bushes. At the boys' school, old newspapers were cut into little squares, pierced with a wire, and hung by the toilet. The Partisans had no newspapers, except a little paper that was saved to roll handmade cigarettes. There were no beds, either. We slept on the floor, on ankle-deep straw, and we were lined up close, like sardines in a can. At the headquarters, we at least had a good wooden floor. Other houses or barns had only a dirt floor. The air in the room was full of smoke from bad cigarettes, and that made me cough. The cigarettes were made from rough-cut tobacco kept in a small pouch, and people made cigarettes by rolling the tobacco into pieces of thin paper, often saved from an old newspaper edge. The Partisans would lick the paper's edges to make it stick and hold the tobacco together. When they ran out of real tobacco, they used ground corn leaves, and the smoke from those cigarettes was even more irritating.

As there was no bathroom, the washing in the morning was done outdoors by the same pump and trough that was used for watering the animals. Usually two people would wash together: one would pump the water, and the other would catch handfuls of water and splash himself. Rags were used as towels, or one quickly put on his shirt, which eventually dried from the body heat. As the season advanced, and the mornings got colder, washing became unpleasant and difficult, and frequently, especially when it rained, it had to be skipped for a day or two.

Going out at night was no fun, either: in the darkness of the room, one would accidentally step on someone's hand or foot, which elicited the juiciest curses I ever heard, all involved with sex, including the weird, with private parts of all sorts, and animals and people all mixed together. These curses were mostly addressed to God and his son or the Holy Mother, and only occasionally to various assorted saints. Some curses were personal; they sent the offender back to his mother's womb. Some curses spoke of weird sex with an owl, a horse's ass, or with the whole wagon and for some reason even the wagon's wheels: "F— your horse's ass and the wagon and the wheels!" or "The barn-owl should f— you in the ass."

I learned the full richness of the folk language. In that department, with the Partisans I got far ahead of the boys in the school. The art of cursing that the boys in the bishopry taught me now seemed rudimentary. Aside from the ornate and convoluted curses, most of the Partisans spoke simply and rarely used any big words that I might not understand. Only the officers and the political commissar regularly used big words that were above my head.

The food was again sparse and bad. A little dry bread, rarely some milk, a small runty apple or pear still found on the tree, and sometimes, as a treat, a piece of dry meat or sausage. I had to unlearn the habit of crossing myself. The Partisans had no God, they said. Sometimes my hand automatically started going toward my forehead to cross myself before eating, and I would quickly scratch my forehead to conceal what I was about to do. A few days after I joined the Partisans, I started having the runs with cramps, and noticed that my excrement was covered with a little blood. This worried me a bit, especially because I felt weak. Commander Štrok noticed my runs and said that nearly everyone had them at one time or another, and that this would slowly pass in a few weeks. He was right. Years later, I realized that what I had was amoebic dysentery; most peasants in the countryside of Yugoslavia had their bowels normally colonized by amoebas, and most had no symptoms from it. Of course, a newcomer to the countryside would quickly get diarrhea. The water we drank came from a courtyard well that was not far from the manure heap by the barn.

I received a little air gun and tried to shoot at birds. I wanted to fire from a real rifle, but it was too heavy for me to hold. I became adept in cleaning and oiling the Partisans' rifles and pistols. I knew all the parts and could take each gun completely apart, clean and oil the parts, and then put it back together. Finally, after I insisted and begged to be allowed to shoot from a real rifle, a kind Partisan gave me a chance: he loaded a bullet into the barrel, leaned the rifle on a low fence, aimed it into the air, and let me shoot. I put the butt against my shoulder, aimed at a high tree branch, and pulled the trigger. I heard the loud "boom" sound, and the next moment found myself on my back. The rifle ricochet hit me hard, and my shoulder was sore for days. Amidst all this, I was useful: I carried messages, walked to the next village, delivered them to a designated person, and safely returned with the answer. Unarmed and without a uniform, a small boy would never be stopped and searched.

After several days with the Partisans, I was told that we would soon be "on the move." On my first march, we walked for several hours on logging roads through the woods, and I was proud to be able to keep up. The commander and a few officers rode horses; the rest of us walked. The supplies and ammunition were carried on several wagons pulled by horses. The road was narrow, rutted, and full of deep, muddy puddles; sometimes it was just a wide dirt path, and in some areas, it was a simple logging road. The Partisans rarely moved on open roads. Occasionally, the horses could not pull the cart out of a mud hole or rut, and the Partisans had to push from behind. On some uphill stretches, they also had to help push the carts, for the horses alone could not do it. I was occasionally lifted on Commander Štrok's horse to ride for a while with him.

On approaching our destination, sentries were sent in all directions, and guard posts were set up first. A password was issued for the night sentries. Then, houses and barns were requisitioned for Partisans to settle in, and finally, when everything was secure, we moved into the headquarters. There was a curfew, and no farmer was allowed to move outside after dark, except for going to do his business close by the house or barn. The password for the sentries and guards changed every day. I learned the routine and became more assured and useful each day, and my days and weeks passed so fast that I did not know what day or date it was. It did not matter: the Partisans had no written schedule to follow. Every few days, we moved to a different village; the orders were given by the regional command through a radio receiver. Apparently, no one knew where the headquarters of regional command were located. The Partisans avoided any head-on battle with the enemy. My shoes were getting tighter, and one day, when we reached our destination and settled in, I decided to do something about it. I had obtained my own pocketknife with a three-inch blade that folded neatly into the wooden handle. With it, I cut a hole in each shoe for my great toe. Commander Štrok noticed this and promised he would try to obtain some leather and have a new pair of shoes made for me by the cobbler in the next village, but there was never time for that, for we moved too often. I looked on other Partisans' footwear. Some had old shoes, some had homemade leather moccasins and some had low boots, the same as the Ustaše, and I found out that they were taken from enemy soldiers. A few had high boots, and I was told that those were taken from Nazi German soldiers.

I did not understand our frequent movements, but I knew that the Ustaše, with the help of German Nazis, were always trying to flush the Partisans out of the villages. We were now further north, and the mountain Kalnik appeared bigger as we were closer. In some villages, the farmers were unfriendly, if not outright hostile, and we would move on, closer to the mountain. It was getting colder. Some days, to keep warm, I took from my bundle all the clothing I had and put it on. I had only a short jacket and short pants. I had my knee socks, which had long ago lost the bottom parts, but I still wore the woolen upper parts that were warm. My feet were now expertly wrapped with foot-wrappers, like those the peasants and Partisans wore. The Partisans were used to living without socks. In the evening, when they took off their shoes and unwrapped their feet, the foot rags made the room stink worse than a pigsty. If someone wanted to open a window, most of the others said, "No way!" Then someone would remind us of the old saying "Many died of cold, but no one ever died of stench," and the windows stayed shut.

We had occasional days of rest declared by the commander, and on those days, the Partisans washed their foot wrappers, underwear, and shirts, and hung them to dry. They sat around the stove in the room. Then I saw that even the biggest macho Partisan had yellow and brown on his underpants, and was therefore, just another "posranac" ("shitnik".) Some of the Partisans mended their shirts and sewed on new buttons that did not match. Then I remembered how orderly and clean the laundry in the boys' school was. Shirts and underwear were changed once a week, always on Sunday, and if one was careful, the shirt stayed clean till Wednesday. The nuns mended any rip and replaced missing buttons with matching ones, and clean laundry was brought back, neatly folded, each Friday. But now I was with people who were fighting for freedom, which was, I was told, most dear, important, and precious to the people, although it was not anything a hungry person could eat. It was not quite clear to me what the word "freedom" meant, but I understood that a dirty shirt collar or cold feet and hands, or hunger, seemed to Partisans quite acceptable if it was to bring them freedom. Freedom, they said, was worth dying for, but I still could not fully grasp what it was exactly about.

One afternoon, the Partisans caught an Ustaša and brought him to the staff house to be interrogated. It appeared that he was a farmer from the area, and he was unlucky enough to have gotten a few days of leave. He was unaware that Partisans were around, and naive enough to wear his uniform while walking home to join his family. Partisans in 1943 had few regular uniforms. Most had only parts of a uniform: a pair of pants or an altered jacket taken from an Ustaša or German soldier. Most Partisans looked like any farmer, except for the hat with three horns. That hat, which would betray them, they kept in their pockets whenever they moved through an unfamiliar area. They also kept their weapons well concealed. Peasants carried with them rolled-up blankets, which were perfect wraps for rifles. Among the Partisans, there were a few women, and they wore pants and did not look or act like peasants' wives at all. They must have come from the city. One of them was clearly Štrok's wife, but most of the time she stayed away from him.

In the headquarters, the captured prisoner was questioned by Commander Štrok and then much more by the political commissar of the brigade. All the prisoner's personal belongings were taken away, and some of his documents and his ID card were laid on the table. They let me look at them because, I was told, he would no longer need them. He was stripped to his underwear and bare feet, and his hands were tied behind his back. He begged the Partisans to let him go home, and promised not to ever return to his military unit. When the questioning was finished, the hapless prisoner was taken by two Partisans out of the house and into the woods. Then I heard a faint shot, and a while later, the two Partisans returned and reported that they made certain the Ustaša would never go back to his unit.

It was the end of November, and the nights were getting chilly. The days were crisp, with a blanket of thick fog covering the fields early in the morning. Frequently, it rained. Partisans had no umbrellas. They just kept walking in the rain as if nothing was happening, but they did put their caps or blankets over their heads. In time, they would dry by the heat of their bodies. I too used my blanket as a cover, and it got soaked, but I stayed warm, if somewhat damp.

One morning, I noticed that Kalnik had a white cap on its rocky top. One could smell the winter in the air. The trees had lost all their leaves. In every village, our unit commissar gathered all the farmers in the biggest barn they had, stood on a wooden box or chair so that everyone could see him, and gave a speech. It was always the same—about the need for brotherhood and unity of all poor, oppressed people, peasants and workers, about the fight for freedom, and the need to resist and fight the enemies of people who caused the war and looted food and livestock from the peasants, and how in the end, only communism would bring equality and well-being to everyone. They should join the fight! Some of the villagers asked questions, the commissar gave answers, and the farmers shook their heads and said that they needed to mull it over.

It was true that the Ustaše, too, often came to the same villages and took away (or "requisitioned") chickens, pigs, cows, horses, and any food they could lay their hands on. Ustaše also asked if anyone wanted to volunteer and join them. The farmers hated to leave their warm homes and their families.

By then, I had noticed that the political commissar, the "politkom," as he was called for short, was the first person to receive all the news and orders from the headquarters, not the brigade's commander, Štrok. The politkom then shared and discussed the news and orders with Commander Štrok, who dealt directly down the line with other officers who were responsible to pass on and explain the orders to all the Partisans. Whenever difficult questions arose, the politkom made the final decision. I tried to ask about these things, but the answers were above my head, and I gave up.

The Partisans in the brigade were mostly Serbian farmers who used to live in other parts of Croatia. Each had a story to tell. Their stories were strange and terrible, but vivid, and though they sounded incredible, others said they were true. These Serbs had apparently escaped the Ustaše, who came to their villages and killed most of the men, and in many places, killed women, and even small children. One said he watched from the neighboring hill as the villagers were herded and locked up in their church, the door was bolted, and the church with all the people inside was set afire. He hid in the woods, found more Serbs who escaped from his and other villages, and found and joined the Partisans. Another Partisan told a similar story. He was in his field working when the Ustaše came to his village. He saw them shoot some men, take the women into the house, and a while later chase the women, half-naked, into the yard and stab them with bayonets. He ran into the woods. At night, when he returned to the village, there was wailing all around by the surviving women who had come back from the fields. His wife and two boys were dead, and so were all the men and most of the other children caught in the village. Some women were only wounded, and they survived. The next day, he buried his wife and children, packed a bundle of clothing and dry food, and went to seek and join the Partisans.

Hearing those stories, I thought of my Mena and Tatek, and I hoped that nothing had happened to them. Only a few officers were with the Partisans from the very beginning of war in 1941. They sometimes told stories from those early days, when the Partisans had no arms, but used pitch forks, sickles, knives, axes, scythes, and spades. Here and there, they ambushed an Ustaša or German soldier, killed him with their crude farm implements, and stripped him of his arms, ammunition, and clothing.

Very few new men joined the Partisans during my stay with them. We were in an area where most of the Serbian villages had already been destroyed. A newly arrived person, before being issued a rifle and ammunition, was first questioned by the political commissar. Times were dangerous, there were spies around, and each new man's story had to be verified and corroborated. Most of the time, I hung around Commander Štrok, and he was never too far from the political commissar. They always worked together. One day, I asked the commissar to explain the meaning of "brotherhood," "unity," "freedom," "communism," and similar big words that he used. Those words were different from simple ones like "bread" or "bacon" or "water" or "dog" that one could eat, see, taste, hear, and feel.

Even the Partisans' official greeting involved big words. The person saluting first said, "Death to fascism!"

The reply was, "Freedom to the People!"

From the stories told by the politkom, I learned that all fascists were criminals and murderers, whether they were German Nazis, Ustaše, or Italians, and thus "fascism" was a mean thing. The commissar explained that "communism" was a good way of life where all people were equal, had as much food as they needed, and everyone could go to school and learn to read and write. With communism, no one was ever hungry or without a place to live, or without clothing; everyone had a job, the workers were well paid, and all people were happy.

Without realizing it, I had had my first lesson in Marxism. In the years after the war, I would learn a lot more about Marx and his ideas, both in theory and, alas, in actual practice. In the next several years, I would also find out what most of the big words that end and rhyme with "-ism" really meant, and this I leave to the reader's imagination.

From what the commissar said, communism sounded like a paradise on Earth, and I thought it would be nice. It sure sounded great. It reminded me of what I learned about Jesus, how he fed the hungry and shared with them everything, and how the first Christians were poor, and they shared what little they had. They had an easy time being equal with one another. But why were these communists against God? Why did they say that there was no God? Why did they not like the priests? Why did they curse the God and the saints? The Partisans' song went:

"Nosim kapu sa tri roga,
ne bojim se niti boga!"
(I wear a hat tripod,
an' don' fear even God!)

The priests, said the commissar, wanted the people to remain ignorant, unable to read and write. They wanted people to be obedient and kept poor, so that they would serve the rich. The priests wanted people to believe that there was another life after death, where they would enjoy plenty of everything they missed on Earth, and the more they suffered now, the better they would have it in heaven. The commissar said that nobody had seen the kingdom of heaven.

Such doubts and sinful thoughts were put into my mind, but I could not believe the least bit of it. The priests at the boys' school were good. Contrary to what the commissar said, the priests gladly taught and gave knowledge to all the boys, and they let me learn many new things. All of this was difficult to sort out, but I had a lot of time to think about it, and my head was churning. I did not dare say it, but Jesus also threw the rich merchants out of the temple, and he wanted everyone to have enough to eat and to be always truthful and good. And he could walk on water. The Christians, too, had to hide under the ground, yes, in the catacombs. Jesus started out as a human, and he seemed to have been preaching and doing things a little bit like a communist, but he was the son of God, and being younger, he had to listen to God the Father and the Holy Spirit, both of whom were older. I believed that the communists were right to fight the Ustaše and Nazis, but that they were mistaken about the God and priests. Still, not everything about God was clear to me, either, and I still had questions. I did not understand what exactly the two older Gods stood for, except that they wanted us all to be good and truthful. And why was the Holy Spirit always shown as a bird that resembled a pretty blue pigeon?

When I had such thoughts, I would go out of the staff house and into the barn where nobody could see me. I liked the barn. Inside, the air was warm from the animals, and there was no smell of cigarettes. I first checked that no one else was there, and then I cupped the first three fingers of my hand, brought them to my forehead, and silently crossed myself.

"In the name of the Father, and the Son, and the Holy Spirit, Amen." I immediately felt better. I believed what the priests had taught me, and I doubted much of what the commissar said. There was relief in placing oneself under the protection of a God so powerful that he was present everywhere at all times. He could be both one and three at the same time (the Holy Trinity), although this was something I could never figure out by looking at my three fingers and one finger all at the same time. Communism, though, did sound close to God, and I could not understand why it would not go along with Him. Was it because some priests and the nuns were occasionally not so nice? I had seen the commissar being very cross with people, and it did not seem that communists were good and nice all the time either. All my doubts and questions had to wait. I was told many times that there were things I would understand only later, when I grew up. Right then, I wished I could see what Mena and Tatek were doing. Did they have enough to eat and a warm soft bed? And oh, I wished I had a few sweet raisins, or a delicious banana to bite into, but there was the smell of the barn animals, and it was warm and calm. There was only a muffled sound of the cows ruminating; there would be milk, and the hens were silently producing eggs. The barn was a nice place, and I began to understand why He was born in a barn.

Then, one day, it was announced that before dawn we would start a very long march, about thirty miles (fifty kilometers), into the foothills of Kalnik. Everyone got ready for the march. On a straight road, Kalnik was quite close, less than ten miles away, but we had to avoid major roads and villages, which were full of Ustaše and their spies. Our plan was to go around and around, marching to our destination through the woods and over hills. The day was long, and I walked most of the time, riding with Commander Štrok on his horse only on a few short occasions. It was cold and snowing, but this was better than the rain and drizzle and mud of November. The ground was hard and frozen, and there was no mud to sink into or slip on. At the end of the day, I had fallen behind and was dragging along with the last group of Partisans, some of whom suffered from old wounds or limped. We arrived at our destination in the late afternoon, when it was dark. As we entered the village, I noticed that the sentries and guards were all in position. I was tired and wanted to sleep, but first I ate my ration of warm soup, dunking in my piece of hard, dry bread.

When I woke the next morning, my feet were burning. I looked and saw that I had lost the skin in several places on my insteps, where the leather shoelaces had cut into my flesh during the long hours of the march. I was too cold and too tired to notice anything when we arrived. The raw wounds were covered by yellow crusts and they still oozed pink and yellow liquid. My feet were swollen, and I could not put on the shoes. I showed my feet to Commander Štrok, and he looked up at the ceiling, then drew a deep puff from his cigarette and blew a few perfect rings of smoke into the air. He kept looking up for a while after the smoke rings disappeared. Did he believe in God a little bit? Finally, he again looked towards the floor, but he did not say anything. He was thinking of something. He seemed different from the political commissar. Then he said I had to stay in the house till my wounds healed, or I would be carried on a wagon with supplies. A little while later, a medic appeared with a white powder that he carefully spread over my wounds. The powder (most likely sulfonamide) stung and hurt me, but

I gritted my teeth and did not cry. Mixed with the wound secretions, the powder created a pasty yellow covering that within a day became a solid crust. When I had to go out to relieve myself in the snow, I wore only the foot wrappers tied with a string above the ankle. Then came the rumor that there would be another very long march in a day or two, and everybody got busy preparing for it. Commander Štrok came to me and said that with my wounds, I could not walk, and the Partisans could not carry me. It was decided, he said, I had to stay back for a while till my wounds healed. The evening before the march, Štrok had me carried into a "safe house," where I would stay hidden. I had to remain strictly indoors, so no one in the village would know that I was there. The house belonged to a farmer who could be trusted. The following morning, while I was still sleeping, the Partisans left the village, and this time, I did not know where they went.

I don't know exactly how many days I spent in that house, but it was at least two or three weeks, and I do not remember the name of the village or the farmer who hid me. They kept me well, though I had to stay all the time inside the house. I was given a little chamber pot, a large metal can from food rations, and that reminded me of my stay in Dragoševci. My wounds slowly healed, and I was able to put on my shoes, but I could not lace them up. The women in the house spun large clumps of sheep wool, and I learned to help spin the yarn. There was no kerosene for the lamps, and there were very few candles, which had to be used sparingly. As it got dark outside, everyone went to sleep early. There was deep snow in the yard, but the room was kept warm, and the food was good. One day, a horse-drawn sled appeared in the yard, and a few minutes later, Msgr. Petranović entered the room. He spoke to the farmer, and then told me to dress warmly, for he was taking me on the sled to go back to the boys' school. On the way back, Msgr. Petranović told me never to tell anyone that I was with the Partisans. If asked by someone who saw me with them, I had to say that I was kidnapped from Lepavina and left in a village. He also told me that the bishop received a message from Commander Štrok, asking that he send someone to take me back to the boys' school as soon as it was possible to travel in the area. I felt betrayed and disappointed, but I knew that I had to show how glad I was to go back to the school. Only a few years after the war did I realize that Commander Štrok, by then an army general, did me a favor when he decided to leave me in the village safe house. It also became clear to me that Štrok was a Jew and that after talking to me and seeing my physical appearance, he must have guessed that I was a Jewish child from the city, and that my Croat name was nothing but a disguise. Štrok must have also understood that Bishop Šimrak presented a better shelter for a child of my age than the Partisans.

A LITTLE FARM HAND IN THE BISHOPRY

When I returned to the boys' school, it was the middle of winter, after Christmas and New Year, and I had missed out on all the celebrations and the days with good food. The boys assumed that I had just stayed a little longer in Lepavina. Some of the boys commented that the food in Lepavina did not seem to agree with me, for I seemed thinner than when I left. I explained that I had a bout of diarrhea, which was true. The wounds on my feet had healed, but I still needed a pair of larger shoes. The scars on my insteps are still there, now hardly perceptible. The nuns eventually obtained new shoes for me, and naturally, they were made much too large so that I would not outgrow them too soon. I had to stuff the entire front of each shoe with rags, and then I had to learn to walk in them without tripping. Anyway, during most of the next spring, summer, and fall, I walked barefoot, like most other peasant boys. I gladly returned to the rules and orderly life of the boys' school. Again, I could freely cross myself before eating, sleep in a nice bed, have regular meals, follow the dorm schedule, and know what day of the week it was. The boys sometimes teased me because they said, I talked and even screamed in my sleep. They woke me up and asked what was the matter. I could not remember anything, but I knew I had bad dreams, and I worried that I might reveal my secret of having been with the Partisans. Cousin Pavle once heard me talking in my sleep and he told me the next morning that all I said was gibberish, impossible to understand, except for a few single words that made no sense. That put me at ease. It was winter, the food in the boys' school was again very meager, and each day it got worse. We got used to feeling hungry most of the time, except for a short while immediately after lunch.

During summer, there were always fresh vegetables, and now and then a piece of pork, beef, rabbit from our own hutches, or rarely, chicken. In winter, however, vegetables were not available, the stock of potatoes was sufficient for once a week on Sundays, and most days it was beans (those elongated brown ones), or turnips, or again beans, and occasionally cabbage. Beans do, of course, contain some protein, but those beans also had with them some meat. Floating among them were little, white, elongated pieces of something that turned out to be worms. With the wormy beans, there were usually pieces of dried pork rind with bits of attached lard, and this gave us calories. The bread was now black, made of coarsely milled mixed grains, which produced a coarse, dark brown flour, with very little or no wheat at all, or we had a yellow cornbread made entirely of corn flour. The older boys decided one day to catch some pigeons in the bell tower. Pigeons are as tasty as a small chicken, and since, unlike the fowl, the pigeons were not counted, it would not be like stealing anything. The boys climbed the bell tower in the late afternoon when it was getting dark carrying long poles with attached nets normally used for picking apples and pears from the high branches of fruit trees. On several tries, there was no luck. The pigeons heard them and flew away.

On one occasion, they caught two pigeons, but found that plucking them and roasting them on an open fire was not easy, and the small amount of meat was hardly worth the trouble.

In the spring of 1944, some of the older boys in the school whispered about good news from the war front. It appeared that the Nazi Germans were being beaten in Russia and had been chased out of Africa. Their ally Italy had given up and capitulated in 1943. The Americans were slowly coming north through Italy. We sometimes saw huge airplanes flying over high up in the sky, obviously on a bombing mission somewhere in Germany. Everyone was asking when the war would finally end. No one knew the answer, and apparently, there was no sign of an end in our area. The bunkers and trenches in the pasture in front of our compound were always fully manned, for there were rumors that the Partisans were seen in areas close to town. I had a hard time keeping my secret, and on one occasion, when we were alone, I told Pavle that I had been with the Partisans. He just told me to keep quiet.

In the meantime, I became a little farm hand. At noon, I carried two cans with drinking water to the hired workers in the fields. I also got a new job. I was entrusted to take the cows to pasture, watch them, and herd them back to the sty for milking. The cows were milked twice a day: early in the morning and again in the late afternoon. They gave much more milk when they spent the day grazing in the pasture than in winter, when they ate just the hay from the loft.

My hands were still too weak and small to milk the udders, but I lingered around during the milking hour and occasionally got a bit of fresh warm milk to drink from the milkmaid. It was delicious. I can remember the names of only two cows, Luna and Beba. Beba had the biggest udder and gave the most milk. Luna was white with large, red-brown blotches, with the horns pointing forward, rather than to the side. She was relatively small and gave no trouble. One day while grazing, however, Luna lifted her head from the grass and looked at me for several moments, then slowly lowered her head. She was about a hundred feet away, and she started walking toward me faster and faster, and then started running. This appeared menacing, and I turned, looked around, and ran for the nearest tree, which was luckily growing on a sharp angle, so that I could run up the short trunk and lift myself up onto the first branch. Luna stopped below the tree, looked up at me, and then slowly turned around and started grazing as if nothing had happened. I was scared. One of the farm hands saw this, came to the tree, chased Luna a bit further away, and helped me down. He then looked at me and said that I should never wear a red sweater around the cows. I learned something. That red sweater would never see a cow again.

I became much more confident and started to play jokes and pranks on the bigger boys. To pay me back, one hot summer Sunday, while I was taking an afternoon nap in our cool dorm room, the boys locked the door from outside and left me stuck in the room for the whole afternoon. They went to have fun somewhere outside. When I woke up, I could not get out of the room and did not know what to do. Suddenly, I opened the large upper door of the stove in the wall and checked it out: my head and shoulders could easily go through. I crawled into the stove, pushed open the door on the other side of the wall into the empty classroom, and I was free. I crawled back into the stove and pulled the dorm side door shut. Then I crawled back out to the classroom and went to the bathroom to wash off the ashes and soot, and went downstairs to the barn. No one had seen me come out, so I stayed and played in the barn storage room for the rest of the afternoon. Late in the afternoon, when the boys returned to the dorm, they unlocked the door, but could not find me anywhere in the room. They searched all the cabinets and chests, the beds, and under the beds, but I was not there. We were on the third floor, and the windows were open. They looked down in the yard, and then went to search the yard. The ductor searched, too. They were afraid to tell the priests that I had disappeared while locked in.

Just before evening, I quietly walked up to our dorm room. The boys were huddled in the middle of the large room, their backs to me, talking excitedly. The one who saw me first opened his mouth, popped out both of his eyes, and remained speechless, just pointing his finger at me. Then the others turned and saw me. Ductor and Pavle jumped at me and hugged me. They wanted to know if I had a long rope to get down through the window. But how would I from the third floor? Did I string up the bed sheets? None was missing. Was there a duplicate key? But that was impossible, for no other key fit, and besides, when a key was turned and left in the lock on the outside, no key could be inserted into the same lock from the inside.

For the longest time, I let them ask and guess—all wrong. When it was enough, I went to the stove, opened the door wide, and leaned in with my head and shoulders. They looked on in amazement. From then on, the older boys had a way to get out of the dorm for a night on the town or a date, even though the priest locked the door from the outside. This could be done only in spring, summer, and fall, when the stove was not used for heating. I unlocked the door for them to leave after the priest had gone; at midnight, they came back and woke me, and I went through the stove, locked our door from the outside, and came back in to sleep. In the early morning, the priest found everything in order and unlocked the door.

One summer night, there was a big storm, and a large old cherry tree fell down. In the morning, the cherries were all for the taking. Normally, the cherries were collected little by little, as they gradually ripened and were divided among many takers. We never had too many. This time there was an abundance of cherries, and I ate all I could, for this was an opportunity not to be missed. By the afternoon, I felt a bit heavy and strange and went to the dorm room to stay in bed. After a while, I felt sick and walked towards the bathrooms. The hallway seemed awfully long, and suddenly I could not hold it any more. I heaved and started throwing up, and all the way along as I lurched towards the bathrooms, the red cherries kept spewing out of me. Just as I turned to pass through the bathroom door, from the corner of my eye I saw the bishop turning the corner and coming down from the opposite side of the corridor.

As I quietly rested in the bathroom, I heard the bishop outside in the hallway loudly saying, "Who could have made this geographic map?"

A nun appeared with a pail and a mop, and the geography I painted on the floor was cleaned up. The hallway tiles shined again.

That same summer, my job with the chickens was expanded. I was taught how to select eggs for hatching chicks. We darkened a room, lit a candle, and looked through the egg towards the light. If there was a solid dark spot inside the egg, it was good to put it under the hens for hatching. The unfertilized eggs were put back into storage to serve as food. The hens sat for about three weeks before the chicks started hatching. After the chicks hatched, they were put into a special, warm, dry room. Soon they would be able to follow their hen all across the courtyard.

There I got the first lesson in bonding, although at the time I had no clue what the word meant. The geese and ducks did not have the patience to sit on their eggs, and nothing ever hatched from under them. The nuns decided to put the eggs from geese and ducks under the hens. This actually worked, though the goose eggs were so big that a hen could sit on only two eggs. We could fit five of the ducks' eggs under one hen. When they hatched, there would be a proud hen walking over the yard with two goslings or four to five ducklings following her. We tried to introduce the ducklings to the ducks, but to no avail. There was a little problem when the ducklings and goslings discovered the pond, waddled into the water, and started swimming. The hens were left standing at the edge of the water. However, as soon as the ducklings came out of the water, they would again follow the hen. This went on for almost three months, until the ducklings and goslings became independent and started associating with their own kind.

Not all of the hens' eggs hatched. Some just spoiled and turned into rotten eggs, or they contained a dead chick that never hatched. The hens' nests had to be cleared of those unhatched eggs. For the cleanup, the nuns had a giant wicker basket into which the spoiled eggs were collected to be carried and thrown onto the manure pile at the side of the barn.

At the end of the hatching season, I had to fill the wicker basket with all the unhatched eggs. I needed the help of another boy, an eleven-year-old, to carry the basket to the dung heap. Both of us were out of breath from the heavy load, and we stood for a while by the manure pile to rest. The white stucco wall on the side of the barn had a round vent hole, the size of a large pumpkin, right in the middle of the triangular space under the peak of the roof. This opening gave air and light to the hayloft. Looking at the round vent hole high up on the wall, we had the same thought: it would be fun to try to toss an egg or two through that hole. One at the time, we threw the eggs toward the hole, but we kept missing.

Soon, the whitewashed stucco wall had green and yellow blotches, with slimy stuff from spoiled eggs oozing down. With our misses we created a nice even pattern around the vent hole, though we had no clue about bell shaped curves or statistics. Meanwhile the runny rotten eggs on the wall began to spread a stench that was worse than the dung heap below. We managed to toss an occasional egg through the hole into the hay, and of course, we carefully kept score. We had emptied half of the eggs from the huge basket when we noticed the bishop approaching from the orchard below us. He was returning from his afternoon walk through the fields, and as he climbed the hill, with every step he swung his walking stick. We quickly grabbed the wicker basket and turned it over to empty the remaining eggs onto the manure pile. I don't know whether the bishop first smelled the eggs, or he saw the colorful design on the barn wall, but he stopped near us and for a long moment he observed the wall. Then he looked at the two of us, and we stood frozen, shivering with fear.

He mumbled something that sounded like, "A nice paint job," and then turned and briskly walked away. To this day, I do not know whether he hurried away due to the stench of the rotten eggs, or because he did not want to reveal that he saw a bit of humor in that whole scene. Now, decades later, whenever I see certain large, "postmodern" paintings made by artists who I will not mention, I am reminded of the lively design moving down that wall. Curiously, we never received any punishment. The following week, after the barn wall had well dried and the stench had largely dissipated, a farm hand with a ladder applied two fresh coats of white paint. Whitewashed with paint, the entire incident was soon forgotten.

The nights that summer were unusually noisy. We kept the windows open to get some cool fresh night air, and we heard sporadic rifle shots, probably from the soldiers in the bunkers, who would see something moving in the dark and out of fear start shooting. We got used to it and stopped paying attention. Other night noises were the rhythmic muffled shouts of hundreds of people. It was rumored that the Partisans, during the night, came to the railroad tracks and with large crowbars lifted the rails off the tracks so that the Ustaše and Nazis could no longer use the rail for transit. To get a better leverage, the Partisans all yelled in unison, "Ho-o-o-rook," and that on the "rook," the rails flew down the embankment. It was also rumored that the Americans were in France, marching towards Germany.

At the end of the summer of 1944, I got a new job helping harvest the honey from the beehives. A man in a special protective suit approached the beehives and opened them one by one. The bees buzzed all around him and slowly left. Then the honeycombs and honey were removed. Putting the honey into jars was a delightful job, for in the end, I could lick some of it. The honeycombs with some honey remaining in them were then placed into the beehives before the bees were let back in to settle for the winter.

With the fall approaching, peasants from surrounding villages delivered cords of firewood to the courtyard to be split and piled up in the storage area of the barn. While I loitered in the yard, a peasant started staring at me. Then he said I looked familiar, and he was almost sure he had seen me somewhere. He kept asking if I was ever in his village. I did not know him, and I said that I never was out of the bishopry or the close-by fields.

All of a sudden, the peasant remembered. He claimed that he saw me with the Partisans in his village about a year before. I said it was just not possible. It was a tense moment, but I stuck to my denial and slowly walked away, out of the courtyard. From then on, whenever I saw the peasants coming to deliver wood or anything else, I went inside the building and watched from the window till they all left. It was a close call. Villagers from the neighboring area couldn't be allowed to see me again.

In the fall of 1944, after the summer recess ended, there were only twelve boys left in the school. Three had finished in the spring and another three had failed to return from the recess, and apparently, no new boys had joined for the coming year. That fall, I was quartered in the smaller of the two dorm rooms, the one with only six beds. There were all sorts of rumors—the war would end soon, the Allies were advancing on all fronts (in Poland, in France, and in Italy, and soon would be on German soil), the Partisans had under their control most of the countryside in Yugoslavia except for a few major towns and cities. Now that the outcome of the war seemed clear, the Croats, it was rumored, were joining the Partisans in great numbers. It was also rumored that some of the older boys who had not returned to school had joined them.

One morning, I woke up from a lot of noise, and when I looked through the window of the dorm room, I saw the courtyard full of German soldiers. The nuns in the kitchen were excited and busy preparing the meals. The bishop had guests; obviously, the German officers were quartered in some of the upstairs guest rooms, next to the priests. The precious little food that was still available was being given to the guests. I was told that guests should always be honored, especially now that it may be the last time we see them. Everyone thought, "Good riddance," but that could not be said. Besides, everyone knew that when the army requisitioned a place, it was better to treat the soldiers as guests. After breakfast, when I went outside, I saw that the orchards were full of German cars, trucks, cannons, small tanks, and armored vehicles, and numerous, large military tents with several hundred soldiers. I loitered around the soldiers' tents and listened. Their conversation was all about getting home soon and safe, and "getting out of this filthy damned land."

They never dreamed that a little boy in the middle of the wild Balkan could possibly understand them. Within two days, the German unit moved on. It took three more days to clean up the mess they left. Quite a few of our chickens and a few ducks were missing, but no one seemed to mind. We were all happy our guests had left without causing more damage.

Not long after that, in the middle of the night, I suddenly woke up. A tremendous noise was coming from outside the building. I listened, and it sounded like a lot of shooting in the nearby fields. The shooting was heavier than ever before. The other five beds in the dorm room were empty. I got scared. Was I having a bad dream, a nightmare?

I rubbed my eyes. This was real! I recognized the "rat-at-at" of the machine gun, and between the single shots from rifles, the "ka-boom" of exploding mortar shells and the "boom" of the small cannon. Occasional stray shots were stopped by the thick outer wall of the building, the one facing the pastures and fields with the bunkers and trenches. Now I was fully awake and all alone in the room. This was a Partisan night attack. They were trying to take the town. I knew the walls were very thick, and the only danger was being hit through the window. The cannon fire had to be coming from the defending batteries. All this flashed through my mind in a couple of seconds. I slid out of bed, crouched down on the floor, and went on all fours out of the room, into the corridor, a safe area. I ran down the hallway, and down three flights of stairs to the basement shelter. The door to the cellar was not locked, as usual. It was wide open.

I ran down the stairs into the basement, and there were all the boys, the priests, the nuns, and the bishop, all giving me that look: where on earth have you been? Obviously, in the rush and confusion, they awakened one another and ran to the basement as fast as they could. It was dark, and no one noticed I was missing. My sleep in those days was very sound, and it took a little extra cannon fire to wake me up.

We all stood barefoot in our nightshirts on the cold basement floor, shivering. Muffled noises from the firefight could be still heard. The storage area nearby was wide open, and we consoled ourselves by eating apples. Gradually, the noises became scattered, never ceasing entirely. Two of the younger priests went up first to see what happened. After a while, they returned. The attack had been repelled, and the town had stayed in the possession of the Ustaše. Our compound had a couple of broken windows, and the next day we saw the gunfire pockmarks in the stucco of the building, but there was no serious damage.

More and more frequently, we saw large allied warplanes flying high over us, carrying out bombing missions north of our area, perhaps in Germany or other Nazi-occupied territories. Then we saw them again flying south, obviously to their base in Italy. They usually flew in formation and very high. These large airplanes had four engines. I was told that those were the bombers. Less often, we saw smaller fighter planes. They sometimes flew low over the hills, buzzing just overhead, scaring us with their noise. These peculiar planes had a double body, their tails joined by a small rear wing. One bright, sunny day, I observed a lone, large, four-engine plane gleaming in the sun, returning south. It was not as high as usual, and it seemed to move slowly. As I watched, four tiny white dots peeled off and floated in the air. After a few moments, four more dots were visible: these were parachutes. The next moment, the body of the plane was afire; the plane turned slowly, twisting upside down, a burning wing fell off, and all started falling, finally disappearing from view behind the wooded hills. The eight white dots slowly also disappeared into the woods behind the horizon.

The next day, an enormous airplane wheel was brought to the main square of the town, a trophy to show that an enemy plane was brought down, but the airmen were never caught, and they were most likely rescued by the Partisans.

Soon, winter was again upon us. The food shortage was worse than ever, and we were constantly hungry. This time, even the nuns exhausted their last reserves of stored food. One skinny cow that was practically dying of old age was slaughtered, but the meat did not go very far, and it was like eating shoe soles. Everyone talked about the war ending, but no one said whether it was won or lost. Somehow, it seemed that no matter who "won", the war had brought losses to everyone.

With my friend at the boys' school, winter 1944/45

Then, one day in the early spring of 1945, we heard that the Partisans had entered the city without a fight. The war was officially still going on, only somewhere else, further to the west. The outer doors of the compound were locked, and everyone was very tense.

A Little Farm Hand In The Bishopry

The next day, someone knocked on the main door. The older boys from our school who had joined the Partisans had come to visit and thank the bishop for his kindness. They showed off to us younger boys with their uniforms and guns. What a change: the Partisans now had regular uniforms and wore their tripod hats on their heads, and did not hide them in a pocket. We all spent a few happy moments together. Now I could say that I was with the Partisans before any of them. There was no food left to offer them, and soon they had to move on with their units, "to help liberate other parts of the country." A few days later, another group of Partisans knocked on the door. When let in, they gruffly asked to be led through the entire compound and they thoroughly searched every nook and corner. Finding no hidden people or food or weapons, they arrested the bishop, who by then was in his seventies and quite ill. He had diabetes and a weak heart. The priests protested and explained that, yes, the Germans did camp at the bishopry, but who could resist or refuse them? They also explained that the bishop did, at great, personal peril during the war, shelter several Greek-Orthodox Serbs who would have been otherwise killed by the Ustaše. The priests said that these same boys had joined the Partisans to fight against the Nazis and Ustaše, and just a few days before had paid a friendly visit and thanked the bishop.

All arguments were to no avail. The bishop was "a collaborator with the Ustaše and Nazis" and had to be taken in for further questioning. It was a "Communist Party order," and there was to be no discussion.

END OF WAR: THE LONG SUMMER OF 1945

We got word from Uncle Stanislav in Zagreb that everyone at home was well, and he would come to pick up Pavle and myself as soon as he could secure transportation. No trains were running, since Partisans had destroyed most of the rails. In the meantime, the school year ended a little early, and the remaining boys said good-bye and went home. Pavle and I were left alone to wait for Uncle Stanislav. The war in Europe officially ended within a few weeks, on May 8, 1945. It was another two weeks before Uncle Stanislav was able to find a small pick-up truck for hire.

When he arrived, we hugged and kissed him, and while our few belongings were loaded on the truck, Pavle and I said good-bye to the nuns and priests. There were tears in parting with the nuns. We had to hurry; the truck was rented only for the day. On the way back, the driver, Uncle Stanislav, and I sat in the cabin, and Pavle rode in the back of the truck with our belongings. The truck was old, and it rattled slowly along the rutted dirt road. About two-thirds of the way to Zagreb, just on the outskirts of the town of Zelina, the truck had a flat tire. The driver had no spare tire and had to go all over town to find one at great expense, and that had to be covered by Uncle Stanislav. Two and a half hours later, we finally reached the paved road and I knew we were close to Zagreb. We arrived home with the first darkness of the evening. Aunt Ester was already worried. She hugged and kissed us, immediately sent Pavle to strip in the toilet, and told him to go straight to the large bathroom and take a hot bath in the tub. I was meanwhile inspected, and I saw the horror in Aunt Ester's expression. I was thin and looked sick, with a large, nearly shaven head. I was dirty, my nails were filthy, and so it went with Aunt Ester's sharp observations. In so many words, it was "a disgrace how bad I looked". I was stripped right in the entry hallway, and all my clothes were put in a paper bag to be thrown away. My protests went unheeded. Aunt Ester kept grousing over my appearance.

"Er sieht aus wie ein Wilder," she kept saying ("he looks like a savage") until Uncle Stanislav told her it was enough. I just thought how lucky Pavle was to be a grown-up. He got to be the first to take a bath, and had for the moment escaped Aunt Ester's sharp eye and tongue. When my turn came for the bath, of course, I was to use Oliver's bath water. Hot water was a sparse commodity; one tubful was customarily used for a two-person bath, one after the other. Aunt Ester gave me a good scrub in the tub using a big brush with sharp bristles. The water after Pavle was gray, sudsy, and not so warm any more, but I was supposed to enjoy it, for it was my "first real bath since 1942." Scrubbing me clean made Aunt Ester happy, but ingrate that I was, I did not like it at all, and I screamed and cried and complained because it felt as if she was trying to remove not only the dirt, but also the skin underneath it.

The next several days were very confusing. I was again Isac—or as they used to call me, "Izzyly"—and Pavle was again Oliver. I tried to forget about being

"Petar" or "Peritsa," but I could not. For a long time, Petar, with all the images from the war would come and inhabit my mind. There was no way to stop him or wipe him out. No wonder: Petar means "the rock."

With time, his visits became less frequent, but I did not mind his presence. Remembering him I felt good. Petar became like an old friend. I did not want to forget him. Quietly and fondly, Petar still resides in me. He will remain a part of me for as long as I live. I am happy to have known him: he helped keep me alive.

Again, like when I was with the Partisans, I tried not to cross myself before eating, but the habit was too strong. I would automatically start crossing myself, and then disguise it by scratching my forehead. Aunt Ester noticed, though, and she would laugh and say I need not worry about it. She told me that all during the war, she, too, had a large picture of the Blessed Virgin Mary with Christ the Child hanging over her bed, and a Christ on the Cross over her night table. When the war ended, she took both pictures off the wall and put them in the furthest corner of the attic storage bin, facing the wall. We did not need to be Catholic any more, and with the communists around, it was better not to show any sign of religion. That was easy to say, and I understood it, but it was hard to stop doing what had become an automatic motion. To erase this reflex, I had to do a lot of hard thinking and concentrate to avoid making mistakes. Forgetting and suppressing religious thought and belief was not as easy as scrubbing the dirt off my skin. It was difficult, because I had to sort out what to do with my beliefs about God, the Holy Trinity, the suffering saints, and the martyrs. What was to become of the celebration on my name's saint's day, St. Peter and Paul, on June 29 of each year? In time, I would sort it all out, but I needed to do a lot of thinking to find the right answers to all these questions.

In the background however, the biggest question on my mind was where Tatek and Mena were, but in those first days at home, I did not dare ask. I knew the trains were still not running, and if I waited a little longer, they might just come back home. One day, Uncle Stanislav said he wanted to talk to me about Tatek. He said he heard what happened to Tatek during the war: a person released from Jasenovac in 1941 knew Tatek and saw him in the camp. One day, a camp guard hit Tatek with a metal bar on the head and after that, Tatek was taken to his cot in a barrack and he lay there for a few days, and then he died. This seems to have happened shortly after the Professor obtained a promise from one of his acquaintances in the government that an order for Tatek's release would be sent to Jasenovac. Uncle Stanislav heard that often, when an order to release a person arrived in Jasenovac, that person would have an "accident." He heard the bad news just a few days before Mena and I were discovered by the Italian militia and sent back to Zagreb, and he did not have a chance to tell this to Mena before. So I realized that all this happened despite the fact that Tatek had changed his first and last name to a Croat one and had become a Catholic.

Since the war had ended eight weeks before, it was now clear why Tatek was not coming back. I asked that the spelling of my last name be changed to the

End Of War: The Long Summer Of 1945

original "Meier," and Uncle Stanislav said he would take steps to do it on all my current documents. Unlike Opapa Meier, who was buried in the Jewish section of the Mirogoj cemetery in Zagreb, Tatek did not even have a grave. The big question now was where was my dear Mena? After the one postcard from Germany, there was no further news from her or Aunt Bella. Uncle Stanislav had already put in a search through the Red Cross, and he had been informed that there were hundreds of thousands of displaced persons all over Europe. Towards the end of the war, many people found alive in Nazi concentration camps were very sick and so weak from starvation that they had to be taken to hospitals. It might be several months before the survivors were well enough to travel home. I worried, because it was also said that some of the liberated people were so sick that they died, despite medical care. I had to wait and hope that Mena had survived and would return. Oh, if only Mena would come back. I thought there was still a chance that she was alive. Oliver, too, was waiting to see if his mom, Aunt Bella, would return, but we did not talk about it.

*   *   *

I want to describe the home of my adolescence, the place I spent the last days with Mena, the apartment of Uncle Stanislav and Aunt Ester, where I lived for the next fourteen years. The apartment lay in a quiet, residential part of Zagreb, on a small street that was not entirely paved. It was a few blocks from the nearest tram stop and a quarter-hour walk from the center of the city. The six-story building was quite modern, completed in 1938, one of the last to be finished before the war. We were on the third floor and had an elevator at our disposal. Each floor had a landing with two mirror-image apartments. Our apartment had three large rooms, an entry foyer, a small "maid's room" with a sink, and a large eat-in kitchen with an attached small pantry, the one in which Mena hugged and kissed me for the last time. The kitchen had a small balcony with metal prongs for drying the laundry, and the family room had a covered balcony large enough to hold a table and chairs. The apartment had one small toilet room off the foyer, and off the family room was a large bathroom with a tub, a bidet, and a sink. The kitchen faced south, whereas the master bedroom and the living/dining room faced north, and since there was no tall building on the north side of the street, there was a beautiful view of the mountain Sljeme north of the city and in the foreground was a tall church bell tower that was a few blocks away. One could look straight through the window and tell the time on the bell tower clock even from the far end of the room, or check if there was snow on top of the mountain. The layout and size of this apartment was very similar to the one I lived in with my parents before the war.

The kitchen had gas for a small two-place burner, and the bathroom had a wall-mounted gas heater providing instant hot water. The cooking was done on a large wood- or coal-burning kitchen stove, which had a steel plate with removable metal rings and a wide edge made of stainless steel that had to be polished daily.

The fire in this stove also served to heat the kitchen in winter, and by the evening, the kitchen was pretty cold. The kitchen stove also had a baking oven, and under it a nook for wood storage. The icebox was kept in the foyer, close to the entry. The apartment was heated by three tiled, wood- or coal-burning stoves, one in each room. The maid's room and the bathroom were heated with small electric space heaters.

Each apartment had in the basement a padlocked stall for storing wood and coal, and a large box for potatoes. There was a similar, individual, locked storage stall for furniture, suitcases, and other items in the attic. In the basement was a common laundry room with a stove that could hold a large cauldron, in which the white laundry was literally boiled and bleached. The laundry room was reserved ahead, and the laundry done once a month in a twelve-hour day, with the aid of a laundry maid. The laundry dried in the courtyard, which had sufficient space and posts for many yards of rope. An ironing maid came after the laundry was dried, and she again spent the whole day ironing and folding.

The apartment building had a flat roof with a terrace on which one could take in a little sun and a shower. The steel and glass entry door from the street was always locked, and there was a bell for each apartment in the entryway. The bells had an intercom that was often not functioning. When someone rang from downstairs, we first checked through the street window to see who was standing at the entrance, and then we went downstairs to open the door. The apartment building was the last one built on our block, and it had the largest courtyard. The adjoining older buildings had their backyards enclosed by tall concrete walls, often with a bit of barbed wire or glass shards on top.

Our building had, in addition to the paved courtyard directly in the back, an extended open area taking up the whole center of the city block, covered with grass and weeds. From that area, we had access to other courtyards on the block, if one climbed over the wall. In one corner of this open courtyard was a low building serving various gatherings or lectures. In the evenings, it became a dance hall with a big side terrace. If one climbed on the wall at the back corner of that building, one could look directly inside the dance hall through an open vent above the stage. The neighborhood boys often climbed up to see what was going on.

Our apartment was furnished with a mix of modern and older, traditional furniture. Most of it was familiar. Right after the war ended, Uncle Stanislav went to my grandparents' house and found most of my parents' and grandparents' furniture. The Ustaše occupants who moved into grandpa's house had apparently fled in a great hurry. Uncle Stanislav took the furniture back and used it to replace his own, which was not in such good shape. I recognized with some delight that in the master bedroom we had my parents' complete bedroom; in the dining/living room, we had the table, chairs, and two ebony credenzas from my grandparents' dining room and two couches from my parents' family room. In the family room, we had a desk set, the upright piano, and the glass display cabinet ("die Vitrine") from my grandparents, as well as a new couch, chairs, and small cocktail table.

End Of War: The Long Summer Of 1945

Grandpa's old display cabinet had beautiful figurines and other crystal and porcelain objects left from Tatek's store, all lined up on several glass shelves. On the walls, I recognized most of the paintings from my parents' apartment, and some from the grandparents' house. Most of the Persian rugs from our home and from grandpa were salvaged and placed in our apartment. My parents' familiar record player with the picture of the dog and a tuba and all the records were also saved.

It all made me feel very much at home, but it also constantly reminded me of my parents and grandparents. An album and a shoebox of my parents' photographs from before the war had been saved in Uncle Stanislav's apartment, and I loved to look at the pictures. Mena and Tatek looked beautiful, and I hoped Mena was alive and would someday return.

Our apartment was occupied to its full capacity: Uncle Stanislav and Aunt Ester slept in the master bedroom, their son Michael slept in the maid's room, Bluma slept on the couch in the family room, and Oliver and I slept on the two couches in the living/dining room. Michael graduated from high school in 1944, and without telling his parents, immediately left home to join the Partisans. He was nearly eleven years older than I was, and he returned home a week before Oliver and I came back from the boys' school. We soon learned that he was in serious trouble. Upon returning home, he took off his Partisan military uniform and stayed in his parents' apartment. He forgot to ask for a formal demobilization and was nearly declared a deserter. Aunt Ester and Uncle Stanislav were quite worried and had long discussions on what to do about it.

Michael had a few Partisan friends who still wore the uniform and were well-connected members of the Communist Party. They frequently came to our apartment and were always offered the best food we had, and coffee and cigarettes, precious commodities right after the war. These friends helped Michael get out of the mess. Unfortunately, Michael's friends also brought to our apartment the same tenants Paul and I were familiar with. No one could tell them to strip, go take a bath, and put on clean underwear. Aunt Ester now had to worry about getting rid of the fleas. There were also a few occasional bedbugs. We got some DDT, and although sometimes we had so much DDT on our bed sheets that in the mornings we looked as if we were working in a flour mill, the pests were never completely eradicated. A year later, a drastic measure would be taken to get rid of this nuisance.

Oliver and I had to make up for our lost formal schooling. Oliver went to the Partisan High School, a special school established immediately after the war for youngsters who were with the Partisans or otherwise detained from school due to the war. That school offered two years' worth of classes in one school year, and if one was willing to attend school throughout the summer, it was possible to make up an additional year's worth of classes. Many of the youth in that school were older and already members of the Communist Party. Many students at Partisan High School formed gangs that roamed the city in the evenings and behaved like hooligans. Gang members used to beat up local youths simply because the locals during the war lived at home and attended regular schools, while the gang members spent time in the woods with the Partisans and fought to liberate the country. The gangs were "well connected," and no matter what felony they committed, the police would not interfere. Graduates of Partisan High School continued their gang activities while attending university, where they used to terrorize and intimidate the professors who failed them on exams.

Regular city schools had the summer recess, and since I was too young for the Partisan High School, I was taken to the home of a local elementary school teacher, Mr. Bubaš, who gave me an exam to determine into what grade I fit. He checked my reading, writing, and math skills.

Before the exam, I was worried and anxious, but once the teacher started asking me to read and answer questions, I calmed down, answered his questions, and passed the exam. Mr. Bubaš told Uncle Stanislav that over the summer, I should read a little about the history of the country and study some local geographic maps, and in the fall, he would accept me into the fourth grade in our neighborhood elementary school. I was relieved on one hand, but also worried. How would I keep up in a class where all the kids attended regular school for previous three years? Would these kids ever accept me and be my friends?

The summer of 1945 was a busy one, and the time passed rapidly. Soon after I came home, Aunt Ester took me to a doctor who took x-rays of my chest and found "a shadow" on my lung. It was clear what that meant. It was the most common illness in the country, the doctor said, and I did not need any treatment whatsoever; I just needed plenty of rich food like butter, milk, cheese, and meat and the shadow would pass all by itself. Nevertheless, Aunt Ester was worried, and she was not pleased at all.

I had TB, and 95% of people exposed to it healed naturally. There was no known medication for TB in 1945 in Yugoslavia. Aside from that, the doctor said that my eyes were red, and the next day I was taken to an eye doctor, who gave me some drops that made my eyes even redder. Aunt Ester threw out the eye drops and gave me plenty of good food.

From the first moment, Aunt Ester was in full command of my medical recovery. She made sure that good food was available, no matter what it cost and no matter how hard it was to find. She also made sure I ate like never before. During that first year after the war, I was often troubled by being favored at the table. Aunt Ester gave me extra food, while others who were older and bigger and had bigger appetites sat at the table and said nothing. Some days, when food was sparse, Aunt Ester first divided it evenly onto everyone's plate, and then she cut off a piece of her own meat and put it on my plate. This was unpleasant, and I did not know what to do about it. At least Aunt Ester was well rounded. She was a real little butterball, but this obvious inequity still bothered me. Being close to Oliver, I asked him about it, and he said that it was all right; my illness required more food, and anyway, after the war no one in the family was nearly as hungry as the two of us used to be in the boys' school.

End Of War: The Long Summer Of 1945

Six months later, the x-ray at my next medical check-up showed that the shadow in my lung had gone away, and there was just a tiny, dense, calcified spot. The doctor was right. I continued to eat well, and a second check-up one year later showed that my lung was clear. I was declared cured. The small, calcified spot in my lung would remain for life, and I was endowed with the sort of immunity to TB that 98% of people in that part of the world acquire by nature.

One day, we had a surprise visit from David Weiner, a distant relative. During the war, he lost his whole family except for one younger brother, and he wanted to know if we were all right. He was in uniform, had a high rank in the Partisans, and was one of those rare people who joined the resistance in the very first weeks of the war, in the spring of 1941, and survived all the battles. He was wounded six times and was blind in one eye. When the war started, he was studying at the University of Zagreb, and in the evenings, to earn extra money, he used to play his violin in the restaurant of the largest hotel in the city. He was among the first Partisans to enter Zagreb, and he went straight for the Ustaše police headquarters to find what was left of the records. He found records of his family and evidence of other Jews taken to concentration camps to be eliminated. The records were well kept, including a photograph of each person. I remembered that at the beginning of the war, we all had an official picture taken to be given to the police for ID, together with our address registration. David took from the police records the pictures of my parents and of myself and brought them to me.

David also found Uncle Ernest's daughter Luisa. During the war, she ran away from home and lived in a small town southeast of Zagreb, hidden in a young Catholic priest's home. When the war ended, she was near-term pregnant with a baby from the priest. She did not dare return to Uncle Ernest, so David took her to stay with him. He eventually married her and adopted her baby son, Krsto.

What happened to the rest of our family? Uncle Ernest survived and continued running his hardware store and forge in Varaždin. Uncle Felix survived in Switzerland, and when the war ended, he returned to Italy and did not wish to come back to Yugoslavia. We told David that Tatek was killed in Jasenovac. The Red Cross had no information about Mena or Aunt Bella. David indicated that he was a member of the Communist Party. He was not stationed in Zagreb, and Uncle Stanislav invited him to visit whenever he could. Within the next year, we heard that Luisa and David had a second son, Živko.

One afternoon, we had another surprise visit. The priest from Lepavina and his sister rang the bell. Aunt Ester opened the door, but she did not know who they were. When they asked about me and explained how they knew me, they were invited to come in and sit down. They brought me several toys and candies, stuff that was, in the first weeks after the war, hard to get. They stayed for the whole afternoon, and Aunt Ester offered snacks and coffee. They had a long story to tell, and it went back to that Sunday morning in the fall of 1943, when I left their house in Lepavina to join the Partisans. That day, they said, they woke up late, for it was the first Sunday since the Partisans left the farm compound. They found me missing and went to look for me in the church, the barns, and everywhere. When they realized I was not on the farm, they roused all the people in the farmhouses and ordered the farm hands to go out into the fields and climb the hill above the farm and search the woods. They were to keep looking until they found me. Even the priest went looking for me. While they were searching the fields and woods, they saw three German planes circling. They watched the planes bomb their compound. The people, the priest, and his sister ran back to the farm and found the church and most of the buildings in ruins. The entire church roof had caved in. If they had been attending Sunday mass, as was the custom at that hour, they all would have been killed. Left without roof and home, they knelt and prayed. They gave thanks to God for having saved their lives. It was clear to the priest and his sister that God had used me for his good purpose, and it was He who made me disappear that very Sunday. It also turned out that someone "related to Satan" had tipped off the Nazis that Partisans had been camped at the church farm, but "God's will prevailed," and the bombing happened just when all the people were safely outdoors searching for me, so no one was killed. Once again, Satan lost, and God won. I remembered that on the day I escaped to join the Partisans, I saw the airplanes flying overhead and heard distant explosions.

The priest from Lepavina also gave us very bad news: the communists kept good Bishop Šimrak in jail for two months. The bishop was released only after several Serbs who were with the Partisans had been alerted and intervened, vouching that the bishop saved their lives. When the bishop was freed, he was so ill that he died within several days. Bishop Šimrak was a good man, and he was a brave man, too. Where was justice and why did God not save the bishop? Those questions bothered me, and for a long time, I could not find any good answers. We all were sick with grief that our "liberators" mistreated the good bishop. Of course, he hosted the German army officers, and in his position, he had to work administratively with the Ustaše government, but he was a decent man who at great risk to himself protected the innocent as much as he could. I understood the meaning of the word "justice," but its presence in the world seemed quite elusive. Perhaps justice was dependent on whoever was administering it.

The communists accused Bishop Šimrak of collaboration with Ustaše, but his testimony and defense statement, given during the interrogation by the communist Secret Service "OZNA" in 1945, indicates that he sheltered at the bishopry a Serbian widow, Mrs. Simić, whose husband was killed in 1941. The bishop also sheltered and protected her three children: I remember well her son, Vlado Simić, who was in the boys' school while her two daughters were kept in the separate girls' school. The bishop also testified to having sheltered and saved quite a few other Serbian people. I remember Nikola Utješinović and Bogdan Jagodić in the boys' school, and Miloš, who lived with his wife and several children in the garden house and tended the farm animals. He, too, was a Serb. The bishop also testified to sheltering two boys named Pavle and Petar Bastašić. [Internet]

End Of War: The Long Summer Of 1945

The entire history of Lepavina may be easily found on the Internet. Serbs who came from Serbia and Bosnia to Croatia to escape the oppression of Turkish rule built it around 1550. The Serbs were welcomed and settled by the Austrian authorities to help defend their borders from Turkish intrusions. That part of Croatia was declared "Vojna Krajina" (the War Region), and it served as a defensive buffer zone between Turkey and Austria-Hungary. Thus, the Serbs built Greek-Orthodox churches and monasteries, helped defend Croatia from the Turks, and lived on the border of Croatia for several centuries. In 1942, the Ustaše killed the Greek-Orthodox head monk of Lepavina; the rest of the monks were expelled into Serbia, and the monastery was handed over to be administered by the Greek-Catholic bishopry in Križevci. After the war, the monastery was returned to the Serbian Orthodox Church. The Internet gives just a terse statement: "The monastery was destroyed by the Nazis on October 27, 1943." Thanks to Google, I found the exact date of that fateful Sunday when I escaped from Lepavina to join the Partisans.

Two months after the war ended, Uncle Stanislav reopened my father's store and my mother's hat store. He found my father's store completely looted, but the space was in good shape. My mother's little hat store was intact and even had some stock left in it. The government trustee must have made good profit from it till the last day of the war, when he hastily disappeared. Uncle Stanislav laid claim to both stores and went to work to provide for his newly extended family. Oliver and I were to remain in his house. The Professor gave Uncle Stanislav the idea for the name of the new store: "Vortex." The name was appropriate, for it would be a general store providing all possible household goods, from brooms and brushes to combs, cosmetics, soap, detergents, pencils, and dry goods, which were in short supply when the war ended. How Uncle Stanislav was able to procure goods for the new store, I do not know, but he did, and both stores prospered. Aunt Ester and Bluma helped in the stores. A person was hired to run the hat store, and Aunt Ester went once a day to supervise. Michael was involved with getting into the university and had no time for the stores. Against his parents' advice, he enrolled into the School of Business, which led to a profession reserved for members of the Communist Party. Oliver and I sometimes helped in the store if we had free time. Within weeks, Uncle Stanislav was earning enough to feed us all, and soon he was able to build a significant savings. As we were all provided for, we could look to the future. What remained to claim and settle were our real estate properties, abandoned by the Ustaše. The procedure for that was complicated, and we had to wait till Mena and Aunt Bella returned home. My grandfather's house had to be divided into three parts, between Uncle Felix, Ernest, and myself. All this took over two years to settle through the courts, and it involved engaging a lawyer. We had to follow convoluted bureaucratic protocols in a land that had suffered a devastating war, a communist revolution, and was in the midst of writing a new constitution.

Right after the war, Uncle Ernest continued to trade with private parties and companies in Zagreb, and before Christmas and New Year of 1945, he sent to us a man with a wagon carrying gifts for seven of his local clients. We received eight packages with slabs of ice around them, and each package contained a whole piglet, clean and ready for roasting. The gifts were precious for that time, something not seen since before the war. Besides, a suckling pig was a great delicacy. Each piglet had a tag with the name and address of the company to which it was to be delivered, and the tags were tied to the piglets' tails. One piglet had Uncle Stanislav's name on it. The others had the names of businesses, and the largest piglet was for a company called "Biserka." Uncle Ernest wrote a note asking that we promptly deliver each piglet to the designated address. The piglet with our name on its tail was scrawny, the smallest of them all, and Aunt Ester felt offended. Was that how Uncle Ernest thought of us? His business associates were more important to him than his family?

Uncle Stanislav was not happy, either. We were to act as messengers, but there was this offensive issue of piglet size, and something had to be done about it. The problem was solved in a way that gave us some satisfaction: the "Biserka" label was tied to the tail of the smallest piglet meant for us, and we kept for ourselves the "Biserka" piglet. A piglet is a piglet, and since the gift recipient would never see the other seven piglets, he would be perfectly happy with what he got, and would surely thank Uncle Ernest for the precious gift. Uncle Stanislav engaged us all, and the business gifts on ice were delivered to their addresses within a day, just as Uncle Ernest had requested. Aunt Ester prepared for us a great feast, and for quite a while, we fondly remembered the fantastic meal that "Biserka" afforded us. That way, Uncle Stanislav and Aunt Ester could also send a nice "thank you" note to Uncle Ernest.

At this point, I might as well bring up something about my family that bothered me very much, an issue that I resented. For as long as I could remember, there had been a rift, a subtle undercurrent of dislike between the two halves of my family, the Silbers and the Meiers. This was evident in the way Aunt Ester occasionally referred to various members of the Meier family. It all seemed to emanate from the fact the Meiers were at home speaking Hungarian or German, a fact considered by Aunt Ester a sign of snobbery and affectation, though in truth, the Meiers never could speak Yiddish. On the other hand, the Silbers spoke at home Yiddish and used proper German only when they had to. Aunt Ester occasionally referred to my paternal grandmother Greta as "the stuck-up Viennese," which, as far as I could remember, was due to Omama Greta's demeanor. She was always very proper and somewhat stiff-necked. But I was a Meier, and I did not like Aunt Ester's tone when she talked about my father's family. On the other hand, twelve years later, when as an adult I finally met my uncles Felix and Ernest in Italy, they expressed complete disdain, mistrust, and such ugly sentiments about my mother's family and especially Uncle Stanislav that I had a hard time keeping cool. As much as the family discord and schism bothered me, I gradually learned to rationalize it away: friends one may choose, but one is born into family and there is no choice.

End Of War: The Long Summer Of 1945

* * *

After my hair grew enough to hide my scalp and my body filled out some, Aunt Ester had my father's old suits taken to a tailor. He took my measurements and altered the suits to fit me. Oliver also got similar old suits turned inside out and altered for him. Now that we again looked "civilized," Aunt Ester declared that Oliver and I could be re-introduced to some of our parents' old friends.

First one evening, the Professor came for supper. He was very happy to see both Oliver and me. Then the Cacciatore family was invited, and we found out that Mr. Cacciatore was in jail. Mrs. Cacciatore came with their two daughters. She was sad, she looked worried, and her facial wrinkles reminded me of Mena's sad, constantly worried expression when she was waiting for Tatek to come back.

Mr. Cacciatore had been accused of "war profiteering," the standard communist accusation for all people who, during the war, remained in their offices, stayed relatively prosperous, and did not join the Partisans. He would be eventually freed, but he came out of jail a sick, broken man. He had been tortured, mistreated, and interrogated, though he did not commit any political act supporting the Ustaše or Nazis. He lived for less than a year.

Despite the fact that many Ustaše left town after the war, there was a tremendous shortage of apartments in Zagreb. Thousands of newly baked communists from the villages moved into the city, where life was more comfortable than in the hills, pastures, and fields. Their slogan was, "Hey, what were we fighting for?" meaning that they fought with Partisans, and therefore had the right to reap the benefits of an easy life for as long as they live.

The apartment opposite ours was found empty after the war. The Ustaša general and his family had vanished. The government assigned it to the extended family of a Partisan from a village in a remote, mountainous region of Croatia often referred to as "Vukojebina" (Wolfukdale). He was a politically savvy Croat who joined the Partisans about one year before the end of the war. He quickly rose to become a member and a functionary of the Communist Party. There were nine people in all, including five grown children, and we never found out exactly what all these people were doing. With them it was, "Hello, comrade," and no other conversation.

Every Friday, these new neighbors had a party, and we heard coarse peasant songs through the wall of our living room, typical of people drinking brandy and getting sloshed. They howled, "The wolf chased a donkey over the fence..." into the wee hours of the night. One day, shortly after they moved in, the apartment janitor rang our doorbell, pale as chalk and staggering on his feet. Aunt Ester invited him in. He asked to sit down, and then he asked for a glass of cold water. After a while, his color returned, and he seemed better. When he caught his breath, he quietly said that he just came out of the apartment across the landing. He was called to fix a drain in the bathroom.

"They have the animals!" he said, and he started retching. Aunt Ester said that we all sometimes keep live chickens or a goose or ducks in a little cage on our kitchen balcony for a day or two before we have them slaughtered and prepared for a meal. The janitor said that our neighbors had sheep and goats; some were in the bathtub, and the bathroom smelled like in a pigsty. What he was really called for, though, was something else.

They had been using the bidet as a toilet, and when its drain was plugged up and the bowl was brimming with excrement, they wanted him to unplug it. They complained that it should function better. The janitor was afraid of the new tenants and did not want to tell them what a bidet was for, nor did he dare tell them what it was not for…

Soon we would find out what happens to the economy when primitive people, the uneducated, and the ignorant run businesses large and small. Such are revolutions. The changes in the society were rapid and were controlled by the functionaries of the Communist Party. The politically savvy profited the most. In Croatia, many of those who in 1941 were openly on the side of the Ustaše began to join the Partisans and the Communist Party.

The advantages were obvious: only trusted communists were put in top positions at factories and businesses. The communist government created new slogans about unity, brotherhood, equality, and equal opportunity. New holidays were declared, based on the significant dates during the "people's struggle for liberation." All government actions were declared "in the name of the People" and "for the benefit of the People." Walls all over the city were, just like in 1941, plastered with posters and proclamations. People who at any time during the war wore a uniform, even the forced conscripts of the Domobrani (home defense militia), had to report to the authorities to be investigated. Through these investigations, many people lost their apartments and jobs in the city, and those apartments and jobs were given to the favored new class, the communists.

New currency, dinars, was issued, and a maximum amount was set for each person and child, so that all families started on equal footing, regardless of how much old money they had to exchange. Polite titles, such as "mister" and "missis," were to be forgotten; everybody was a "comrade," children were "pioneers," adolescents were "communist youth," and everyone was addressed as "thou," regardless of age, title, and position. Religion and religious people were shunned; God did not exist, the communists said. In the meantime, food in Zagreb grew harder and harder to get.

What saved us for the moment was that the U.S. Army in Europe was being dismantled and as soldiers were shipped home, huge supplies of food were left behind. Some of this food was distributed to countries ravaged by the war, and the Yugoslav communist government received and distributed packages of K-rations and other food to the hungry citizens. However, we had to pay for food that was given and delivered to Yugoslavia for free. We were told the payments were to compensate for "the cost of transportation and distribution." Nevertheless, for a while we had good canned food, meat, cheese, sardines, chocolate, and even chewing gum. After several months, that supply was exhausted, and we again

End Of War: The Long Summer Of 1945

had to scrounge for food. There was a black market, and with the money earned in our stores, we could obtain all the food we needed. The bread was again all yellow, made of corn flour. When the bread ran out, Aunt Ester bought corn flour and made "polenta" (grits), and that was our breakfast for the next several years, sometimes with a little milk.

During that first post-war summer, I was overwhelmed with all the new circumstances, the new facts I learned, the news I heard, and all the new people I met. I even had to get used to the members of my own family and get to know them all anew. They, too, appeared "new" to me. I had to adjust to a new lifestyle and find out what was expected of me. At the same time, images from the past three years kept passing through my mind, and older memories came, images of when my parents were still with me. In those moments of "absence," one or another of my cousins or Aunt Ester would ask what I was thinking about. "Nothing," I would say. I just wanted to be left alone.

Some nights, I had dreams of the past, some of them frightful, real nightmares, and I talked or screamed in my sleep. Aunt Ester would wake up, come to me, and calm me. She would ask what I dreamt, but I could not remember. She thought I was stubborn and did not want to tell her. She did not believe me. I would overhear her the next day, talking to Uncle Stanislav about it, wondering what was wrong with me, whether I was "normal," or should she take me to a doctor, a psychiatrist. That made me even more withdrawn, and I began to wonder whether I was all right.

That first summer after the war was hard and long, and as it drew towards the end, the thought of going for the first time to a regular school made me only more anxious. I was nearly ten years old, savvy and street-wise on one hand, but shy and unsure of myself in my new surroundings.

THE FIRST YEAR IN SCHOOL AND LIFE IN MY NEW HOME

When in the fall of 1945 school finally began, I was preoccupied with trying to catch up with other children. It was my first time in a regular classroom, and I was going straight into the fourth grade. My interaction with other children in the class was at first limited, partly because they all knew each other from the previous three years and had already formed friendships, and partly because I was shy and tense. Nevertheless, my progress was steady, and within a couple of months, I was more comfortable and made friends with a few kids in the class, though I still did not have a "best friend." The teacher, Mr. Bubaš, was always very kind and understanding and his demeanor was very soothing. Only towards the middle of the school year, did I finally settle down and learn to be more relaxed.

There were two other boys in class, David T. and Mirko R., who helped me to relax in my interaction with other kids in the class. They were first cousins and were introduced into the class several days after the school year began. They were just as tense and anxious as I was in my first few days in school, and they struggled to catch up in making friends with the other children. Both of them spoke Serbo-Croatian haltingly and with a foreign accent, and one stuttered so that it was hard to understand him. It appeared that both had spent the war years somewhere in a camp for refugees in Switzerland. They were Jewish, and their parents were able to leave Zagreb just in time to avoid being sent to concentration camps. The two cousins clung to each other, and it took them even longer to become comfortable enough to actively interact with other kids.

Once, Mr. Bubaš took our class on an outing to the city zoo. It was my first zoo visit since my parents took me there before the war. For some of the children, it was their very first visit, and for once, I felt on a familiar ground. It was early spring and still quite cold, and the monkeys were in the cages inside the monkey house. The air inside was warm, but it had an awful smell. I looked for Štefek, but he was not there. He must have died during the war. I heard that during the war, the zoo animals were not well fed or cared for, and many had died.

The kids crowded around the teacher, who stood right in front of the cage explaining something about the monkeys. Being among the smallest kids, in order to see some action, I had to stand further in the back, where I could see at least the upper half of the cage, above the heads of the taller kids and the teacher. A small monkey was high up, holding onto the cage wires and looking down on the heads below him. He was right above the teacher. Suddenly, he started to urinate. A single fine stream came silently down, straight onto the teacher's hat. The hat had a wide, turned up rim, and it held the urine pretty well until the teacher tilted his head and spilled it down his shoulder. It was fun to watch, and I had the best view in the house.

I was a B student and quite satisfied, and so was Aunt Ester. For the first year in school, she commented, B was a sufficient grade, but she hinted that later she expected a better performance.

In the spring of that year, after a string of head colds with fever and swollen tonsils, Aunt Ester took me to our family physician, who immediately said that my tonsils had to come out. An appointment was made, and on the given day, I was taken to the doctor's office. I was covered with a white gown and some white sheets, and a male nurse took me to sit in his lap, holding me steady with his arms wrapped around my arms and chest. The doctor came in holding a large white oval cover made of gauze and poured some liquid onto it. The doctor told me he would put the cover over my face and I should close my eyes, breathe normally, and count slowly to thirty. The cover had an awful chemical smell that caused me to retch, but I followed the instructions and counted aloud. By the count of about twenty, I could no longer remember anything.

I woke up with a slight soreness in my throat and a strange feeling in my head. Aunt Ester had a taxi waiting, and we went home. When the elevator stopped on our floor, everything in my stomach continued to go up, and I threw up a cupful of dark blood. Aunt Ester said that that was usual after the ether anesthesia, and I went to stay in my bed. For the next two days, I was allowed to eat only ice cream, and that felt good. When I was to go back to school, my cheeks appeared swollen, and I looked like a squirrel with a mouthful of acorns. Aunt Ester took me again to our doctor, and he said I had mumps and had to stay home for at least a week until the swelling was down.

After a week, I noticed itchy red dots all over my skin, and I was taken back to the doctor. This time, he said it was chickenpox, and I had to stay at home for at least two weeks. I missed four weeks of school, and when I finally did go back to school, I worried how I would make up for it. The teacher, Mr. Bubaš was very kind and patient and I made up the lost time without any problem.

Toward the end of the school year, it was customary that the children and their teachers prepare a small, end-of-year performance in the school gym, with singing and reading of their compositions in front of the parents. After that, the children would return to their classrooms, and the teachers would distribute the certificates with grades. There was a class contest for the best-written short essay. The teacher offered several themes, and the children were to choose one theme. I chose to write about Maxim Gorky, a Russian writer whose stories became very popular in Yugoslavia after the war.

It was my misfortune that Mr. Bubaš chose my essay, and I had to read it on a stage in front of the full gym of parents. I had nightmares about it. The closer it came to the last day of school, the more scared I became. I wished and dreamed that the school year would never end. Finally, that day arrived, and we all stood on the stage and first sang the national anthem: "Oh, Slavs, still alive...," which was easy, for among so many voices, mine could easily hide.

After a few children from other classes read their essays, Mr. Bubaš, standing behind the side curtain, signaled me to step to the center of stage and begin reading my essay. In those days, microphones were sparse, and there were none in a grade school. In front of me, hundreds of people sat in rows of chairs, and as I stood in the middle of the stage, there was an increasing sense of silence in the large gym. Hundreds of eyes were upon me. It was frightening. I started to read, but my voice was so thin and small, I could hardly hear it myself. My mouth was dry and my throat seemed constricted. I felt like choking. For a long moment, I looked at the paper in my hands, though I knew the text by heart, and then slowly, trying to produce a louder voice, I began anew. My voice faltered again.

"Louder!" whispered the teacher, who stood behind the curtain.

On my third try, my voice returned and I started to recite the text by heart. My voice became stronger while my eyes were glued to the paper in my hand, without consciously reading from it. On and on I went, mechanically mouthing the words I knew by heart, as if I was in a trance.

The end of the essay came suddenly, and I was in a daze, my mind having wandered somewhere far away from the large room with the people and the essay in my hand. I ran out of words to say, and just stood staring into the void in front of me, forgetting that I was to bow. My mind snapped back into awareness of where I was. Again, I saw a mass of faces and eyes in front of me. What now? An old reflex came to my aid: I crossed myself, right in front of all the people. Mr. Bubaš jumped from behind the curtain and pulled me back. There was a moment of silence in the hall, and then a muted applause. For a moment, I had lost my head.

The school performance continued with the next student's recital, and when it was over, we all went to our classrooms to collect our certificates with grades. For many weeks after, I was embarrassed and ashamed, and whenever I met any of the kids' parents on the street, I blushed and could not look them in the eyes. Anyway, I graduated from elementary school.

On a recent visit with David T., my classmate from 1945/46 who now lives in Switzerland, he suddenly stopped our conversation, looked at me, and after a short pause asked if I still remembered crossing myself on the stage in front of all the parents.

"How could I ever forget?" I asked and added, "That embarrassment haunted me for months, and it took nearly a decade before I could think of it and silently laugh."

During my first year in school, there were a few new events in our family. Michael was not getting along with Aunt Ester. He said he was "too old to be under parental supervision," and he moved out to stay in a sublet room in the apartment of a widow, Mrs. T., who was Aunt Ester's acquaintance and a "close friend" of Uncle Ernest. Michael came home to eat, and in winter to study, for his sublet room was not heated. He was doing very well in the School of Business, but a degree in business was good only for Communist Party members who would receive jobs as managers of various government enterprises. The following year, he switched to the medical school, which required much more study, but led to a far more practical profession. There was a great shortage of doctors, and one did not need to be a Party member to get a job. Aunt Ester and Uncle Stanislav were delighted. About that time, I also met Bluma's boyfriend Karel, a university student in the School of Chemical Engineering. He was handsome and charming. I sensed that Aunt Ester did not like him, though she tried to conceal it.

On most evenings, our apartment was full of young people—Michael, Karel, Oliver, and their many friends, mostly students at the university. Most of their girlfriends studied languages, while the boys studied medicine or engineering. Rarely, a few boys from the school of business, Michael's old acquaintances from his time with the Partisans, came to visit, but with them around the atmosphere turned "dead," and soon everyone left. The business school students were all members of the Communist Party, and all normal conversation ceased. No one could relax: one had to watch every word. Having fun seemed to be a sin around communists, but on most evenings without the communists' presence, I sat in a corner of the family room, happy to be allowed to listen in and observe the grownups.

The university students usually brought with them modern records and put them on our old turntable, wound it up, and lifted the carpets off the parquet floor to make room for dancing. For the first time, I heard popular Italian songs and dance music from the forties. Couples formed and danced. This was new, and it was fun to watch. Aunt Ester did not seem too happy, but she tolerated it.

"Young people have to live," Uncle Stanislav would say. He and Aunt Ester stayed in the dining/living room, behind the closed French doors, and I enjoyed observing and learning the ways of young grownups.

Aunt Ester was usually on top of everything, and she craved to know what went on in town, in the country, in the world, and above all, in our family. She played the role of our "commander-in-chief," and Uncle Stanislav gladly let her have that role. After a hard day's work, he would just as soon be left alone reading the newspaper or listening to the news on the radio. If Aunt Ester did not know something about our family, she would ask, and we had to answer until she was satisfied. Within the family circle, Aunt Ester called Uncle Stanislav by his original name, Moritz, using the Yiddish version of "Moische." She played a good game of chess. I learned the game in the boys' school, and it took me several years at home before I could beat her.

Aunt Ester cooked, cleaned, directed, and micro-managed all of us, and she did it with passion. She had a special thing about cleanliness: if there was dirt or dust anywhere in the apartment, she claimed that fleas or other pests would hatch directly from it. Everyone in the house had to wear slippers. Guests were an exception, although, if they came more frequently, my aunt taught them to take off their shoes in the foyer, or to step around on special, thick pieces of cloth she provided, and on those they had to shuffle around the parquet floors.

In the spirit of cleanliness, Aunt Ester organized every year the great spring-cleaning that we named "the hurricane." It was a grand affair that lasted three full days and was fully orchestrated by Aunt Ester, with a hired maid and all the rest of us helping. Furniture was moved from its usual place toward the center of the room, so that the floor underneath and the walls behind could be cleaned. All the heavy oriental rugs were lifted, rolled, and carried into the courtyard next to a tall goal-like metal post. Each rug was unfolded and hung over the post, first with the right side up and then with the underside up, and each side had to be beaten with a rug beater until not a speck of dust came out.

The job of rug beating belonged to Oliver and me. Aunt Ester showed us that the wicker rug beater was vastly superior to the Electrolux vacuum cleaner which despite all the weekly cleaning still left a lot of dust in the rugs. She supervised, and when a rug was declared clean, we rolled it up and carried back to the apartment. The entire apartment was dusted, up to the last little figurine in the glass case. The parquet floor was waxed with a smelly wood paste and then polished by the maid "dancing" around on two thick rags. Then the rugs and the furniture were put back into their places, and at last, the hurricane was over, till the next year. We all dreaded the three days of the great spring-cleaning.

When one of us did something wrong, Aunt Ester would berate him (or her), and continue on his (or her) case for several days, on and on, to rub it in, to teach us never to make that mistake again. Making the same mistake for a second time appeared to aunt Ester so abhorrent that we understood it as a mortal sin. I learned this lesson so well, that it took me several decades to unlearn it.

While she was a great cook, Aunt Ester's "tongue soup" could drive one crazy. My dear cousin Oliver got into trouble most often. Being older than I, he would disappear to spend time with his friends, come home too late, not finish his home work, have a tear on his shirt sleeve, a missing button on his jacket, or he would be caught smoking in the bathroom. Bluma mainly got in trouble if she came home late from a date with Karel, or if she left her clothing in disarray, did not study enough, or did not properly polish the stainless steel edge on the kitchen stove. I made my pants or shirt "excessively dirty," brought mud into the entry hall, kept my shoes not polished well enough, and my hair not combed right (it was supposed to be slicked down). We were repeatedly reminded that these rebukes and admonishments were meant "for your own good."

Pretty soon, when one of us was caught doing something wrong, we jokingly said, one was "posted on the bulletin board." The rest of us quietly laughed, though we knew that in a few days it would be someone else's turn to be the guilty party and be "posted on the bulletin." Bluma was caught and ordered to polish the stove just as she was ready to go out on a date. Oliver and I got used to this; the boys' school also had rules, and when we were caught there, we sometimes had to kneel on dry corn. Michael was too old for this, and he protested loudly, for he would not have anyone tell him what to do. That is why Uncle Stanislav had to let him move out and pay rent for a sublet room. Luckily, with business in the stores going well, this was affordable.

Uncle Stanislav would come home, and get to hear the whole "bulletin" lament from Aunt Ester forward and backward a few times. He wanted to relax and bury his head in the newspaper; instead, he had to pay attention and react to the bulletin. Aunt Ester spoke Yiddish to Uncle Stanislav, and in no time, Oliver and I learned to understand it. Yiddish was just archaic, fifteenth-century German with a generous sprinkle of Hebrew and Slavic words, and we understood German. Besides, we had already heard Aunt Ester's plaintive bulletin in Serbo-Croatian three times over.

As soon as another family member showed up at home, the whole story would be repeated. Oliver would quietly raise his hand and indicate with outstretched fingers how many times the story had been told. We had to suppress our laughter, and it was not easy. Frequent guests and friends also had the privilege of hearing Aunt Ester's bulletin, and it was hard to tell whether they were more embarrassed by listening to it than we were.

Uncle Stanislav, now again Moritz, was the man from whom I learned the meaning of the word "phlegmatic," just by observing his conduct. He was the paradigm of a calm, cool, phlegmatic person. None of Aunt Ester's ramblings disturbed him. He read his newspaper, gave a little smile, and occasionally mumbled, "Everything will be fine; you'll see."

Occasionally, when he had enough of the background noise, he would just say loudly in Yiddish, "Genick shojn" (enough already), and Aunt Ester would finally cease her lamentations. My uncle was an optimist, a sun-shine of a man, and we all loved him. He spoke little, but when he did talk, we listened, for it was meaningful. When we had a problem, it was a pleasure to go to him and hear his advice, always measured, calm, patient, friendly, and soothing, and above all, reasonable. And he would not repeat it five times over. He was conservative, of course, for he was a man from the nineteenth century. For him the "good old times" meant the time of the Austrian-Hungarian Empire, in whose army he served during the First World War. I enjoyed hearing him reminisce and tell funny stories and episodes from his army service in the most backward regions of Bosnia and Montenegro. He used to say, "Peeing onto a shoe and peeing into a shoe are two very different things, very different," and this was meant to back up his conviction that a boy may go around and have fun with girls, but for a girl to have fun with boys, well, that was not at all proper.

In all those years, only once did I see Uncle Stanislav get really mad, raise his voice, and look ready to strike, no less than with a chair in his hand. On that one occasion, he was so provoked by the vile mouth of his own son, Cousin Michael, that he grabbed a chair as if it were a baseball bat. Seeing the chair in the air above his head, Michael stopped his ranting.

When Aunt Ester rambled on, we learned to simply tune out. That sometimes led to more trouble: between her ramblings, Aunt Ester occasionally and without

The First Year In School And Life In My New Home

warning changed her theme and mentioned something important. Tuned out, we missed it. Later, all hell would break loose, for we "again did not listen" to her. To make things worse, Aunt Ester never learned to speak Serbo-Croatian properly. Her command of the language was fluent, but she had a funny accent, and she was daring and inventive enough to make up her own words, words that no one ever heard before. On top of it, she completely mangled the grammar and syntax. The biggest problem Oliver and I had was keeping a straight face while we were being "polished." When out of her earshot, we repeated her kinky new words and phrases and rolled with laughter.

Through it all, though, we knew that Aunt Ester truly cared for us, but this care was expressed in her own peculiar way. We thought it was like a "machine love." Whatever she did, she did with an iron will and determination. A couple of years later, when Oliver finished the accelerated Partisan High School and wanted to enter the university to take some "blow-off" course, like geography or meteorology, Aunt Ester put her foot down and said, "No way, not in my house will you ever be allowed to become 'ein Luftinspektor' " (an air inspector).

In those times, an "air inspector" was a person who went around the town just breathing in and breathing out, smelling the air, "shooting the breeze," and doing nothing productive.

"Either you go and become a doctor, like a decent person should" (it seemed every other calling was indecent), "or you go to work, my dear, to work! In my house I am not supporting any stupidities!" Anything she did not agree with was "a stupidity," and the related people were "useless," "clowns," or "charlatans," but some were "thieves" or "robbers," or mere "cretins" and "idiots."

Uncle Stanislav, however, with his kindness and calm demeanor was much better able to drive a point home. After having a couple of long discussions with Uncle Stanislav, Oliver thought it over and finally, he agreed to go to medical school. Eventually, Oliver did get his MD degree, though he was forced to apply some extra long and hard effort.

The Rubin household had many books, and among them, I discovered the Yugoslav Encyclopedia. It was first issued in the late thirties, and only the first four volumes came out, up to the beginning of the letter E. The war stopped the rest, and it would never be completed. We had the first three volumes, and I liked to pull the books from the shelf, sometimes two at the time. They were huge and heavy, and I would lay them on our dining room table on top of the a thick rug-like cover. I would kneel on a chair, lean my elbows on the table, and hover over the wonderful books, looking at the beautiful pictures. I first read the captions, and if my interest was aroused, I read the entire article and marveled at the new and amazing world that the books revealed. I spent hours with the encyclopedia, and I learned a great deal. As I moved from subject to subject, I would slip between the pages anything within my reach, so I could return to the same page later.

I read about different subjects and jumped from one to another with voracious curiosity. If I was interrupted and forgot to put the books back in place, I was not allowed to take them out the next whole day, and this was a real punishment. I loved those books. In them, I saw all kinds of new things and fantasized about them.

As much as I loved the encyclopedia, at one point, it caused me great anguish and calamity. In the spring of 1946, while I was still in elementary school, Aunt Ester lost her two precious nail files. She looked everywhere and asked everyone, and no one had seen them. Only Bluma and Aunt Ester used them for fixing their fingernails. These were precious, prewar files, and such things were unobtainable in the years after the war. It was vexing: one day we had two long metal nail files in the house, and the next day, both had disappeared. After long discussions with everyone, it was concluded that I must have hidden the files, for they had last been seen on the table where I read. After all, I could have many gripes for being punished for all sorts of little transgressions, I was known to be stubborn, and sometimes I acted "strange" and "absent."

I had no idea where the files were, and I earnestly helped to search for them. Just then, I did something silly; I cannot even remember what it was. Aunt Ester was at the time at her wits' end with Bluma and her boyfriend, with Oliver, and with who knows what else, and she gave me a real spanking. While she was at it, she got madder and madder, and said that some of it was also for the missing nail files. That infuriated me, and knowing that I was not guilty, I tried to hit her back, so I got some more beating. To get out of her reach, I threw myself on the floor, but she started kicking me with her feet. I yelled that I hated her house and only wished that my mother were there to protect me. That stopped the beating, but I was miserable and sobbed for a long time. We eventually made up. She said she was sorry, and me, too, and all was well.

In the meantime, I began to wonder whether, in my absentmindedness, I really had taken the nail files and put them somewhere. Shortly thereafter, some other item in the apartment was lost or misplaced, and it was declared "disappeared." I no longer remember what the item was, but I was again pinned on the bulletin board. Aunt Ester questioned everyone, and they all denied knowing anything about the missing item. This time, I overheard Aunt Ester tell Uncle Stanislav that perhaps I was a kleptomaniac, and "maybe the poor child needs help."

I had to find out what that big word meant. To the dictionary I went. Aha, that was it, and Aunt Ester said she would take me to a psychiatrist. That was for me the worst of shame. Not only my cousins and family, but also Karel would hear about it. I knew I had nightmares and talked in my sleep, I knew I daydreamed, I knew I was forgetful and a scatterbrain, and I crossed myself at the school performance. I began to wonder if I was capable of doing things unawares. That was frightening!

Aunt Ester, though, was not wasting any time: she made an appointment with Dr. J., a well-known senior attending psychiatrist, and took me to his apartment. He first spent some time with her alone, and then it was my turn. Aunt Ester wanted to be present, but he sent her to sit in the foyer. He asked me all sorts of questions and spent with me what seemed a very long time. He was kind and

The First Year In School And Life In My New Home

patient. He asked me about the missing nail files and other issues. I had no idea who took the nail files, and I certainly did not have them.

In the end, he said that I was all right, and that all would be well. Then he again spent some time alone with Aunt Ester, while I waited in the foyer. On the way home, Aunt Ester was unusually calm and thoughtful and told me we did not have to go back for another visit. According to the doctor, I was not a kleptomaniac, and all seemed well with me.

My life slowly settled back to normal. One day, I took out my beloved encyclopedia and put it on the table. When I opened it, I let out a scream. One of Aunt Ester's precious nail files was between the pages of the book. I leafed frantically through more pages and found the other file. I remembered then that I had stuck them in there to hold the pages, but I must have been distracted and forgot about it. Lucky for me, Aunt Ester was in the room when I found the files, and she saw my happy surprise. She understood that I did not hide them on purpose; I had just forgotten about them. She used to leave them lying around on the table, and she was happy to have them back. She admitted that it was, in a way, her fault, and she henceforth always put her nail files away.

The psychiatrist was right, she declared, as if she had some doubt about him before. I was, after all, "normal." I was relieved. At least some of my insecurity was wiped out. It would take a while before I became more confident. In the meantime, I learned a new big word: kleptomaniac.

A few years later, the name of my good psychiatrist popped up in the news. He was a prewar communist, one of those good-natured, naive people who sincerely believed the communist literature. He, his wife, and two sons spent the war years with Partisans, and his older son lost an arm in one of the major battles of the war. After the war, Dr. J. was chief of a large psychiatric institution near Zagreb, and he unwisely criticized a management decision at his work. The communists had no tolerance for criticism and promptly reprimanded and demoted him. Despondent and disappointed, Dr. J. put a bullet through his head. He was a well-known and well-liked person in Zagreb, and the news of his death was quite a shock for many people. I will never forget how kind he was towards me when I was in distress. His disappointment with communism was made worse by the fact that his younger son had become a rabid communist, denounced other people, and committed all sorts of malfeasance on behalf of his Communist Party bosses.

In the summer of 1946, it became clear that Mena would not return. She was no longer alive, and we did not know where or how she died. Like Tatek, she would never have a grave, and like millions of other Jews, she was just another victim of Ustaše and Nazi crimes. Oliver's mom, Aunt Bella, did not return, either. The Red Cross had no information to give us. I never stopped trying to find where my mother was taken. Over the years, I have tried through several Jewish agencies and the Red Cross in the U.S., but all my inquiries have ended without any clue.

Nazis were meticulous, both in pursuing their victims to death and in keeping good records. Those who should be able to find the proper information long ago decided to keep all records and information away from the public. The archives of the Nazi concentration camps in Bad Arolsen, Germany, were opened to public inquiry only recently, and when I wrote asking for information about my mother, they answered, "Records are made available only for persons born in Germany." The vast majority of the victims of Nazi concentration camps were not born in Germany, and I am left wondering about the meaning of "the archives are now open."

One day, Uncle Stanislav called Oliver and me to have a serious talk. He asked whether we would like to be adopted by him and Aunt Ester. We did not have to think long. It was logical, and we agreed. However, Oliver and I did not want to give up our family names of Silber and Meier. After adoption, Oliver and I never called our uncle and aunt "Father" and "Mother," nor did we ever refer to Bluma and Michael as sister and brother. We avoided the issue by calling our cousins by their proper names, and we continued to call our uncle and aunt just the way we always did—"Uncle" and "Aunt." The adoption had one practical value: from a legal standpoint, it was easier for Uncle Stanislav to become the executor and trustee of the inherited real estate properties transferred from my mother and paternal grandfather to me. Obtaining the required proof that my parents were dead and getting the deed to the properties took about two years. By then, the new communist constitution and laws stated that no one individual could posses more than the equivalent of four rooms, whether it be two two-room apartments, or four one-room studios, or a single four-room apartment. The properties were divided among us three inheritors, Aunt Ester, Oliver, and myself, so we could retain at least some of the small apartments; I chose to own two small apartments from grandfather Meier's house (sharing with Uncle Felix and Uncle Ernest), and Aunt Ester and Oliver each took two small apartments attached to the large real estate with factories. The factory buildings that were the major part of our property, were nationalized, but we were allowed to use the adjacent land, the orchard, and the meadow.

One more thing happened in the summer of 1946: we got news from Boris and Željko that their stepfather, Uncle Ernest, was arrested. His business and properties in Varaždin were taken away, confiscated by "the people," and Uncle Ernest was accused of war profiteering and collaborating with the fascist enemy. Friends he helped to escape into the Partisans had to be located, and strings were pulled to get him out of jail.

He was a diabetic, and by the time he got out six weeks later, he was in bad shape. He was released in Zagreb, and he stayed at the apartment of Mrs. T., a widow who was his mistress after his second wife died. After a few months, Uncle Ernest recovered, regained some strength, and decided to escape into Italy. The borders were closed, as we were behind the Iron Curtain, and he had to cross the border illegally.

Uncle Ernest was in correspondence with Uncle Felix, and he wanted to join him in Italy. His two grown stepsons, Boris and Željko would go with him, and in Italy they would all work together and start a new life. Uncle Ernest arranged

The First Year In School And Life In My New Home

for the escape, and towards the end of 1946, all three successfully crossed the border into Trieste, which was at that time a special autonomous territory under American administration. [19]

Shortly thereafter, Uncle Ernest sent a messenger to Uncle Stanislav with a letter asking him to go to Uncle Ernest's estate in Varaždin and dig up a box containing jewelry from his wife and a bag with gold coins, which were all his savings. The box was buried far out in a field that had belonged to his estate. This was a dangerous undertaking, for Uncle Ernest's property had been confiscated by the communist administration. Uncle Stanislav made the journey, hiked over the old estate, located the right spot in the field, dug up the box containing the valuables, and delivered everything to Mrs. T. She was to keep the jewelry from Ernest's wife for herself and give the gold coins to the messenger, who was to deliver them to Uncle Ernest. No receipts were exchanged, since all this was confidential and illegal. If caught, everything would be confiscated, and someone would end up in jail. The communist authorities forbade anyone to possess foreign currency, gold, or other valuables without registering them with the government. Those who registered had it requisitioned "in the name of the people."

During the war the Ustaše had issued orders requiring that Jews hand over all their gold and valuables. After the war, the communists were more equitable: they wanted everyone's gold and foreign currency. After a while, Uncle Stanislav received a letter from Uncle Ernest inquiring about his gold coins. Uncle Stanislav wrote back that he handed everything over to Mrs. T., but she wrote to Uncle Ernest that she received only the jewelry. What became of the gold coins? This issue will be revisited later, when I describe my meeting with Uncle Ernest and Felix many years later.

The relationship between Uncle Ernest and Uncle Stanislav came to a bad end: all ties between them were severed. For many years, I had no news from or contact with my uncles, my father's two surviving brothers. A minor consequence was that Cousin Michael had to find another sublet room; Mrs. T. was no longer a friend of our family.

Bluma had a difficult year behind her: she had to pass the final high school exam, the baccalaureate. It was hard, especially the math test, and she had to take it over. Aunt Ester, of course, blamed her boyfriend, with whom Bluma "spent too much time."

When she passed the exam, Uncle Stanislav rewarded Bluma with a week's rest in the Slovenian Alps, on Lake Bled. I was allowed to come along to help my lungs in the clear mountain air, and so in 1946, I had my first postwar vacation in a beautiful Alpine resort. Uncle Stanislav brought us there by train and left us in a little "pension," where the room and meals were included in the plan. At the end of the week, he came again to take us home. He and Aunt Ester had to stay in Zagreb and mind the stores. Bluma's boyfriend Karel came to visit once and spent a day with us. It was a very relaxing vacation. I still could not swim, but I was able to use a tiny wooden raft made of an old door, and I was allowed to go on it all over the small lake, even to a little island in the middle.

It was the end of summer, and the water was warm, so I could take a dip in the shallows. That summer, I saw Marshall Tito for the first time. While I was on my little raft, he slowly glided by in a boat with several people, and a second, larger boat with armed men followed them closely. They all stayed in a big hotel on the other side of the lake. One day, Bluma and I climbed the mountain above the lake and enjoyed the views of the Slovenian Alps.

After returning to Zagreb, I was ready to go to junior high school, and Bluma started her first job as a clerk in a bank. Bluma and Karel wanted to get engaged, but since he was still a student without any means, Aunt Ester said that the engagement had to wait until he graduated from school and got a job. Karel was falling behind in his studies, and instead of studying and passing his exams, he was having lots of fun with his friends at the boat club on the river and all over town.

Karel's best friend was an older student who had earned the title of "eternal student," and was appropriately nicknamed "Otata" (grandpa). I was not sure whether his nickname stuck because he was completely bald, or because he was the oldest student at the school of chemistry.

PART II

LIFE UNDER COMMUNISM

JUNIOR HIGH: LITTLE PRANKS AND NEW AWARENESS

Junior high school was a new experience. For the first time, I felt that the school was a level playing field. I was no longer the only "new student" in class. Everyone was new because we all came from different parts of the city, and only a few children knew each other from before. I finally found a good friend, a boy with whom I instantly felt comfortable. We had immediate, mutual magnetism. He was tall and slim, with strawberry blond hair, green eyes, a handsome face, and an easy, mellow demeanor. He invited me to play at his home, which was not far from mine. His mother was very kind and pleasant. Their apartment was full of dark, heavy, traditional furniture, very much like that in the house of my grandfather. Ivica M. and I soon became best friends, and for the next fourteen years, all through high school and university, we spent innumerable hours together, including summer vacations on the Adriatic Sea.

Since the end of the war, most high school buildings were occupied by the army and used as barracks. Many schools were relocated to various makeshift locations. Our school was in a building requisitioned from the nuns, in a space that was formerly a school for nuns. It was relatively far from our apartment, and I had to walk for over half an hour to reach it. When it was cold or rainy, I used the streetcar most of the way. In 1946, more than a year after the war ended, no new high school textbooks were available. For most subjects, we had to listen to the teacher, take notes, and learn to write very fast.

For a few subjects like math, we could use the antiquated textbooks, published before the war. The government banned textbooks printed during the war because they were replete with political propaganda dictated by the Ustaše government. Wartime textbooks were also written in a new Croat language style, where both the spelling and pronunciation were artificially altered to make the language appear as "pure Croatian" and thus prove that it was different from Serbian. (In fact, some of the local dialects spoken in parts of Croatia were for us much harder to understand than the language spoken in Serbia.) In line with postwar political slogans of "brotherhood and unity" for all people in Yugoslavia, the communist government wanted to bring back the traditional Serbo-Croatian language as it was spoken for centuries, and as it was originally defined by linguists. Along with the Latin script, the teachers were directed to teach us also the Cyrillic script, which was used in two-thirds of the country and was similar to Russian.

The first "free" elections in Yugoslavia occurred in 1946. Zagreb was plastered with large posters on every wall and corner. All the posters urged people to vote for the Communist Party. No one should want to go back to the prewar government system. The communist government wanted everyone to vote. Those who would refuse to vote were considered "enemies of the people," and so most people felt obliged to vote. My uncle and aunt took me to the voting place, which was in a meeting and dance hall on the corner of our street. They each received a ballot in the form of a little black rubber ball that easily fit into a closed fist. To vote, one placed the fist through an opening in each of the two available ballot boxes, and released the rubber ball into the box of one's choice. The election was supposed to be secret. However, when the rubber ball was released, on the way to the ballot box, it went bouncing through a long wooden channel, and everyone in the room could clearly hear it bouncing. The election commissioners, all members of the Communist Party, were watching, listening, and keeping a record of the few people who dared to drop the ballot into the box for the king's return.

The election poster I remember best was the one with a fat goat dumping pellets from her behind into a box labeled with the name of the king. Of course, the election was "won by the people by a landslide," and the king had no chance of returning. The government was busy writing a new constitution, and thus Yugoslavia, like most communist countries, got a new name with four words in it: Federal People's Republic [of] Yugoslavia. With a name so rich in words, both its legitimacy and nature were firmly defined. The news media proclaimed that we were to build socialism and communism, and since any building is a process, it naturally should take some time. No one dared ask how long a time.

The newspapers told the public to be prepared to overcome some hardships. For the next decade and a half, I witnessed several more elections, but always with only one party and one candidate running. Such landslide victories have never been seen in the decadent capitalist and imperialist countries that claimed to have a democracy. It was, as some irreverent people dared joke, like a horse race with only one horse running; there was no chance to make a bet. Anyway, in those first few years of communist rule, betting was considered a decadent capitalist activity and not allowed.

The communist government declared new national holidays based on dates commemorating significant events in "the people's struggle for liberation." Each block in the city organized a local Street Committee composed of members of the Communist Party, and a few days before each holiday, the communists went from door to door and rang the bells of each apartment to "remind" the occupants of the coming holiday and to tell everyone to decorate their windows.

On national holidays, the people were expected to hang nice carpets out of their apartment windows, and the neighborhood communists watched who did, and who did not decorate the windows. The government also organized the workers in factories and offices to march to the central plaza of the city (then renamed the Plaza of Marshall Tito), and to stand there and listen to the speeches of local communist officials. Individual communists were always dispersed within the crowd to give the cue for 'spontaneous' applause. The crowning event was a recording of Tito's speech blaring from multiple loudspeakers all over the central square, and only when that was finished and the last big hollering and clapping applause ceased, everyone was allowed to go home.

These mass demonstrations of the people's joy were supposed to be voluntary, but people felt pressured and were scared not to participate. Another communist

Junior High: Little Pranks And New Awareness

novelty was the organization of voluntary work actions, whereby city dwellers were supposed to sign pledges to perform voluntary labor, which meant they would help construct new apartment buildings and roads. Whole families would participate, and children, "the pioneers", were welcome, too.

The Street Committee kept a record of how many labor hours were given by each person and family. At the end of each year, the communists would publish the names of those who gave over five hundred hours of work, and those lucky citizens were proclaimed "national heroes of labor" and given the medal of labor. Out of fear, most people donated at least some token hours.

All members of our family, Aunt Ester included, donated each year some hours of volunteer work, carrying bricks at a local building site or similar manual labor. Though we disliked it, we were afraid to stay away from the voluntary effort that was supposed to show our devotion and support of the beloved people's government.

In our neighborhood, I met several boys with whom I used to play on the street or in our courtyard. Sometimes the boys brought a ball and we played soccer. The soccer ball was heavy and did not bounce because it was made of a heavy cloth and filled with rags. A real leather soccer ball was unobtainable. I also participated in some silly pranks with those boys.

Our courtyard was enclosed, and many people kept their chickens in it. One of Michael's friends had given me a small silk parachute about five feet in diameter, obviously the kind used during the war for shooting night flares to light up the area during night raids. I played with it, letting various objects drop from our third-floor balcony. One day, the idea came to me that I could also drop a basket with a chicken hanging under the parachute. The chicken that was easiest to catch belonged to a tenant in our apartment house who lived on the ground floor below us. I tied the chicken securely inside a small basket and let it slowly float down with the parachute. All my friends watched with great delight.

The chicken must have been frightened flying without being able to flap its wings, and it made loud squawking noises. A neighbor came out on her balcony, saw the spectacle, and promptly reported it to the owner of the chicken and to Aunt Ester. Aunt Ester confiscated my parachute. The silk could anyway be put to better use by making out of it ladies' underwear, she said, since underwear was in terribly short supply. I also got a good tongue lashing, but no spanking, for Aunt Ester and Uncle Stanislav regarded the incident with a bit of humor.

Uncle Stanislav could not suppress a good laugh over the whole affair. My worst punishment was the embarrassment I had to suffer when Aunt Ester made me go downstairs, ring Mrs. Božić's doorbell, and tell her how very sorry I was for mistreating her "little chicky."

Another prank I remember from that time was the idea of one of the neighborhood boys. He obtained somewhere a load of used, discarded, negative film. One could wrap a length of the film with paper into a tight roll, close one end, light the other end with a match, extinguish the fire, and throw the roll in the air. The smoldering film would smoke intensely, and the smoke coming out of one end of the paper roll made it fly like a rocket for quite a distance. We had quite a bit of fun with the film rockets, and then one boy had a new idea. On an early summer evening, we shaped a nice big roll of film into a rocket, and two boys climbed onto the brick wall of our courtyard. They stood just below a large round vent, looking at the backstage of the neighborhood dance hall. The film was lit, extinguished, and tossed through the vent over the stage where the musicians were playing. We heard the music stop, and then the screams of people leaving the hall and running through multiple open doors onto a large side terrace on the other side of the building. The boys jumped off the wall, and we all disappeared from the courtyard to the safety of our apartments.

In my first year of junior high, I had a clash with a boy, Zvonko Ž., whom I actually liked. It was an argument over some silly issue that I no longer remember. Since we both had an aversion from being punched in the face, we decided to settle it in a "more civil way," by wrestling till one threw the other one to the ground. During the school recess, we went into the cloakroom behind the classroom, and some of our classmates were delighted to form a human circle around us and watch the fight. We wrestled, puffed, and moaned for quite a while, and neither of us could push the other down. We were getting tired, and finally our legs entwined and we both tripped and crashed onto the floor. Each of us thought he won, and we were happy to stop wrestling. Our classmates declared it a draw. Zvonko was bigger than I was, and I was satisfied with the outcome. I held my ground.

The next day, he did not show up in school, and a day later, when he did appear, he had a cast on his left arm. For the next two weeks, I felt pretty bad having to look at that cast, but he was nice enough not to show any hard feelings, since it was clearly an accident. He and I remained friendly, and though we later attended different high schools, we stayed in touch and used to meet occasionally. Many years later, in the late sixties, while walking the streets of Toronto, I met Zvonko by chance and we chatted for a while.

I continued to be a good student, with a B average. I had my favorite subjects, where I excelled, but I also had subjects where I was just mediocre. One of my favorites was ancient history. At home I found an old book from before the war, a book belonging to my older cousins. The book was not the text required by the school, but it had more than enough information, and as a bonus, beautiful pictures and stories about the Stone Age, Bronze Age, and Iron Age, about the Egyptians, Babylonians, Assyrians, Phoenicians, Persians, Greeks, and Romans, about India, China, and Judea, and it was all just fascinating. Reading that book was a real escape.

In subsequent years, when I learned the history of the middle ages in Europe and especially local Balkan countries, it could never match the magic of the ancient people of Egypt, Greece or Rome. In fact, the closer history got to current events, the cruder and uglier it seemed to become. By 1947, we finally got new history textbooks sanctioned by the communist government. The new books were verbatim translations of Soviet Russian textbooks, and they were heavily invested with the communist slant and propaganda.

According to these books, everything that ever happened in the world was done and caused by the people. The people made history happen, not kings, or emperors, or other leaders. Well known historic persons played only secondary roles, because they really followed the will of the people. A few exceptions were people like Spartacus and the leaders of the French Revolution. Aside from this biased political slant, it still appeared that the condition of the people in the world after the fall of the Roman Empire grew worse by the century. First, there were hundreds of years called "the dark ages." Then, after an improvement during the Renaissance, came an event much applauded by the communists: the French Revolution. The French Revolution may have had a positive effect on mankind, but its execution and aftermath was murderous, cruel, and unjust. The guillotine killed many innocent people. Next was the Industrial Revolution, which brought benefits to the middle class, but enslaved workers with inhuman labor conditions, including child labor. Finally, came the First World War, which when I read about it, appeared the culmination of human savagery. At that time, the Second World War was not yet history. We had just finished living through it, and it was not yet in our curriculum. I learned about the Second World War mostly at home.

Every now and then, I heard Uncle Stanislav talk about the war and the politicians who instigated it, and about the kind of people who wanted to be involved in it. Uncle Stanislav knew people in Zagreb who during the war actively collaborated with the Ustaše. Several months after the war, he saw the same people working for the communist government; some had even become members of the Communist Party. Politicians were filthy, dishonest people who were not to be trusted, Uncle Stanislav calmly declared. Politicians, he said, came from the ranks of people who turn with the wind and who for personal gain were capable of committing any crime. The new communists may have liberated the country from the fascists, he said, but now they were behaving nearly as badly. The only difference between the fascists and communists was that the communists, at least for the moment, did not stand for any ethnic or racial bias. Uncle Stanislav always cautioned us never to get involved in politics and never to associate with any politicians, lest we be badly burned.

In the fall of 1946, Aunt Ester decided I should receive some cultural education by studying to play the piano. We had at home the upright from my grandfather's house, and soon I had a music teacher, Miss Mary H., who gave piano lessons for a reasonable fee. She lived a little further out, near my grandfather's house, and twice a week I walked to her house and spent an hour learning piano technique and music reading. She was a very kind and patient teacher, and I enjoyed the lessons and being able to read sheet music and play songs. Bluma was receiving music lessons in violin from Mr. T., a member of the opera orchestra, which at the time was renamed the "People's Opera."

Bluma had no ear for music, and Mr. T. grew exasperated. Her screeching and off-key notes made one's hair stand on end. Uncle Stanislav loved music, and he was very disappointed when Bluma (or the teacher) finally quit the lessons.

I remained his only hope for musical education, and I continued practicing and playing piano for the next eight years, throughout high school. I was supposed to play only classical music. According to Aunt Ester, popular songs and jazz were "just trashy noises, not worth wasting your time with."

About that time, nearly a year after the war, I saw a movie for the first time. It was Disney's *Fantasia*, and I was enchanted by it. It left a lasting impression on me. Next I saw *The Great Dictator*, with Charlie Chaplin, twice. Then the *Great Expectations*, with Estelle, who was so beautiful that I saw her regularly in my dreams, although that movie also gave me nightmares from the horror of the opening scene at the cemetery, with the disfigured convict catching the little boy. I was on the way to becoming a movie buff.

At home, Aunt Ester grew tired of our "tenants." No matter how much she cleaned, vacuumed, and dusted with DDT, the bugs kept reappearing. Finally, she hired a company to perform "cyclonization" of the entire apartment. Cyclone was the name of a poisonous gas, very similar to what the Nazis used to suffocate their victims in the concentration camps. We had to seal all windows and balcony doors of the apartment with paper tape, and then we had to move out for three nights and stay with any friend or neighbor we could find.

The chemical company crew, wearing gas masks on their faces, put a large canister of poison into each room of the apartment. As soon as we left, the canisters were opened, and the entrance door was sealed with tape. Large signs with a skull and bones were glued to the door of the apartment. On the third day, the apartment was opened, the poison canisters were closed and removed, the rooms were aired for eight hours, and then we were allowed to move back in. The fleas, bedbugs, and lice were dead, and we no longer had to sleep on bed sheets full of DDT powder.

In the summer of 1947, our family was doing very well. We had a relative abundance of food, and our two stores prospered so that Uncle Stanislav was able to put aside significant savings for the future. We could also afford a vacation on the Adriatic Sea. The government of the people owned all hotels; that is, the hotels were poorly managed. At least it was possible to book a room and get basic services. Everyone in the family was scheduled to get a short turn in the resort of Opatija in the northern Adriatic, near the port of Rijeka. It was beautiful at the seashore, even though the water had oily black blotches on the surface, and one came out with a greasy ring around one's neck and gray specks on one's skin. It was said that the oil refinery in the nearby city of Rijeka spewed the pollution, but no one paid much attention to so small a nuisance.

After only four days, my turn at the Adriatic beach was cut short, due to an accident. Bluma's boyfriend Karel and his friend Bobo were vacationing on the nearby island of Mali Lošinj. While learning to ride Bobo's motorcycle, Karel

Junior High: Little Pranks And New Awareness

slipped, fell, and slid across a dusty gravel road, scraping the skin and flesh off his right shinbone. He was brought by boat to the hospital in Rijeka with an infection and a raging fever. Hard-to-find antibiotics had to be obtained quickly. Strings were pulled, money was provided, and penicillin was found. I was sent home, and Bluma came to stay at our hotel so that she could spend time with Karel and nurse him. His recovery was slow, and he barely survived. It was two months before he was able to come home to Zagreb, and he forever had a tender scar running from his knee all the way to his ankle, and his lower leg had to be kept bandaged up.

In subsequent years, I got to know Karel D. and his family quite well. His older brother Zoran used to study law, but he interrupted his study to go to work and support the family. Karel's father used to work for the city as a manager at the zoo in Zagreb. After the war, he retired, and he liked to go around the pubs drinking and having fun with his friends. He lived with a mistress, and gave hardly any money to support his family. After Karel and Bluma were engaged, Karel's father started paying friendly visits to our apartment, usually in the early evening, at suppertime. Many times, he arrived tipsy, and this was to me amusing.

Aunt Ester always played a generous host, although underneath she resented his visits, for it was clear that the man was abusing his position of the future "in-law" and was coming just for a free meal. When he was well plastered, his visit only added to Aunt Ester's aggravation. Karel also had a younger sister, Barica, who was about Bluma's age. Barica's boyfriend was Bobo N., and he owned the motorcycle that Karel rode in the accident. Bobo did not go beyond high school education. He was interested in cars and motorcycles and preferred to work in his father's shop as a mechanic.

Karel was enrolled at the University of Zagreb in the School of Chemistry, but he was behind in his studies. He eventually did get a chemical engineering degree, but it took him seven years instead of the usual four. His school record, however, did not matter because he was handsome and charming. It was always fun to be with Karel; he knew so much about life, especially things that interested an eleven or twelve-year-old boy. I really liked him and would ask him questions and listen to his explanations and opinions. He seemed particularly knowledgeable about love, sex, sports, and other such important subjects.

Karel was also good at organizing Sunday picnic excursions, usually to a remote bank of the river Sava. Those outings were made on bicycles with his colleagues and a whole group of other young people. Our family had two bicycles, and in those days, they were our principal means of transportation, other than city buses and streetcars. At first, I was too small to ride a big bicycle, but in a year or two, I learned to ride the girls' bicycle. Sometimes Karel and Bluma took me on their picnic excursion, and on those occasions, Karel had me sit sideways on the bar of his bicycle. It was not a very comfortable ride, but I would do anything to be allowed to come along with the big boys and girls. They played soccer with a real soccer ball in ankle deep water, in part of a quiet side arm of the river. Both men and women played in their bathing suits, and they often slipped and fell into the mud under the surface of the shallow water. At the end of the game, they were all covered with black mud, and it was great fun to watch. Afterwards, they swam in the deeper part of the river to wash off the mud. I could not swim, but Karel would put me on his back and swim with me holding onto his shoulders. Then we would sit on a blanket and have our picnic lunch in the shade of a tree or next to a large bush. Afterwards, everyone would rest for a while before taking the long journey home, bouncing over the rough, dusty, country roads.

Two years after the war ended, in the fall of 1947, our class was held for the first time in a proper school building not far from where we lived. The army units that used to occupy the school had finally been demobilized or moved into army barracks. Everything was getting back to normal, and the memory of war was slowly fading.

For my twelfth birthday, Karel gave me a book by Karl May: *Winnetou*, a monumental work in three volumes about the American Indians (the term "Native Americans" was not known to us). In that book, I again discovered a new world. At the same time, I became better adjusted and happier at home and began to enjoy school. It felt as if I was beginning to acquire the life of a normal child my age, in a family that, though it was a little different from conventional families, was nevertheless my own. In school, I experienced my first "falling in love," though it was much more a child's fantasy than real love.

The school was co-ed, though the classes were divided into either all boys or all girls. In the parallel class, there was a girl I began to like, though I saw her only during the five- or ten-minute recess in the hallway and never dared speak to her. I somehow managed to learn her name and eventually her address. Armed with that knowledge and a talent for daydreaming, I remained in love with her for about two years. My love life thus happily solved, I could concentrate on novels and short stories, and all the other interesting people and events around me.

That fall, Aunt Ester allowed me to have a real birthday party and invite six friends from my school class. I remember my first post-war birthday party very well. My friends arrived with modest gifts. Aunt and Uncle went out and left Bluma home to supervise us. Bluma asked Karel to come over and keep her company. While we boys played in the family room, Bluma and Karel stayed in the living room, behind the closed French doors, listening to quiet music. We played various games and made a bit of noise, not enough to bother Bluma. At one point though, during the game of blind man, it was my turn to be blindfolded and to try to tag the next guy. The other boys dodged me as silently as they could. All of a sudden, the silence became absolute, and while I was blindly trying to tag the next guy, I heard strange noises from the other room. My friends started laughing loudly. I took off my blindfold and looked around, and my friends made funny signs with their hands, pointing to the other room, and laughed even more. I chose not to notice anything.

A few minutes later, Karel came out, passed through our room, and went home. Bluma came out a little later and asked if we were all right. Of course,

Junior High: Little Pranks And New Awareness

we were, and we continued to play our games. Afterwards, I showed my friends one of the books I discovered on our shelves: *The Perfect Marriage*, by Van der Velde. It had many very "educational" illustrations from married life that would be of great interest to twelve-year-old boys, most showing the act of sex, but naturally only the marital kind.

There were two more episodes I remember from the time I was twelve. In the neighborhood were many boys with whom I played soccer on the street. One of these neighborhood boys was a little older and a full head taller than I. He met me once on the street and found some pretext to push me to the wall of a building and start slapping me in the face. I looked for help, but there was no one on the street. I tried to push him away, without success. In desperation, I kneed him in the groin. He fell down and started writhing in pain. I just walked away. That fellow never came near me again, and I gained a bit of confidence.

The other episode happened in class. I shared the bench with a student from Belgrade, a Serbian whose father was a high-ranking officer of the Yugoslav army. He was tall, blond, and a little shy, perhaps because he spoke with a Serbian accent. We got along quite well, and I sometimes went to his apartment to play or finish our homework. The math professor that year was a stern older man, and all of us were a little scared of him. He had a reputation for hitting the students.

Towards the end of the school year, while this professor was examining a student at the blackboard, my bench mate turned to me and quietly asked something. The professor saw and heard him, and was furious that he wasn't paying attention to the proceedings. The professor approached our bench and ordered him to stand. I froze in place, looking straight ahead. Then I heard a hard slap. I looked up and saw my friend holding his face, blood streaming out of his nose. The professor was walking back to his desk. I took my friend by the hand and we went to the bathroom to clean up, after which he went straight home. He was missing from school for a few days, and by then it was the end of the term.

About a week later, Uncle Stanislav received a certified letter from the local court requesting that on a certain date the following week I come to school early in the morning. No reason was given. I was frightened, for I knew there would be an investigation of the incident. My friend's father was a well-connected communist. When I appeared in school, two other students who sat in class behind my friend and me were also present. We were called, one by one, into the professors' conference room and questioned about the incident. The school director was there with two professors and a third man, a detective who recorded what was said. I testified that I heard a slap, but I did not see it. The detective asked repeatedly how could it be that I did not see the slap. Sitting with my head facing forward, I could not see anything above the professor's waist in front of our bench. It turned out that the two students who sat in the bench behind me also heard a slap, but did not see it. Our testimony was sufficient, and the next school term, the brutal math professor was transferred to a small provincial town. He deserved to have been booted, and we were all relieved. My friend and his family, meanwhile, moved out of town.

At home, I met a few more members of our family. Uncle Stanislav had a younger brother, Uncle Bernard, who left his native Romania at the age of eighteen and settled in France. He worked nights and attended school in the daytime, and became a chemical engineer. Being both bright and diligent, he eventually patented a process for producing a major agricultural nitrate fertilizer. During the Second World War, his wife was killed in an allied air raid on Avignon, France, and he was left with two young children. In 1947, he married a young French woman, and wrote to Uncle Stanislav that he would like to spend his honeymoon on the Yugoslav coast and visit with us.

The two brothers had not seen each other for over ten years. It was arranged that Oliver and I would sleep at our friends' apartments, so that Uncle Bernard and his new wife could have the master bedroom, and Uncle Stanislav and Aunt Ester would sleep in the living room on the couches that were normally used by Oliver and me. Only the younger of Uncle Bernard's two children, ten-year-old cousin Sara, came along. We had a week of festivities, good food, and lots of fun.

During this visit, Bluma and Karel again asked her parents to allow them to be engaged. Uncle Stanislav and Aunt Ester wanted to postpone it, but with family in the house, they finally gave in, and so we celebrated the engagement of Bluma and Karel with Uncle Bernard's family.

Uncle Bernard's new French wife spoke German, so we could all talk together, but Aunt Ester was suspicious, wondering how and where she learned to speak German with such a good accent. Michael had learned quite a bit of French in high school, and he could speak to his new aunt in French. His knowledge of French, unfortunately, caused a misunderstanding.

One afternoon, while Michael was talking to his new aunt in the family room and Oliver and I were studying behind the closed doors in the living room, we heard a hefty slap. Then there was silence. Later, we noticed that Michael had one red cheek. Thereafter, he avoided his new aunt. Otherwise, we all had a good time with our French relatives, and I often played with Sara, who spoke both German and Yiddish.

After about ten days, Uncle Bernard's family packed up to go to the Adriatic seashore, and we saw them off to the train station, gave each other lots of hugs and kisses, and promised to see each other soon. Ten years would pass before I got out of Yugoslavia and visited Uncle Bernard's family. Stuck behind the Iron Curtain, Uncle Stanislav did not see his brother for an even longer time.

Bluma and Karel married at the end of 1950, before Karel finished his studies at the university. Uncle Stanislav found them a sublet room in the apartment house next to ours, so that they could easily come to our apartment and eat with us. Times were hard, and Bluma's bank salary could hardly pay the rent for their sublet

Junior High: Little Pranks And New Awareness

room. In 1951, Karel finally graduated and became an engineer of chemistry and started his first job at the new film factory Fotokemika.

Karel, unfortunately, had a chronic weakness for chasing other women, and he kept this habit well after his marriage. Film manufacturing has to be done in the dark, a fact that was partly to blame for Karel being caught with a female co-worker "in flagranti" (in the act), that is, in a very embarrassing position. He had to look for another job.

One night in 1951, Bluma came at two a.m. to our apartment and woke her parents crying, worried that Karel had not come home. Karel had apparently left in the afternoon to get some exercise at the Rowing Club on River Sava. Michael offered to walk to the house of Bobo N., by then the fiancée of Karel's sister. In the middle of the night, they both went on Bobo's motorcycle to search for Karel at the Rowing Club, far on the outskirts of the city. They awoke the club attendant, who claimed that Karel had not been there in a long time. Michael returned home in the morning very angry. Karel came back to Bluma later in the morning, safe, sound, and very happy. He had spent the night "celebrating the graduation of his best friend." Telephones were at the time not common, and few people except members of the Communist Party had one.

There was one more person in my extended family—Karel's sister Barica. She was a very pretty young woman. At her engagement party to Bobo, there were many guests, and among them was a young Italian boy, Gogo R., whose father worked at the Italian Consulate. Gogo was distinguished by the fact that he had a real novelty in town, the first Vespa scooter in Zagreb. He was pleasant, polite, and on the quiet side.

At the engagement party, Barica asked Gogo if he would give her a ride on his new Vespa. They soon became good friends, and Gogo would frequently visit her and take her for a ride all around town. When her fiancée got wind of these afternoon rides, he was not so pleased. He did not think a Vespa, a mere scooter, was better than his BMW motorcycle. There was trouble, and soon we heard that Barica's engagement with Bobo was broken. Then, within a very short time, Barica announced a new engagement, this time with Gogo. Gogo's mother was from Greece, quite conservative, and for some reason she was not happy with her son's new liaison. Pretty soon, Gogo's mother came to call on Aunt Ester, asking for her opinion about Barica's family. I do not know what the two ladies talked about or what they concluded, but in any case, nothing could be done because "the children were in love." So, despite Gogo's parents' tenacious objections, Barica and Gogo were married, and Barica thereby achieved the dream of many girls who studied languages at the University of Zagreb. No, she did not really care so much for the Vespa; it was the Italian passport she was after, and with it the chance to go abroad and live in the West. And so, by marriage, our extended family was enriched by Italians and Greeks.

My last year in junior high was 1948/49. For my thirteenth birthday, Karel gave me *Anthony Adverse,* by Harvey Allen, a book about an orphan born and raised in Italy, ending his life in the New World during Spanish, English, French, and Dutch colonization and the horrors of the slave trade, before the era of United States. I loved that book, and read it repeatedly. For that same birthday, Uncle Stanislav gave me my first fountain pen, a Parker with a gold nib, a symbol that I was ready to approach the world of adults. I would rather have had a novelty recently invented in France, a ballpoint pen. Aunt Ester talked me out of it: ballpoint pens leaked, and their greasy ink smeared all over the paper, messed up people's hands, and left marks on shirt pockets. Uncle Stanislav owned one of these novelties; Uncle Bernard gave it to him. Since no refills were available in Yugoslavia, Uncle Stanislav had to throw the ballpoint pen away when it ran out of ink. Aunt Ester was happy because it would no longer mess up his shirts and jackets.

At the end of my last year in junior high school, Uncle Stanislav had a worker's employment coupon for a two-week vacation in a typical, government-run facility on the Adriatic coast, in the Dalmatian town of Omiš. He gave it to Bluma, who was working in the bank and had not gone on vacation since 1946, and Bluma would take me along. That summer, Bluma's fiancée Karel had an internship in Dugi Rat, only a couple of miles from Omiš, at a chemical factory producing plastics based on polyvinyl chloride. This was nice because he and Bluma could spend time together, and I had relative freedom. The local sandy beach was known for long stretches of shallow water, just three to four feet deep, and there, with the help of good ocean buoyancy, I finally learned to swim. I tried and tried, till I succeeded swimming a few yards without any aid. I was exhausted after just a few seconds of keeping my chin above the water. Later that summer, back in Zagreb, I joined a swim club on River Sava, and there I was taught to swim properly, with my head submerged and my mouth coming up only quickly to breathe in the air. In fact, I joined the swim team.

As I found out a few years later, the plastics factory in Dugi Rat exposed local workers and their families to a known carcinogen, from which scores of people in that region subsequently died, most of them from liver cancer.

Our apartment was stacked with books. Uncle Stanislav and Aunt Ester were avid readers, and so was Michael. I, too, began to read voraciously. I particularly liked novels about travel to exotic lands, Russian stories from the Arctic, Amundsen, stories by Erich Kästner, Jules Verne, Zane Gray, and the Russian "stories about things," especially the story of the development of the clock through the ages. I also perused the public library in the city, which was free and just a few blocks from home. I used to immerse myself in reading, fantasize about the world, and forget about the time or anything around me.

My older cousins brought home some documentary books describing "the war of peoples' liberation," fought by the Partisans in Yugoslavia. In those books, I read detailed descriptions of events during the war in Croatia and Bosnia and the rest of Yugoslavia. It reminded me of the tragic stories I heard while I was with the Partisans. However, the extent and horror of the events described in these books was much greater than I realized. Only then did I begin to grasp the scope of killings that took place in Croatia and Bosnia during the war. Certain units of the Ustaše had with them a photographer who took pictures of their exploits. The records of those actions and the photographs of the deeds eventually came into the hands of the Partisans and were published. The pictures in one of the books were particularly gory. They showed Serb civilians being stabbed with bayonets, mutilated bodies with cut-off noses and ears and gouged-out eyes, an executioner holding a severed head, bodies of dead women and children scattered on the ground. There were also scenes depicting mass conversions of Serbs to Catholic religion.

Not long thereafter, I went to see a Red Cross movie showing Nazi concentration camps as they appeared immediately after liberation in 1945. Live people, thin like skeletons, were barely moving, as if the film was made in a slow motion. Some were not moving at all. Heaps of corpses, dead people—their stiff bodies piled up like logs. Bulldozers pushing the bodies into deep pits used as common graves. People with masks and protective suits were seen pouring white liquid over the bodies in the pit. I left the movie in a daze and then I thought of how lucky I was to be alive, and how grateful I was to the Professor and the good Bishop Šimrak.

Only recently did I feel an urge to gather and again read the books I read when I was thirteen years old. I obtained most of the books and additional ones documenting events from the war in Yugoslavia, Croatia, and other parts of Europe. Between 1939 and 1945, millions of innocent civilians, most of them Jews, were killed in concentration camps and many other locations throughout Nazi-occupied Eastern Europe. The fate of my parents and other members of my family in Croatia was similar: on orders given by local government leaders, my parents were taken to concentration camps and murdered. In the next few pages, I wish to summarize what I found in multiple reliable references.

Over three hundred thousand people belonging to minorities in Croatia and Bosnia, mostly Serbs, Jews and Roma, were murdered between 1941 and 1944 in Croat concentration camps and occasionally in their villages, rounded up by units of Ustaše, or in Bosnia by the volunteer units of the Muslim Division. The local government and military leaders including several thousand individuals who facilitated or directly participated were responsible for deliberate mass killings of innocent people, including women and children. Many of the victims were abused as slave labor and brutally tortured prior to being killed. All this was done as a part of ethnic cleansing.

Toward the end of the war in 1945, units of Partisans murdered several thousand Italian prisoners of war in Istria. An unknown number of Ustaše were caught trying to escape the country in 1945, and Partisans in Slovenia executed many close to the Austrian border. Most Ustaše who surrendered in Slovenia were marched back to Croatia under deplorable conditions. During and immediately after the war, hundreds of civilians accused of collaboration with the Nazis and Ustaše were jailed, and the communists killed many of them. I could not find any reliable documentation with a list or a number of victims of the Yugoslav communists in 1945, but in any case, the latter number amounted to a fraction of victims who were killed between 1941 and 1944. [1, 2, 5, 6, 8, 10, 13, 16, 17, 18, 21, 25]

The events concerning the Jews in the Independent State of Croatia may be summed up as follows: within weeks of establishing the new government in April 1941, Ustaše leaders issued orders to round up the Jews and send them to various concentration camps, mostly Jasenovac and other camps in Croatia, and later also to Nazi Germany. Most statistics show that there were about 70,000 Jews in Yugoslavia before the war; only about 10,000 Jews were identified after the war. At least 30,000 Jews were eliminated within the territory of the Independent State of Croatia. Some of the wealthy Jews in Croatia were arrested early, and their property and assets were taken away in exchange for their liberty.

In 1941, in the very first days of the war, the Catholic Church and its leaders gave their full support and blessings to the Ustaše and their leader Pavelić, and the Catholic clergy throughout Croatia and Bosnia organized and helped the Ustaše disarm local units of Yugoslav army and take over the power.[11]

By 1942, after many atrocities and killings of minorities in Croatia, some Catholic Church leaders began to protest to the authorities, but to no avail. In the case of some of the Greek-Orthodox Serbs, the Catholic Church accepted and in some instances advised conversion to Catholic religion, and the Serb converts were thus able to save their lives. Jewish converts were not so lucky: their fate was sealed by the plan to exterminate ethnic Jews, regardless of their conversion to Christian religion.

In the course of the war, however, some of the clergy, while nominally supporting the Ustaše regime, secretly protected Serbian and Jewish minorities. I personally know several such members of clergy, and I am grateful to the Professor, who was an ordained Catholic priest, and to Bishop Šimrak and all other clergy who knew my identity and saved my life, as well as the lives of several members of my family, at grave risk to themselves.

In 1941, as news about Ustaše and Nazi atrocities spread throughout the Yugoslav population, a growing number of people joined two major resistance movements, one led by Tito's communists, and the other led by Četniks, the ultra-nationalist Serbs who operated mostly in the eastern half of Yugoslavia. Četniks' leader was Draža Mihajlović, a former officer of the prewar Yugoslav army. When Tito's Partisans began to gain the dominant role in the resistance movement, the Četniks switched sides and began to fight for the Nazis and against the Partisans. The Četniks also began to terrorize, plunder, and kill people they considered enemies. After the war, the Četniks continued their guerilla fight until 1946, when Draža Mihajlović was finally caught, tried for war crimes, and executed by the communists. [10] However, for more than five years after the war ended, there were small groups or individual Četniks hiding in the woods and living in caves in remote parts of Yugoslavia, aided and supported by their families and Serb nationalists. At the same time, there were also a few remaining groups of Ustaše hiding in the countryside of Croatia, aided by their families and Croat ultra-nationalists hoping to someday start an uprising against the communist government.

Nazis in Germany first decreed the elimination of Jews in order to achieve a pure Aryan race. The leaders of the Independent State of Croatia made a similar decree. Along with that, Ustaše followers spread the theory that Croats were not of Slavic origin—that they descended from the Persians and thus were Aryan. The Ustaše adopted and zealously applied most of the racist Nazi propaganda, dogma, and laws. In a similar manner throughout Nazi-occupied Europe, from France to Ukraine, Poland, Slovakia, Lithuania, Belarus, Holland, Belgium, Latvia, Hungary, Norway, Romania, Greece, Czech Republic, the new local governments, aided by thousands of collaborators, rounded up the Jews and sent them to Nazi death camps. In many places in Ukraine, Poland, and Lithuania, local collaborators volunteered and participated in mass killings of Jews, burying them in shallow graves outside their towns. The plunder of properties was an additional motive in Croatia, Bosnia, and the entirety of Nazi-occupied Europe. [23] Most of the plundered properties have not been returned to the surviving owners or heirs. [20]

While the Jews suffered the Holocaust, thousands of other innocent people from various nations were also destroyed during the Second World War. As for the victims, statistics show great variation in estimates. When one reads published reports, the quoted numbers of innocent victims killed during the war in Europe vary widely. However, the number of Jews who perished in Europe is counted in millions, and in Yugoslavia, the number of Serbs killed are counted in hundreds of thousands, and Croats and other nationals in tens of thousands. In each case, the exact number of victims will never be ascertained. When it comes to murder of innocent people, whether it is expressed in millions or thousands, every life destroyed is a crime against humanity. The enormity of the crime transcends the relevance of an exact count and deprecates a discussion about numbers.

Even in the twenty-first century, I noticed that despite all the documentation about the Holocaust, some deniers still attempt to show that members of their nation committed fewer killings than reported by most sources. The desperate efforts of Holocaust deniers appear futile: the truth has and will come out. Some Holocaust deniers intend to revise their own national history. These revisionists are trying to cover up and diminish the crimes committed by their own citizens, at the same time that they vastly exaggerate the number of victims in their own nation. By distorting and concealing the truth, revisionists aim to save their national conscience and protect their children from the truth about the misdeeds committed by their ancestors.

In at least one European nation, Germany, the truth has been brought into the open. Knowing the truth has given the German people a chance for healing. Within the last few decades, whole classes of high school children in Germany have been taken to museums set up in former concentration camps, to learn about that dark period of their history. The Germans have thus achieved a balanced and healthy attitude without the need for further guilt and recrimination. Most other European nations, whose citizens during the war actively participated in the Holocaust, still do not own up to *the truth. Sometimes it takes a nation more than a hundred years for negative historic facts to be recognized. A case in point is the steadfast refusal of the Turkish government to admit the massacres of Armenians committed one hundred years ago, though it is a well-known and well-documented fact.*

SENIOR HIGH SCHOOL – FURTHER AWAKENING

Education on the European Continent was at the time radically different from that in English-speaking countries. In general, there were no colleges on the continent, and therefore the senior high school played the role of a liberal arts college. After junior high, those who did not wish to attend senior high school went to various trade schools to become carpenters, plumbers, masons, builders, and electricians. The senior high school curriculum was strict and rigid, demanding that all students take all subjects without exception. One foreign language was obligatory during all five grades, Russian. One also had to take a second language for three years, and one could choose between French, English, German, or Latin. Written tests were few: only math, a few required essays in Serbo-Croatian language, and simple translations in foreign languages. The test methods were such that more than eighty percent of grades were based on verbal answers to professor's questions in front of the class, and in math at the blackboard. This was particularly difficult for shy students who sometimes froze and remained speechless, even when they knew the right answer. This system was known in Germany as "Gymnasium" and in France as "licée," or "liceo" in Italy. At the end of high school, there was a rigorous examination, verbal and written, leading to the baccalaureate degree. After that, one could go on to higher education at a university or take a job in civil service or in a business office. Those who wanted to go to a medical school in Yugoslavia had to be A students with a baccalaureate degree and have some knowledge of Latin. Other schools within the university did not have special requirements, except that for some of them, one had to pass a general entrance exam in addition to having high grades on baccalaureate. Those who were well connected easily bypassed these requirements. Entering the university required a token tuition, equivalent to about one dollar per semester. University education in Yugoslavia was accessible to anyone with good grades, and it was affordable to anyone in Zagreb who could simply live at home. Students from out of town had to have some modest means to live in a dorm, but even that was, in a communist economy, inexpensive, and it was often subsidized by the government, which granted special stipends.

In the fall of 1949, at nearly fourteen, I entered senior high school. School space was in short supply, and our high school building was shared with another high school, so that on any given day, one school had a morning session from eight a.m. to one p.m., and the other school had an afternoon session from two to seven p.m. The remaining half of each day was left for homework. To be equal, the school sessions alternated, so that one week we had school every morning, and the following week every afternoon. The school week was six days, only Sunday was considered a weekend, and the normal workweek at that time was six days. We walked to school or took the streetcar or a city bus. A school bus did not exist. For those who lived far from the school, it was tough luck. They had to walk to school, whatever time it took, or they could use public transportation if it was available.

The high schools were crowded: there were over forty students in a class, with two to three parallel classes in each grade. The professors were mostly older, and most were skilled professionals, strict and demanding. A few young new professors were obviously members of the Communist Party, and they usually read their lectures from notes and were far less skilled, if not outright clumsy. Since the choice of attending senior high school was left to the students and their parents, the student body in the senior high school was, by the government standards, predominantly "reactionary"—that is, children from families educated and well off from before the war. People who did not join the Partisans or the Communist Party were designated as reactionaries, people disposed to be against communism and the government.

"If you are not with us, you are against us," was the communist slogan. The government made sure that at least several students from communist families enrolled in each class of senior high school. The communist students were the snoops who spoke with a different accent and dressed expensively but without taste. Most of us recognized them and knew that one had to watch every word and not say anything that might be construed as critical of the government or daily events. With all the nonsense coming from within the framework of the communist doctrine, it was hard to keep our mouths shut and refrain from laughing or making fun.

Our high school class had evolved into little groups, or cliques of friends who, during recess or outside the school, socialized and did homework together. A group of several boys from the Greek-Catholic boys' school in Zagreb, sons of formerly rich peasants ("kulaks") always stuck together. Several loners kept to themselves, and no one knew what they thought or how they felt. The few communist students, when their attempts to mix with others failed, ended up forming their own little group. We were polite and spoke with one another when it was necessary and appropriate, but deeper social contact outside the school barely existed. As Ivica M. and I were already close friends since junior high, we became part of a small group with five other boys in our class. Ivica came from a well off family of educated people. His father was a prewar member of the Communist Party, from a time when many educated people naively believed the myth of social justice as it was described in the Utopian Marxist texts. In 1945, when the communists took power in Yugoslavia, Ivica's father was soon disappointed, but he knew how to keep quiet about it. The friendship between Ivica and me blossomed over several years. On many a Sunday, the two of us went together and trekked the path up the mountain of Sljeme, had lunch with his family on top of the mountain, and went down again by ourselves. On some of those Sundays, we braved the steep, muddy, slippery paths and the bad weather and cold. To get extra pocket money, we occasionally did odd jobs; for example, we once gathered and sold old bottles from the storage bins in our apartment buildings.

Many times, Ivica and I went for a walk in the city, stopped for a pastry in our favorite pastry shop, or went for an ice cream. One morning, we both came

Senior High School - Further Awakening

to school pale and tired from a sleepless night, as both of us had been throwing up all night. The next day, the press wrote that over one hundred and ten people in the city had to be hospitalized with a gastric infection from bacteria isolated from the ice cream in our favorite ice cream parlor. We remembered that the boy serving us had a bandaged hand, and the bacteria most likely came directly from his infected wound. A large family from Kosovo ran the ice cream parlor, and it was closed for a couple of weeks and then re-opened. The lawyer who defended the owners and helped them reopen the store was none other than the father of one of our classmates, Josip C., a member of our group in class.

The other four boys in our group were Ante E., Stjepan Z., Marko N., and Tomislav X., the son of a merchant whose father before the war owned a store near my father's store, and our fathers knew each other. Marko's father was the curator of a small museum, and his mother was a high school professor of English and German. As soon as I met her, I knew she was of Jewish origin, but Marko never mentioned it. A few years after the Holocaust, people were still afraid to reveal their Jewish heritage.

Stjepan Z. was the son of a university professor. His mother died when he was a small child, and his father married a younger woman. The seventh member of our group, Ante E., lived in an apartment alone with his older brother, a university student. His parents were divorced, and his mother, who lived in France, supported both of her sons. Ante's father was a lawyer who was jailed by the communists for having served as an official in the Department of Justice under leader Pavelić. However, Ante's father had a brother who joined the Partisans and helped him get out of jail. Ante's father then escaped from Yugoslavia and ended up somewhere in the U.S. Ante had a stutter that got worse when he was excited or upset.

We were a diverse group of boys, but we had a few things in common. We all came from families that cherished higher education, we all strove to achieve, and we all wanted to get somewhere. We all grew up in Zagreb and spoke the local dialect with a familiar accent. We often went to one another's apartments to do homework together, and we helped each other on many occasions. Aside from this group of boys, in the next two years I also became a good friend with Ivan U., a classmate who was quiet, kept mostly to himself, acted reserved, and was a bit of a loaner. Ivan was, throughout high school, one of the top students in our class, and with him I shared the bench for two years (most classrooms still had benches for two students). Ivan stayed away from sports. He supposedly had a mild heart condition following a childhood illness. He lived with his widowed mother, and they had a hard time making ends meet. He regularly tutored a younger, less gifted student, whose widowed mother eventually had the pleasure of initiating him.

Ivan carried a tragic aura around him, and most likely, this had to do with the fact that his older brother had disappeared in the last days of the war. Despite being fairly close to me, Ivan never spoke about his brother, and I found out about his fate much later, when we were students at the university. These were the major friendships I had during high school. I kept in touch with a few other friends that I met at sports clubs, the music school, or earlier in junior high and elementary school. Since a large part of our class went to medical school, I was able to retain most of my high school friends at the university.

However, all through my adolescence, I felt most attached to Oliver. He was not only my first cousin; he was my best and dearest friend, my greatest support. Though he was six years older, we understood each other very well and always helped one another. Together we survived the war at the boys' school. We were Paul and Peter. For ten years, we shared the living/dining room of our apartment as our common bedroom. For all those years, we exchanged the last words late at night, just before falling asleep, and the first words in the morning after waking up. Sadly, soon after Oliver's engagement and marriage, our friendship vanished, evaporated. We never had a quarrel.

Our estrangement was at least partly due to a mistake I made unwittingly. Oliver started dating a girl who would become his future wife, and once early in this relationship I cautioned him to beware, for I had the impression that she was "not too nice" a person. Oliver had dated many girls before, and we always freely discussed those relationships. We were as open as two brothers, but I could not predict that his latest fancy would become his one and only. Oliver obviously shared my remarks with his wife. I can only say that I was young, and whatever I said to Oliver was because I loved him and cared for him.

My remarks on Oliver's future wife were partly based on an impression of her aloof and "uppity" demeanor, and fueled by an unpleasant experience I had with her younger brother. He once "lent" me a photoflash to use to take some pictures and then claimed that the flash was rented. He demanded a considerable sum of money for the rental. I paid him fully, but the episode left me with a bad taste. Now I am old enough to know that one should not form an opinion about people based on one or two incidents or observations. What was done was done. Oliver slowly drifted out of my life. Nevertheless, the memory of Oliver and Pavle (Paul) forever remains in my mind as one of the fondest of my youth.

I tried to contact Oliver by phone in 1970, when I was attending my father-in-law's funeral. On that occasion, his wife answered the phone and told me that Oliver was "resting and could not come to the phone." I let it go at that. We had not been in touch for over four decades. Curiously, after his marriage, Oliver also severed his ties with the entire Rubin family. Years later, on a visit to the U.S., he did not even want to see Uncle Stanislav and Aunt Ester, who were living in Michael's house. Oliver has severed all connections with Cousin Bluma, too.

* * *

By 1949, our family's financial situation had become quite difficult, and Michael had to move back into our apartment. He was still attending medical school. I never developed a good rapport with him. He was moody, had a volatile temper, and was a difficult person. He got into fights with everyone, including Aunt Ester and Uncle Stanislav. I was no exception. Being smaller and younger, I got the short end of it. Once, when just the two of us were home, Michael ordered me to do something, and I refused. He lashed me with his belt, so that for a while I wore blue welts, marks from his belt buckle, on my back. I managed to kick and punch him a few times in the belly, but it did not seem to do him much harm. From that moment, I avoided contact with him as much as I could. My relationship with Michael would remain in the form of a sparse, polite discourse. He was my elder cousin and brother by adoption, so we had to have formal contact, but I tried to keep our conversations to a minimum.

Encouraged by the professors of literature, I began reading classical literature: Balzac, Tolstoy, and other well-known French, Russian, and English writers. These classic works, besides teaching me the art of good language, also revealed a fascinating new world of human characters, relationships, politics, and intrigue. My vocabulary broadened. I discovered a trove of new words, like "cynical," "hypocrite," and "perfidious," words fitting for conditions I had been seeing in the communist system. The life and political system I was familiar with could now be described with proper adjectives. I knew there would be plenty of use for the new expressions in the real world, but I restrained myself. I was content to think in real terms without saying anything.

The government press was full of half-truths and deceit, mixed with smidgens of irrelevant truth. I began to see that the world in which I lived did not care for or tolerate the truth. Neither truth nor justice existed. The politicians representing the government trampled on the truth. Justice was not just blind; it did not exist. The politicians ranged from scoundrels to thieves and robbers, and some were responsible for murder. Most people, instead of trying to make the wrongdoers accountable, joined them and enjoyed the spoils of power. Uncle Stanislav was right about politicians: it did not matter whether they were fascists, Ustaše, Nazis, or communists; they were all similar.

At that time, yet another event in Zagreb shook me up and upset me. A large cache of jewelry, gold chains, wedding rings, and gold teeth was discovered in the crypt of a small Catholic church in the old "upper town," a few hundred feet from the Cathedral of Zagreb, the seat of the archbishop. The criminals who hid the loot did not even have the time to melt down the gold. The items were obviously plundered from victims in Croat concentration camps. Wasn't a priest for several months the commander of the notorious extermination camp Jasenovac? Catholic Church authorities later defrocked him. The news about the cache of loot reminded me of the awful events during the recent war.

By 1949, it was common knowledge that most of the top Ustaše leaders, those who spawned the orders for mass killings and those directly involved in the murders, had escaped at the end of the war into Italy. As they claimed to be refugees from communism, they were charitably hidden and sheltered in special safe houses in Rome by the Vatican clergy, which helped them to immigrate to South America, Canada,

Australia, and the U.S. Some of the worst Nazi war criminals and Nazi collaborators from France, Holland, Ukraine, Poland, Lithuania, Latvia, Slovakia, Hungary, and other lands continued to live quasi-normal lives with the aid of their sympathizers at home, or in emigration, using the money and loot they plundered from their victims.

Over the next few years, I uncovered more facts about what politicians and many ordinary people did during and after the war. Knowing that the criminals got away with their crimes without any trial or punishment, gave me a bitter feeling. Bitterness gnaws on one's inside; it is not a good feeling, and it took several years before I was cured of it. I worked as hard as I could to drive the ill feeling out of my mind. Being cognizant of the evil caused by politicians both during the war and after, my belief in government authority and justice was badly shaken. With all this evil, injustice, and dishonesty around me, where was God while crimes and mass murder were being done? With all His omnipotence, absolute goodness, and omniscience, how could He have allowed evil of such magnitude to reign? Did God lose his fight with Satan? If so, the devil will take the whole world with him to hell and fire. Many adults who claimed to be religious were obviously just pretending, for their behavior betrayed their lack of respect for truth, goodness, and honesty. These hypocrites would readily go to confession to obtain the absolution of sins for the price of a few prayers, and then continue to behave in their usual depraved manner.

Children and adults who were truly honest and pious trusted in God; the rest of the people seemed to have turned to Satan. God appeared to have forgotten millions of his children, including people like my parents, my family, and the Jews at large. Such thoughts led me to question and doubt God's existence. I noticed that Aunt Ester and Uncle Stanislav did not practice any religion. When I asked them about God, they said that each person, while growing up, has to meditate and decide for himself. When I asked Oliver about believing in God, he just laughed and said, "Who knows? Do you know anyone who saw him lately?"

I gave God's existence the benefit of doubt. If He existed, His presence was a lot different from the way He was presented in the religious books. Maybe God was just an invisible spirit, an unattainable ideal. If God did not exist in the form in which he was described in the books, at least love existed, for love was something I felt coming from all those who loved me. Love, too, was an ideal. I was taught that God loved us all, and maybe God was Love itself. In the world of my fantasies and daydreams, the girl I was "in love with" was perfect, divine, just like God. I believed that someday I would find such a real girl, and I would want to marry her. Often in the evenings, when I had trouble falling asleep, thinking of that perfect, ideal girl, seeing her image in my mind, allowed me to drift to sleep in a most pleasant way.

In my early years of senior high school, my daydreams and fantasies began to include a vague idea of what I wanted in my future: someday, I would grow up and have a family, children—my children. Above all, I would do everything possible to live in a place where my family would be safe from war. I needed to find such a place. It had to be as far as possible from where I was and where I suffered so much loss, far from the place where my parents were taken away from me. I kept remembering how my parents wistfully spoke about "Amerika."

The state of Israel had come into existence in 1948, and being a Jew, I certainly considered it as a possible destination, but something did not feel right. Five thousand years ago, it may have been the Promised Land for Moses, but in the twentieth century? Instead of "milk and honey," it was a country at war. I'd had enough of war. I wanted to live in a place where there was peace and safety, as far as possible from any war. I had already paid my dues to war.

Emotionally, of course, I was attracted to Israel, but the more I read about it, the better I understood that this new Jewish homeland, Israel, was not a solution for me. As much as I was drawn to Israel, I also felt I had to resist it. I deserved to live in a happy place. Perhaps my desire was selfish, but after what I went through, I wanted peace and security. I wanted to live a full life, to make up for all the time my parents did not have. I thought about Israel and here is how I saw it at that time:

1) The state of Israel was established by the UN upon a final, decisive, tie-breaking vote from the communist Soviet Union, by order of a tyrant, Stalin.

2) The state of Israel was given only a sliver of Palestine, from which the British carved out Jordan, where majority of people were Palestinians.

3) It was known prior to the UN vote that if Israel were to declare its own state in Palestine, six surrounding states would declare war against it.

4) Israel was one of the two states in the world officially established as a theocracy. *At that time, Pakistan was the other one.*

No matter how much love, attraction, and sympathy for Israel and the Israeli people I felt in my heart, I did not want to live and have a family in a country at war. I also could not imagine living the rest of my life under a theocracy any more than under communism. Israel was not a place where I saw my future.

As later events would show, Israel was capable of winning a number of wars and battles, it developed a burgeoning economy, and reclaimed parts of the desert and turned it into green, fertile land, but despite all the economic success, it has not won the peace. The track record of the UN regarding peace between the Arabs and Israel has been very bad, and both the actions and outrageous inactions of the UN in troubled areas of the world have not been any better. [22] For fifty-odd years, there have been a few truces between Israel and Jordan and Egypt, but there has never been a time of real, lasting, guaranteed peace. Some Muslim nations do not want to make peace with Israel and say so openly. The most radical Palestinian and Muslim leaders have declared that "the Jewish entity" should be eliminated.

From what I knew about the imaginary "Amerika" of my parents, and from what I gleaned by reading literature and hearing the news on Western radio stations, the U.S. was a decent and safe place. Gradually the U.S. became the dream of my future.

For more than a century, thousands of Europeans have emigrated to the U.S. My secret adolescent dream gradually transformed itself into a desire, a determination, and finally a plan that I would not reveal to anyone. I made a firm decision, a sort of personal oath in honor of my parents: when the time was ripe, I would escape from Yugoslavia and go to live in the U.S.

I began to read all sorts of books to find out why Jews were so hated, why anti-Semitism in Europe was so widespread. The vast majority of my friends were Catholic, and after the war, I grew up in a predominantly Christian society. With my Catholic friends, I felt completely comfortable. Having spent three years in a Greek-Catholic boys' school, I was thoroughly familiar with Christian religion, and I was even more knowledgeable about it than most of my friends. On holidays like Christmas or Easter, which were not recognized by the communist government, I used to visit my friends, wish them and their family a Happy Easter or Merry Christmas, and participate in the festivities as if I were one of them. Of course, because of the communist intolerance towards religion, those festivities were held quietly and privately at home. For Christmas, however, I used to join my friends at midnight mass, which was given in the cathedral. They sang beautiful carols, and I enjoyed participating. Never, in all those years, did I feel any anti-Semitism from my closer friends, though I believe that at least some of them have been exposed to it within their own families. My friends never made any anti-Semitic comment, and I am inclined to believe that this was not only due to personal friendship, but because they truly resisted such feelings. And yet, in the broader society, both anti-Semitism and intolerance towards anyone foreign—Serb, Roma, Sloven, etc.—was widespread. The intolerance was evident in common expressions and vernacular as well as occasional "slips of tongue" or even deliberate outbursts, using derogatory names like "Čifut" (kike), "cigan" for Roma, "Šiptar" for an Albanian from Kosovo, "Srbenda" for a Serb, "Kranjec" for a Slovene, etc.

During those first years of communist rule, offensive remarks or verbal abuse of any ethnic or national group or minority were officially forbidden and punishable by law. However, in everyday life, little outbursts against a minority could be heard frequently, particularly from persons who thought that they were safe, believing that they were "among our own kind." As long as such verbal abuse was not directed at me, I learned to just swallow hard, keep quiet, and slowly walk away. I learned in my youth that tolerance and love had to come from the heart and could not be enforced by law. On the other side of the coin, I took pleasure knowing that the communists had no control over what people thought, and as long as I did not say it aloud, I could think or believe whatever I wanted.

Both from reading on the subject and from my personal experience, I found that in Europe, the main sources of anti-Semitism were the church and the home. The priests disseminated anti-Semitic invective straight from the pulpit. Christians grew up being taught as small children that Jews had crucified Christ, were evil, and that they were an "alien race." Even Jews who assimilated and accepted Christian religion were still considered foreign, unsavory, and untrustworthy. A Jew was greedy, money grabbing, and dishonest, a peddler who did no regular work, or a scheming merchant out to cheat the Gentiles. Even in literature, there was Fagin, Shylock, and many more.

What I experienced in my adolescence was confirmed throughout my later life. Many years ago, on a visit to Italy, I saw in the little Museo Diocesiano in Trento, Italy, a small sculpture of an infant called St. Simonino, taken from a local church altar and described as "the infant martyr who was sacrificed by the Jews," on account of a local baby found dead near a Jewish house around 1505. A Franciscan priest spread the news of that infant martyr throughout Italy, and it sparked widespread killings and persecution of Jews. On the Internet, it is easy to find the picture of St. Simonino by a search on Trento Museo, St. Simon, and clicking on "Anti-Semitism in Art: The Middle Ages," which lists and shows little St. Simon and multiple examples of similar myths used as a pretext for killing Jews.

In the middle ages, the Christians fabricated myths that Jews sacrificed the babies of the Gentiles in their religious rites. Russian anti-Semites fabricated The Protocols of the Elders of Zion, *a scathing accusation against Jews, whose fake origin and pure anti-Semitic intent was later proven beyond doubt. [12] The Vatican's own publications show that orders and instruction for the treatment of Jews came straight from the Pope to the bishops and then to the individual clergy. [3] Over many centuries, the Church has built a widespread prejudice against the Jews, embedded in the story of the Passion and the rest of Christian beliefs. [15] Religious belief or persuasion unfortunately leaves no room for logic or critical thinking, nor does anti-Semitism.*

Where I grew up, generations of people have been taught in their homes, from parent to child, and by the church that Jews are an evil lot, that they committed an unforgivable sin. Two thousand years ago, the Jews not only failed to recognize Christ as their Messiah, but they caused the Son of God to be tortured and nailed to the cross, and thus He gave His life for the salvation of the people. It is said that Pontius Pilatus, the Roman governor of Judea washed his hands, as if he had nothing to do with the decision to nail the Christ to the cross. For that sin, the Jews, God's Chosen People and all of their children's children, would receive eternal punishment and revenge and be vilified and persecuted for as long as they existed.

I also noticed that among Christians, there existed many individuals who were decent, had open minds, did not succumb to prejudice, and were not anti-Semitic, but what was the percentage of those people who, despite their upbringing, remained free of prejudice? Such people were a minority where I grew up, and from reading recent history, the ratio of people free of prejudice was not much better in most parts of Europe, except in Denmark and Bulgaria.

Aware of anti-Semitism, I developed a chip on my shoulder. When I grow up, I thought, I won't be a merchant or a businessman, or a politician or a lawyer or banker, and I will at all costs stay away from those professions for which the Jews were so reviled and criticized by the Gentiles. Of course, I saw all this as a perpetual injustice: the Gentiles were well entrenched in commerce, and they could freely indulge in finance, banking, usury, and all those trades that they accused the "evil" Jews of practicing fraudulently. Jews represented a minority of people, and therefore they could be easily dispensed with, as was done on countless occasions through the centuries. Jews had no choice but to bear this injustice as they best could. There was a Latin proverb: "Quot licet Iovi, non licet bovi!" (What is legitimate for the god Jupiter is not for the oxen!) How did one deal with this? One could try to disguise himself by assimilation, as was done by hundreds of thousands of European Jews. The problem was that assimilation takes at least two or three generations. A whole lifetime is not sufficient for a Jew to become assimilated; it may be only an investment towards the safety of future generations. The other alternative was to leave Europe, find a more open and tolerant society, and move there. That would work, and it was my choice.

After the Second World War in Yugoslavia, only about fourteen percent of Jews survived and returned home. In Zagreb, they restored the Jewish Community Center, but did not rebuild the temple, and in a communist system, there was no rabbi. For ten years after the war, the Jewish temple that Ustaše destroyed was left in ruins, hidden behind a tall fence in the central part of the city. Most of the younger people and many adults did not even know what was behind the fence. One day, the fence was taken down, the lot cleared of debris, and a small, state-owned department store was built in its place.

For several years after the war, Uncle Stanislav and my remaining family never went near the Jewish Community Center. The reason was simple enough: in 1941, the leaders of the Jewish Community Center, including the local rabbi, gave to the Ustaše government the list of all people of Jewish origin. That list included not only current members of the Jewish community of 1941, but also all those former members, who had opted out and converted to the Catholic religion.

On a few occasions, Uncle Stanislav gave me serious advice, both for school and for life. With my Jewish background, he would say, I should strive to be about two times more knowledgeable in school, and three times more productive at work than the Gentiles were; only then might I expect to be rewarded on a level equivalent to Gentiles. This was a "Jewish ghetto attitude." Being practical and realistic, I understood and accepted that principle. Then I also came across some "friends" who, after getting to know me a little better, "complimented" me by saying how they "never would have guessed" that I was Jewish, for my behavior was so contrary to what they knew about Jews. One such friend, I found out, had never met a Jew before, but somehow knew "how they were."

At the age of fourteen, I was becoming cognizant of the world I lived in. Influenced by classic literature and having read ancient Greek philosophy, I began to search deeper inside myself. "Know thy-self," I learned. Without knowing yourself, life has no purpose. Little by little, I found out the traits I did not like—rash response and anger. I looked at myself, and I saw that I occasionally acted in a rash manner or got angry. Michael and Aunt Ester often acted rashly, but Uncle Stanislav and Oliver were calm and gave a slow, measured response to any problem. Uncle Stanislav told me that my maternal grandfather Silber was volatile and "had a temper." My mother, as I recalled, was always calm. I became critical of my own behavior. When I noticed rashness or the feeling of anger towards people, I immediately stopped talking. I wanted Oliver and Uncle Stanislav to be my models.

I worked hard to control and to suppress my temper, and if it showed its ugly head, I did not let it come out. I trained myself to hold my breath and keep my mouth shut whenever there was an unpleasant event, or if harsh words came across my ears. Breathe, concentrate on your breathing, count slowly to ten in your head, and if you still have something to say, do it in a cool and deliberate voice! Control yourself! It took a while before I learned to keep cool even under pressure, but when it worked, I felt a lot better about myself. I could control myself; I would not lose my temper or act foolishly. The result was that I rarely got into conflicts or fights. If there was a potential for disagreement, I knew how to withdraw without giving up much ground.

Gradually, I realized that under pressure I was able to perform better than under normal circumstances. This control also served me well during the oral exams throughout my schooling: when the professor asked a question to which in the first instant I seemed to have no answer at all, I did not panic. I would calmly think, and the answer would just pop into my mind. Much later, in my professional life, whenever I had to handle a difficult situation, a calm, deliberate response won me respect from my peers and my bosses.

Privacy, or rather the lack of it, was an issue I became aware of at home. Aunt Ester had an insistent curiosity and needed to know everything about all of us, even our innermost thoughts. She would ask, "What are you thinking about right now?" and I would evade the answer. I caught aunt Ester reading Oliver's letters and some of my own notes. I decided never to keep a diary, for it would not be safe. At the time, I was too young to understand that Aunt Ester was doing this out of love and care for us, to protect us. She used to tell us that everything she was doing, was "for your own good," and "to save you from your own stupidity."

Aunt Ester took good care of us, but growing up under her care was not easy. In those days, I really resented her ways. I understood her, but I could not agree with her. Here again, I have to digress. Guess whom I enjoyed the most in the well-known TV series *Seinfeld* from the nineties. It was neither George nor Kramer, nor the hilarious Elaine. It was George's mother. She even looked like Aunt Ester, only with a different hair color, and she acted very much like Aunt Ester. Now I know that there are a few Aunt Ester doubles floating around. Seinfeld did not invent the character of George's mother. He must have known such a person. Aunt Ester's meddling taught me that in her presence it was best to either keep quiet or use as few words as possible. Aunt Ester interpreted whatever was said in her own way, and her conclusions were often right, but sometimes she was dead wrong. In her presence, I learned to speak only if asked a question, and my answers were short and to the point, without gratuitous comments. To avoid misunderstandings,

I learned to keep my thoughts to myself and stay quiet for long periods. When I was with my friends, though, I could be lively and natural. Depending on the company and the subject, I learned to be relaxed and open, or if needed, very much on guard.

Though I did not like Aunt Ester's poking into our private lives, there was one occasion when her insistent pursuit and dogged devotion probably saved Oliver's life. It all started in the summer of 1947 when Oliver complained of feeling weak, and Aunt Ester found that he had a fever of about 100.2°F (38°C). Oliver was immediately examined by our family physician who could not find a specific cause of fever, considered it due to a virus, and advised a few days of rest at home. After one week there was no improvement, and Oliver lost some weight. He was then admitted for observation at the Hospital for Infectious Diseases. The hospital physicians could not make any definitive diagnosis, and they suggested that the fever would just run its course, and with time, Oliver would recover. After a week in the hospital Oliver's fever continued, and he was in bad shape. When Aunt Ester saw him all weakened and emaciated but still without a diagnosis, her hackles were raised, and she was ready to move the mountains. Without a moment's rest she ran all over town seeking the best physicians. She kept repeating: " Ich muss ein Consilium aber nur mit den besten von Internisten haben" ("I must have a group consultation, but only with the best internists"). Within two days Aunt Ester found, persuaded and recruited three experienced internists to jointly give a private consultation on Oliver's case. The consultants convened at the hospital, looked at Oliver and his medical records, and suggested that he had a smoldering infection in the area of appendectomy which he had received four months earlier. Oliver was put on hard to obtain antibiotics, his abdominal scar was surgically explored, an abscess (pocket of pus) was found and drained, and his fever soon abated. He started gaining weight, got back his strength, and a week later he came home. Thank you, dear Aunt Ester!

THE GLORY OF COMMUNISM: UNDER THE TABLE AND THE HOME MANUFACTURE

By 1947, the Yugoslav communist regime was well established, and the "people's government" gradually started to implement Marxist communist theories and principles in the economy. The government maintained that no one individual should be allowed to own any land at all, nor any substantial real estate, nor should anyone own a private business employing other people. Only the government or government-run companies were allowed to employ workers. The communists wanted to prevent the "exploitation of people by people," which, they said, was practiced by individual employers or private companies in the capitalist system. Consequently, at the beginning of 1948, private businesses were gradually taken over by "the people"; that is, they were nationalized and owned by the government. Every small or large business was now run by the state. The government employed salaried managers and workers. All business revenue went to the government. Commercial buildings (factories) and large houses with apartments were also nationalized. Most of our inherited real estate, except for a maximum of four rooms per one owner, was taken over and nationalized. Even if an individual owner had retained a four-room house, the land under the house belonged to "the people," that is, to the state. As no one had any real estate to speak of, taxation became unnecessary, and so we lived in a paradise free of taxes.

By the end of 1948, the nationalization process was completed, and practically all private enterprise ceased to exist. The upper management, the executives who now ran the businesses, needed only one qualification: membership in the Communist Party. The new managers had no clue how to run a business. Because of the ineptitude of the new communist managers, most stores soon had empty shelves. No consumer goods or food was imported from abroad because the communists had other priorities: all foreign currency was used only for the government's "strategic" purposes. Communism brought the entire economy to ruin, and here follow a few examples.

New aluminum factories were built far from the source of the ore, and even further from the source of electric energy needed for aluminum extraction. New dams were built on land so porous it could not hold water. Goat and sheep herders from the barren mountains were relocated to work on collective farms on fertile land in the valleys to cultivate crops with which they had no experience. In a time when renowned film factories (Kodak, AGFA, Gevaert, Fuji) had the power and know-how to supply the entire world with film, Yugoslavia, according to Marxist principles, had to become "self-sufficient" and have its own film factory. Naturally, the industrial products of Yugoslavia were of inferior quality. Photographs taken with film and black and white photographic paper made in Yugoslavia appeared foggy. X-ray film had so many unintended spots that one never knew whether a spot was caused by the patient's illness or it was a simple film defect. The products made by the Yugoslav industrial plants had no market except within the country or in undeveloped countries. A few communist Eastern European countries were politically compelled to become trading partners. Cheap Yugoslav hammers, screwdrivers, drills, and badly made radio receivers were bartered for small runty bananas from third-world countries whose leaders were friendly with Marshall Tito.

Perhaps the most catastrophic of all measures was the introduction of the collective farms. All farmers were forced to join collective farms modeled after the Soviet Russian communist example. Farmers had to work the common land around a village, and an executive, imposed by the government, managed all products. Each farmer waited to see how much work his neighbor would do; no one wanted to do more than the other. The farmers' productivity spiraled downward. At the same time, the government rationed the prices of all farm products so that farmers were forced to sell their products at rock bottom prices. With no profit, the farmers' productivity spiraled even further down. They produced just enough food for their own needs. With no surplus to sell, produce, meat, dairy and other farm products disappeared from the city markets.

The Yugoslav agriculture, it was said, was reminiscent of the fabulous wazu bird, which with its long neck resembles the flamingo. Have you ever heard of the ancient wazu? No? The wazu bird may be recognized by a very peculiar habit: it flies in circles with an ever-decreasing radius, in spirals that become smaller and smaller and smaller, until the bird ends up flying into its own ass. So the story went, and thus went the farm productivity in the communist system. Food markets in the cities closed. All this happened despite the fact that collective farms utilized tractors and other mechanized farming equipment. Those familiar with the prewar economy remembered that Yugoslavia used to produce ample food for export from private farms cultivated using wooden ploughs pulled by oxen. We were told that building socialism and communism was a gradual affair, a process that would take a few generations, and we had to be patient.

So it happened that three years after the war, we were again starving. Since the shelves in the stores were empty, we had no clothing or shoes. We were issued coupons for food rations, clothing, and shoes. The food coupons had different values, so the amount of food allotted an individual depended on his or her physical activity. A worker in a mine or factory received a larger weekly ration of meat or bread than a professor, lawyer, or physician, and the least was given to a lowly office clerk who sat all day in a chair. A child received more milk than an adult did. We were also allotted coupons for shoes. Each person got one pair per year. If one grew out of the shoes, tough luck. We each got coupons for a few yards of cloth per year for clothing needs. In those days, clothing (shirts, underwear, suits, dresses, overcoats) were still made by individual tailors. Cobblers made shoes, but first one had to obtain leather for the sole and the upper part. Then there were the ubiquitous queues. As soon as there was a rumor that a certain store had food or any other items obtainable with or without coupons, a queue formed. People lined up and patiently waited until the store ran out of supplies. Sometimes we waited for an hour only to be told that the shelves were emptied. We would go home and hope that next time we had better luck. Meanwhile, the members of the Secret Service and top members of the Communist Party and military were able to buy food, clothing, and other necessities without restriction. For them, everything was available in special stores that imported from abroad any supplies they wanted. Those stores had windows painted white, so one could not see what was inside; they had no signs or markings on the outside, their doors were locked, but there was a bell to call, and one could enter only with a proper ID. Ours was a society with communist equality, where the top communists played the role of "the first among the equals."

For our family, the application of communist theories in economy meant that, as of 1948, we had lost our source of income. Overnight, our two stores were nationalized, and Uncle Stanislav had to seek employment as a salaried middle manager in a government-owned business office. He worked in the office of a chain store, where all decisions came from somewhere higher up. Since there was no food to be found in the open market, the government organized communal kitchens, especially for people who lived in the cities. We were forced to go once a day to collect prepared food for the main meal of the day from public kitchens that functioned like an army mess. We lugged home tall stacks of army-style metal containers with rations of beans, cabbage, beets or potatoes, soup, and sometimes pieces of tough beef or pork, and once a week, even a dessert. The food tasted awful, but when one is hungry, anything goes.

I still remember the stew made of salted air-dried fish called "bacalar" (cod). It stank to high heaven, and I remember Oliver forking it into his mouth with one hand and holding his nose tight with the other. The beans, as usual, had the bonus protein, little worms that came out in the broth during cooking. Some of the larger communal kitchens also had dining halls; on Sundays, we usually went to eat there. On one occasion, Uncle Stanislav put on his reading glasses to see what was floating in his soup. I could see already that it was a well-done cockroach. He indignantly called the waitress to remove the soup, and she just shrugged and brought him another bowl.

On another occasion, a waiter was carrying many bowls of soup on a large serving tray, balancing it with one hand over his shoulder. As he leaned to lower each bowl onto our table, from the corner of the tilted tray came a stream of soup right down Oliver's neck and shoulder. Uncle Stanislav's comment was that the soup was mostly water, and Oliver need not worry; it would not leave a greasy stain on his jacket. This lifestyle went on for several years. For breakfast we usually had home cooked polenta (corn grits) with a little milk. There was a shortage of bread and flour. For supper, we had an egg obtained on the black market or home baked bread smeared with cooking fat and sprinkled with salt. If one found and bought on the black market a can of vegetables or Spam, it was considered great luck.

In the winter, on special occasions, we had a few slices of sausage or ham from "our pig" for supper. What ham or sausages? What pig? Well, we retained the right to work the inherited land next to our former real estate buildings. That land yielded fruit from the orchard (little, round, yellow Mirabelle plums, blue Italian plums, cherries, apricots, peaches) and corn. The former meadow was tilled, corn was planted, and we gave the entire corn crop to a peasant in a neighboring village. In exchange for the corn, the peasant kept and fed for us one piglet. The rest of the corn he fed to his pigs. Year after year, this barter saved our family from starvation. By December each year, the piglet grew into a pig of nearly two hundred pounds, and then it was slaughtered and butchered. We would go to the village and with the help of the peasant's horse-drawn wagon, bring home the hams, various cuts of meat for drying, the remaining meat for sausages, and all the lard for making cooking fat. The blessed pig helped sustain us until the next year.

Much of the fruit from our orchard was made into preserves and compotes for winter. Fresh fruit or vegetables in those days were available only in the summer. Chilean or South African fruit in the middle of winter was not known to us. For winter, Aunt Ester prepared jars of boiled and marinated vegetables bought when they were in season. We harvested the fruit from our own orchard, and Aunt Ester washed, cooked, sweetened, and preserved it in large glass jars sealed with wide rubber bands. The oblong, blue Italian plums from our orchard were used to make a huge amount of jam that lasted us all winter. The preparation of jam was an ordeal usually done on a Sunday, when the whole family was home and could help. Washing the plums and removing the pits was easy. Then the plums were put into a cauldron with water and sugar on top of our wood burning kitchen stove. The plums had to be vigorously mixed with a long, wide, wooden spatula that was almost as big as a baseball bat. As the cauldron's contents grew hotter, its bottom had to be scraped to prevent burning the fruit. The surface of the hot jam would bubble and squirt hot droplets of jam into the air. To avoid being burnt by the flying droplets, we had to stir and mix with the spatula as fast as we could. Mixing the plums was hard work and tiring; we took short turns and then rested our arms. It took a good hour before the jam was uniform and dense enough to be declared done. Uncle Stanislav presided as the referee, and on that occasion, he taught me a bit of the Old Testament.

Towards the end of cooking, my arms were hurting from mixing and my hands had little red burn spots that I earned every time I slowed my motion with the spatula. I repeatedly asked Uncle Stanislav, "When will the jam be finished?"

Finally, he explained that the jam is done when it becomes so dense that one could drag the spatula from side to side across the bottom of the cauldron and see the bottom clear for a split second. "It should be," he explained, "just like when God opened the Red Sea to let Moses pass."

When that moment finally came, the cauldron was pulled to the cooler side of the stove and hot jam was quickly ladled into the jars, which were sealed. The next day, we had to repaint the ceiling and the wall above the tiles over the stove. This ritual of jam production was performed in our household every summer that I can remember.

Speaking of home production, in the first few years after the war, there was a tremendous shortage of ordinary coarse soap, the kind used mostly for laundry. We used the laundry soap also for washing our hands and bodies. Aunt Ester had acquired the knowledge and skill to produce soap during the war. Once every few months, Aunt Ester would obtain unusable fat, bone, gristle, and bad meat from the slaughterhouse, and after cooking it in a cauldron with some chemicals, she made soap. Hot, fresh, liquid soap was poured into large, flat molds, and when it cooled off, it was cut into rectangular bars.

In the Rubin family, yet another little festival was held each summer: the dumplings. Aunt Ester made fresh plum dumplings with potato dough, and we all loved them, especially when they were covered with breadcrumbs doused in melted butter and sprinkled with sugar. In fact, this festival made Aunt Ester so famous that my cousins' friends and my friend Ivica would appear at our apartment on the designated day. Aunt Ester would make more than a hundred dumplings, and all would be eaten in one day. When the plum harvest was meager, Aunt Ester substituted the plums with small apricots. Ivica and I used to come in for an early lunch, and in no time, the two of us would polish off the first thirty dumplings. Aunt Ester was happy and proud.

Uncle Stanislav's office salary was too short to support us, and it was clear that the savings from our former businesses would last only for a limited time. There were seven mouths to feed, and there had to be a way out. On the city outskirts was an area where in prior years the peasants used to bring their horses, cows, pigs, sheep, and goats to sell. With the new communist economy, there was no longer any livestock for sale; now the fairgrounds were transformed into a giant flea market. People gathered and brought whatever used clothing or miscellaneous items they had in their houses to sell or barter for other items they needed. They lugged their wares in a small cart and set up little stands displaying what they had for sale. Many people also had items from the black market that could not be openly displayed. While displaying old pants and jackets, the seller of black market goods would ask in a low voice, "Do you need coffee?" as long as the passer-by was assessed as harmless. The seller had to beware of government informers. Aunt Ester started going once or twice a week to the flea market, and my job was to help her in the wee hours of the morning to carry her wares to the fair grounds. This effort brought in very little money, and within several months, we had exhausted all unwanted items from the apartment and our storage stall in the attic. Our savings were rapidly dwindling. As one would expect in such an economy, the black market was flourishing, and everyone, including government agents, knew about it. One could buy leather, textile, food, or household items, but it was all sold from under the table. If a person was caught buying or selling black market goods, he or she faced a short jail sentence and all merchandise and money was confiscated on the spot. Those were the risks of the black market.

Nevertheless, Aunt Ester and Uncle Stanislav decided to try their luck. From a moral standpoint, most people felt that the black market was supplying items unavailable in government stores, and therefore it was a valuable service and not a crime. People did not agree with the communist notion that only the government should be allowed to procure necessary wares, particularly when that government supplied everything only for top communists, and the rest of the people were left without sufficient food or other necessities of a normal life. Most people also felt that it was wrong for the government to forbid citizens to conduct private business and own stores. We could not freely buy clothing, shoes, coffee, sugar, flour, rice, meat, or soap, not even talcum powder, not to speak of chocolate, bananas, oranges, or lemons. Those and many other items were only available on the black market. Cigarettes were plentiful, and one could buy a cheap homemade radio receiver to listen to government propaganda. It was rumored that many black market items were coming from those unmarked, special stores with painted-over windows, and that a hefty profit was enjoyed by the inner circle of the Communist Party, those who had unlimited access to the imported goods. For the vast majority of people, communism and its practices were a disaster. Its theorists, Marx, Engels, and Lenin were long dead and never experienced the product of their utopian ideas. Tyrants like Stalin and his cronies, and our local leaders, however, enjoyed the spoils of communism. Marshall Tito, usually addressed as "our beloved Comrade Tito," was a national hero. He had a Swiss bank account, a yacht, and villas and castles in several choice places throughout the country. Perhaps he deserved it. As they said, he fought for it.

Uncle Stanislav still had connections with his previous contacts in neighboring Austria. Among other items, the wristwatches in Yugoslavia were nowhere to be found, and on the black market, they would fetch a good price. Uncle Stanislav invited one of his Austrian contacts to bring in some cheap watches so we could try to make a living. The watches were relatively small and easy to smuggle, and selling them quietly, one at the time, would bring a nice income. Of course, the supplier wanted to be paid in dollars. Buying or selling foreign currency, or even possessing it was a crime punishable by jail and confiscation of property. Only the government was allowed to possess and deal in foreign currency. Uncle Stanislav first had to find the dollars and buy them from reliable friends. One of his old friends, Božo V., a jeweler by profession, always had dollars, gold coins, or diamonds for trade. Božo frequently spent time at our home, and in his leisure he showed me how to tell a gold-plated coin from a real one and how to recognize impurities in a cut diamond by looking through a small magnifying lens. His trade, however, was risky. In the early fifties, Božo was caught in possession of dollars by the Secret Service. He was jailed and severely beaten to find out if he had more hidden foreign currency, gold, or diamonds. He recovered from this bad experience and eventually escaped Yugoslavia to live a normal life in Caracas, Venezuela. With Božo's help, we were able to start the black market venture.

The Glory of Communism

Uncle Stanislav's contact from Austria would come for a brief visit to Zagreb and bring a dozen or more wristwatches in his briefcase. We would go to the fair grounds and sell them one by one. While selling old household items on a little bench, Aunt Ester would quietly ask passing people if they needed a wristwatch. If someone said yes, he would be told to come back in ten minutes. In the meantime, Oliver or I walked around with several watches in our pockets and passed Aunt Ester every few minutes. If she had a customer, we left one watch with her. That way, if her client were a government agent, she would have only one watch, and could claim it was her personal property. When left with just one watch in our pockets, Oliver and I would also try to sell them.

One risked being robbed, and a few times a prospective client looked at the watch and suddenly took off with it. Even so, we were ahead in the game. Between Uncle Stanislav's office salary and selling watches on the black market, we could make ends meet and did not starve. There was enough money earned to buy food and other items on the black market. Our stomachs were full. Bluma's fiancée Karel, who was still "ein ewiger Student" (an eternal student), sometimes pitched in to sell a few watches. After all, he regularly ate at our table, and he liked to make a little extra profit for his own pocket.

This black market business picked up nicely, and it came to a point where the Austrian contact would smuggle in and leave a whole briefcase full of cheap Swiss wristwatches at our apartment. Anker was the popular brand name, but occasionally, on special order, we also sold more expensive brands, like Doxa, Omega, or Schaffhausen. We did quite well, and in the fall of 1949, even Michael, who was still a medical student, wanted to help. He figured we could do better by selling a larger volume with a smaller profit per watch. Among his friends, he found a client who wanted to buy three hundred watches all at once. Michael was absolutely sure that his friend was reliable. The transaction would require more than one briefcase of watches, and it required a large sum of dollars for the purchase. It would take a while before the required amount could be procured.

One morning, in the spring of 1950, while I was doing my school homework, our apartment bell rang and I answered the door. Aunt Ester was working at the fairgrounds with Oliver's help, Michael was attending medical school, and Uncle Stanislav was at work in the office. I was home alone. At our door were three men, and one of them, a piece of paper in hand, announced that they came from the internal security service to check out our apartment. I was not too surprised. It was well known that many people periodically suffered sudden apartment searches for illicit black market wares or foreign currency, all of which we kept so well hidden that I did not need to worry. A malicious tip given by a communist neighbor or a false friend usually caused the search. In Serbo-Croatian language, the word for these events was not "the search," but *premetačina*, which literally translated means, "a throw-about." It was a good word, because after a search, everything in the house was left in complete disarray; the contents of the furniture were left literally thrown about on the floor.

I let the men in, and upon their request, I showed them through the whole apartment so they could see the layout. Then they went to work. They started in the master bedroom, taking the clean linen and clothing from the drawers and armoires. They shook each linen piece and then dropped everything into piles on the floor. They uncovered the bedspreads and threw all the bedding covers and pillows on the floor and the mattresses on top. The pillowcases were unbuttoned and removed in a hurry. Feathers went flying. The mattresses had to be thoroughly searched inside, too, and in the end, they were left a bit ripped up. To inspect the contents of the night table drawers, they were turned over and emptied on top of the heap of bedding. I knew we had hidden dollars, but did not fear, for they were either under certain parts of the oak parquet floor (which we knew how to remove and put back in perfect order), or buried in the clay ground under the potato storage bin in our basement stall, tied in a condom. At the time, the watches were also not home: they were being sold. The men went from room to room, leaving each in a state as if a hurricane had passed through. In the large living/dining room, our two couches were lifted and their boxes emptied of bedding. I was worried about our large, round dining room table, which contained all our black market food supplies. The table rested on a single, central, wide, square, wooden column with a somewhat wider foot support on the floor. That massive column was about two feet wide, and its hollow inside could be reached by spreading apart the two top halves of the table. In it, Aunt Ester kept sugar, coffee, rice, tea, and similar rare and precious food items. The snoops glanced at the table and its heavy rug-like cover without realizing that the massive central column was hollow and contained a storage space. Instead, they emptied the contents of the shelves and drawers of the two credenzas. Next was the family room, with its desk and couch. They worked in silence and with relative speed. They appeared to be an experienced team. The desk drawers were emptied on top of the desk and what did not fit fell on the floor. The couch was lifted to see into its box. Again, they found nothing illicit. By the time they reached our foyer and started searching and emptying all the furniture contents there, it was clear that they would come out empty-handed. These internal security men were former peasants or factory workers who had no clue about city apartments or furniture and lifestyle.

My anxiety was slowly turning into quiet satisfaction. I began to feel joy that these gangsters were unable to find anything. They ended their search in the kitchen and pantry, and when it was obvious that there was not much left to do, I became a bit exuberant. Pretending to be friendly and inquisitive about their work, I asked the leader of the group, using the nicest tone possible, whether I could ask a question.

"Go ahead, ask what you want!" he said dryly.

"Comrades," I asked, remembering the proper protocol, "I would like to know whether in your line of work you get paid by the hour or by productivity?"

There was a silence, and the three of them looked at one another. I quickly added that I hoped they were satisfied there was nothing wrong to report in our apartment.

They looked around a little more, then had me sign their paper, mumbled a greeting, and left. I closed the door behind them and then tried to dig up my homework and books from under the pile of things dropped on the living room floor.

When Aunt Ester came home, she had a fit. I told her what happened and laughed about the goons having found nothing, but she was not in any laughing mood. I helped her put at least a few larger items back in order. It took several days to fix the apartment and get everything in its place. It turned out that Aunt Ester did have a few dollars left in the pocket of her house gown, but the slobs did not see them. House gowns were not a part of the attire they wore in their homes, and they did not think to look for the sewn-in pockets.

The day was not over yet. I had to eat a quick lunch and go to school for the afternoon session. When I came home in the early evening, Aunt Ester projected an air of gloom and despair. Office work hours in those days were from seven a.m. to two p.m., but Uncle Stanislav was still not home. No one had seen him. Michael was also not home, but it was not unusual for him to come back late at night. Oliver spent the afternoon at the medical school and came home for supper, but he did not see Michael all day. With grim foreboding, Aunt Ester went to the police, but in the evening, they had no information to give. She was told to come the next day, early in the morning, during office hours. Uncle Stanislav and Michael had not shown up even after midnight, and this was very worrisome. We had just received a large shipment of watches that Michael was to sell to a single client, and Aunt Ester began to suspect that this might have been the day of the transaction, and that things may not have gone right. That would also explain the sudden search of our apartment.

Aunt Ester was right. Uncle Stanislav and Michael were arrested and sitting in jail, and of course, the watches were confiscated. Aunt Ester hired an attorney. We went through a few aggravating weeks until the affair was sorted out. Uncle Stanislav, not directly involved, except for being close to Michael during the transaction, received only a one-month jail sentence, but Michael, who arranged the deal, was sentenced to sit for three months, considering that it was his first offense. The sentences were short, thanks to the successful and pricey intervention of the lawyer. Michael's reliable friend and client was an informer working for the Secret Service. Michael perhaps learned that greed is not a good thing, but he did not learn that in a communist system one cannot trust anybody. A year later, Secret Service agents arrested him again, and that time, he sat in their interrogation jail for only eight days. On that occasion, in a meeting of his class at the medical school, he had criticized some organizational changes initiated by the Communist Party. A friend heard his remarks and denounced him to the Secret Service. While in jail, Michael asked for a lawyer, but his interrogator said, "We are the law, and we are the lawyer!"

He finally learned that the Secret Service was above the law and that he had to keep his mouth shut. More than ten years later, in the U.S., Michael told me that the communist snitch who denounced him in medical school somehow managed to sneak through U.S. immigration and was working as a physician in White Plains, N.Y. Michael also knew of another of his former medical school colleagues, a well known Communist Party member highly connected with the Secret Service and who had committed all sorts of malfeasance in Yugoslavia. He also managed to cheat his way through the immigration system and be admitted into the U.S. to do research at a medical school. It was not clear how those communists managed to deceive the U.S. immigration service and be admitted into the country.

More recently, I heard from a colleague of mine that the individual in White Plains together with his physician wife committed a double suicide and left behind two little sons. It was not clear why this tragedy occurred. The other individual, the researcher, eventually published an autobiography, disingenuously denying his former communist allegiance, pinning some of his own acts of malfeasance on other people.

Right after our apartment search, we began to notice a man standing in the doorway of the apartment house kitty-corner across the street. It was a plainclothes man, and we knew we were being watched. Now we had to look out for the next visit by our Austrian contact and turn him away before he was caught. We still owed him part of the money for the large delivery of watches that ended with the catastrophe. One day, the Austrian came and rang the bell downstairs at the main apartment entrance. As usual, the intercom was out of order, and I ran down the stairs. I recognized him through the glass door, and without opening the door, I signaled him to go away. He understood, turned, and walked away. The spy across the street did not have a chance to catch on. Our black market venture was over, and we had to find new ways to make a living. One of Uncle Stanislav's favorite sayings is appropriate for the end of the black market trading in our family: "Nichts dauert ewig; sogar der schönste Mann wird schäbig!" (Nothing lasts forever; even the most handsome guy turns shabby!) When our businesses were taken over by "the people" and the communists nationalized our real estate, Uncle Stanislav just said, "Yes, yes! Nothing lasts forever..."

While in jail, Uncle Stanislav lost his office job. When he came home, he began to look for a new job, but given his age and recent jail record, it was not an easy task. He decided to try his luck in home manufacture. In our communist paradise, individuals were not allowed to employ other workers, but people were allowed to practice a trade within their own household and with the aid of the members of their own family. The items that one could make in a home manufacture were many. There were shortages of everything, but there was also competition, and one needed to pick something that would succeed and turn a profit. Home manufacture of all sort of items already existed, and the products were carried to sell on the fair grounds. Uncle Stanislav and aunt Ester noticed that house shoes (slippers) were nowhere to be found. This was an item widely used by city dwellers in their apartments and homes. We still lived in a culture where one would not walk inside the house with shoes that were worn outside. This culture evolved in Europe for practical reasons: to save on cleaning, and for hygienic reasons, to prevent the introduction of all sorts of bugs and infections that were present in the outside world.

Uncle Stanislav, at the age of fifty-four, went to learn how to make house slippers. There was a shortage of leather, and he learned to make the soles from rope and the upper parts from cloth remnants. From a cobbler he bought a series of wooden foot forms (models) in different sizes, and then he obtained cloth rests and odd pieces from tailors and from a textile factory. The leftover pieces of cloth came in all shapes and sizes, in flannel and satin, and they were very inexpensive. Coarse string or rope was also cheap and easy to find.

We had at home an excellent old Singer sewing machine with a large foot pedal and a shiny flywheel. Aunt Ester cut the cloth pieces for the upper parts against a cardboard model and then sewed them together with a double layer of lining. Uncle Stanislav made braids for the shoe soles out of coarse rope. This hard work caused calluses on his fingers. Oliver and I helped to braid the rope. The braid was first flattened with a hammer, and then it was wound around three steel nails on the sole of the wooden form until it formed a thick sole of the future slipper. Then the sole was sewn through from side to side with a heavy needle threaded with strong twine. The sewn upper parts were placed on the wooden model with a little starch paste smeared between the two layers of the liner to harden and retain the shape of the slipper after it was taken off the form. The upper (part) was sewn onto the sides of the sole with strong, heavy, nylon thread. A final thin decorative rope braid was again sewn all around the sole to hide the stitching of the upper cloth part. The steel nails were pulled out of the wood form, and the slipper was free to be taken off. Finally, an insole made of cardboard and covered with cloth was glued to the inside of the slipper to cover the rough rope sole and provide a smooth surface for the foot. Voila, one slipper was finished. Now a matching one had to be made to complete a pair.

Was this description boring? Well, if it was, imagine how boring it was to manually make the slippers one by one, at first very slowly, day after boring day. But we wanted to eat, and so we endured. For the next three years, right in the family room of our apartment, we made many hundreds of pairs of slippers of all sizes—men's and women's. We sold them one by one at the fairgrounds, and eventually we sold many dozen pairs to the government-owned city department store called The People's Store (NAMA). Uncle Stanislav had found a means of survival. Nowadays, when I see the little local town fairs at which people derive an income from selling homemade crafts and artifacts, I am reminded of our home manufacture of slippers. Is this what is meant by global leveling?

During my first year of high school, in 1949/1950, I was involved in a violent incident. I used to occasionally play soccer on the street around the corner from where we lived. In those days, there was little street traffic: very few cars or motorcycles. Of course, the communist operatives had a few cars at their disposal. They mostly obtained them at the end of the war while they still wore military uniforms: they simply commandeered and requisitioned any private vehicle they encountered. New luxury automobiles were later imported for the VIPs in the government. There was sparse vehicular traffic in Zagreb, but only on the major city roads. Most city corners had no lights to regulate traffic, and most people used either public transportation or bicycles, or simply walked. We could play soccer in the middle of any small side street, placing temporary goal posts at each end. On one of those afternoons, while I was running to retrieve the ball, which was kicked far behind our goal, a large group of boys ranging from between twelve and eighteen years of age appeared out of nowhere. It was a mean street gang from another neighborhood. The boys in my soccer team saw the gang approaching and they ran to safety in the nearby apartment hallways. The gang was known to be violent, but I had never encountered them before. By the time I turned to go back with the retrieved ball, I was standing in the street all alone, facing the gang. I looked them over and was happy to recognize a familiar face, a boy who had been a classmate of mine two years earlier, before he dropped out of school. I said, "Hi Tom!"

He stepped forward, and as I opened my mouth to ask him a question, he stared into my eyes and then punched me in the mouth. I felt the salty taste of blood on my tongue. The liquid slowly filled my mouth and ran down my chin. With the tip of my tongue, I felt a deep gash in my upper lip, an imprint of the cutting edge of my front teeth. I rocked a little on my legs, but remained on my feet. The soccer ball dropped out of my hands. The blood slowly dripped from my upper lip down my chin, and I wiped it with the back of my hand. There was a moment of silence.

I heard a bigger boy say, "That's enough; let him go!"

Then I heard a male voice from a window of the neighboring building shouting loudly at the gang. One of the gang members picked up our ball, and they all retreated down the street. I was very lucky, for they could have beaten me badly. I went to Bluma's apartment, and she put a cold compress on my swollen upper lip. It took more than two weeks for the gash to heal into a thick, permanent scar. Just as I relaxed, I had to learn to be vigilant and cautious, even while playing soccer on the street.

In the summer of 1950, our family received a voucher for the annual vacation. Travel, vacation arrangements, and hotels were relatively inexpensive, as the government regulated the prices. This was commensurate with the extremely low salaries that the government was giving to all but the inner circle of communist officials. Vacations were affordable, despite the fact that most people lived from hand to mouth and often could not afford enough food in the last few days of each month (salaries were received at the end of each month). We were assigned to go to the Adriatic shore for two weeks in a little "pension," in which the room and board were provided for a very reasonable price. Train transportation was also discounted with a special annual coupon. We rotated the family members, always in a group of two or three in the assigned one room, and I got my one week in Dalmatia in a town called Makarska. The pension was a small guesthouse, right on a clean pebbly beach, and it had only eight rooms, all rented to families from different parts of the country. The food was adequate, and it was served outside on a little terrace. It virtually never rains in summer in that part of the country. On the beach in front of the pension, we met some pleasant people, the ocean was crystal clear and warm, and I practiced swimming. There I met an eighteen-year-old girl from Zagreb who was involved with the rare sport of fencing. I did not even know that women fenced, let alone that communists would tolerate such a bourgeois sport. Anyway, there was Lovorka with a pretty face, dark eyes, long black hair, and legs with the muscles of a gladiator, or at least a male soccer player.

How do I still remember her name? She and I were the only young people around, and she most likely, out of sheer boredom, talked to me. Within a couple of days, naturally, I fell in love with her. That she was four years older did not bother me in the least, and that sweet idea of "love" again lasted me a good while. We all returned to Zagreb recharged, and I was ready for the new school year.

Nothing exceptional happened during my second year of senior high school. The only important change was that my grade average started to creep up from a solid B average to an A-minus. Grades were important if I wanted to have my choice of study at the university. Our professors ascribed my improvement to the good influence Ivan exerted on me, for that year, for the first time, the two of us shared the same school bench. However, the material we studied, especially math and physics, got each year a little harder, and the old established class "elite," the guys who came from their junior high as straight-A students, little by little started falling behind. My grades improved only by default. I was just holding steady. I also became more confident. I had acquired a broader vocabulary and better language skills, and since most of the exams were oral, this worked to my advantage. A similar improvement followed in my written essays. I began to enjoy the subjects we were taking in the higher grades. I had no trouble with math, but I did not find it exciting, either. I liked chemistry better, especially in areas where it supported or bordered on the principles of physics, my favorite subject. I also loved geography. At home, we had some wonderful old prewar maps and a large atlas of the world. I spent many hours looking at the maps and learning the names of odd places, rivers, oceans, mountains, and countries, and it all tied in neatly with the travel stories I liked to read.

Another subject I greatly enjoyed was history, especially of Europe, how it evolved through the middle ages and the Renaissance into modern times. Reading local history, I finally grasped how the Slavic people moved into the Balkan and succumbed to the rule of the Austro-Hungarian and Turkish Empires. Thus, I began to understand the roots of the political issues in the Balkan, the small and complex backwater of Europe where I lived.

Outside the school, I developed a new interest: photography. Karel taught me to develop prints from negative film (only black and white or sepia brown prints were made in those days). I joined a photo club on the corner of the block where we lived and obtained an obsolete prewar camera that used glass film plates as negatives, one photo at a time. In my free time in the late afternoons or evenings, I practiced the art of photography. In the club's dark room, I learned to develop the negative film plates, dry them, and then make the prints on paper. The photographic paper from the local factory was of poor quality, but obtained in bulk, it was very cheap. The paper was in the form of large rolls that had to be cut to proper size in the dark room. While I cut hundreds of pieces of paper to an exact size, my eyes acquired a perfect memory for sizes, a skill that would serve me later in other areas. Within a few months, I started producing some very nice photographs of flowers, trees, and landscapes. Later, I practiced with portraits of people, family members, or friends in school. As soon as I could, I purchased a used camera that used rolls of negative film, and thereafter I used the ancient large glass plate film only for portraits. This hobby eventually turned into a source of income, and I started paying for my piano lessons with my own money.

In 1951, I started meeting young members of the tiny Jewish community in Zagreb. I knew a few young Jewish people in the city, and some of them persuaded me to visit the Jewish Community Youth Club. The club was located in a townhouse near the center of the city, formerly owned by the prewar Jewish Community Center. After the war, all leaders of the Jewish Community were members of the Communist Party. There was no rabbi and no religious service of any kind. It was more of a social club for young people of similar backgrounds. The club had several rooms on the main floor, a small library with some books, an automatic record changer with a few new long-play records, and a few records with old tunes sung in Yiddish. There was a group of young people who seemed likable, and I started visiting regularly about once a week. Many members of the Jewish club were children of mixed marriages; one parent was Christian, usually of Croat ethnic origin. After several months, I was invited to perform with other Jewish club youths in a play to be given in the drama theater of Zagreb. This sounded exciting, and I accepted. The play was a simple story about a Jewish family with children who were with the Partisans during the war. I could easily identify with playing a Partisan child. I was happy to participate, but I had to overcome stage fright, and this took many evenings of practice and rehearsal. With a limited audience for such youth plays, the performance was given only a few times. I was happy to have had the experience of being an "actor" in a drama, although my role was relatively small. There were two other Jewish club members in that drama, a brother and sister, both younger than I; their parents, too, were killed in the concentration camps during the war.

In the summer of 1951, I was accepted for a month-long vacation in a student camp on the island of Krk, in the northern Adriatic, along with several classmates. The camp was run by the communist youth, with a few lectures aiming at indoctrination, but otherwise, it was meant to help kids from the city "get out into the fresh air." Our housing was improvised in a school building during the summer recess. The system of admission was supposed to be a lottery, but judging by the students who were accepted, at least half were chosen from communist families, and for the rest of us there was a lottery. Only two other members of our little group in the high school class got in. The camp had a schedule, and we had to help with simple chores, but there was plenty of free time to enjoy the beach and have fun. I frequently enjoyed the company of older students. At the end of that year, I was going to be sixteen years old, and I felt more and more like an adult and naturally preferred to be around older boys. Even physically, I felt grown up.

In the third year of senior high school (1951/52), my grade average again improved, and for the first time, I became a straight-A student. Only then did I know I would be able to choose my university courses. I was able to follow all school subjects with pleasure, and during class, I sometimes felt bored, especially during other students' oral exams. I kept a book hidden under the bench and quietly read. Sometimes I whispered quietly with my neighbor. That led me to the discovery that I could follow two conversations at the same time. Each time the professor called my name and asked me to continue the on-going discussion, to catch me as "inattentive due to chatting" and give me a penalty in the "comportment" grade, I stood and picked up the discussion exactly where the other student left off. This drove some of the professors up the wall. I felt ready for the university, but I had to endure two more years of high school. Accelerated classes did not exist. That year, I also developed a deep interest in physics. There was something exciting about a subject that required logic, was backed up by math equations, and postulated that every action had a reaction. There was magic in the revelation that a mass always attracted another mass, that there was a wondrous gravitational force, and that a magnet could induce electricity and vice versa. Physics appeared capable of explaining the riddles of the cosmos, Earth, and life, and it reinforced my feeling that God was a separate, abstract concept.

At the University of Zagreb, Professor Supek had written a textbook of physics, including all the latest knowledge and discoveries. I got a hold of it and read it more than once from cover to cover, particularly the chapters about the atom. The atom and its orbiting electrons seemed to have a parallel in the solar system. The burst of energy emanating from the change in the orbit of an electron or a split of the atom—the energy contained in invisible rays, the speed of light, the conversion of mass and motion into energy—all this held the hope of some day deciphering the origin of the universe. Perhaps it could elucidate the relationship between the matter and the spirit. What came first?

Einstein believed in the existence of a spiritual order of nature that could be said to approach the concept of God. Niels Bohr did not believe in any such spiritual concept. Either way, electrons and protons were real and evident; one did not need to "just believe" in them. Even Greek philosophers could not have improved on the atom. Armed with knowledge and concepts of modern physics and aware of the principle that everything flows and changes all the time, my view of the world rapidly evolved, and I was getting ready to accept big changes within myself as well.

NATIONALITY: THE CONFLICT OF BEING

Towards the end of 1951, on my sixteenth birthday, I was due to get my first ID card, something everyone in Europe had to have. To obtain it I had to fill out an application form and provide a photograph. However, a question on that form gave me a pause. I had to declare my nationality. The communist system did not recognize religion and did not ask about it. About my nationality, I had to stop and think, and this one question would delay my application for several weeks. The choices of nationality offered in Yugoslavia were "Croat," "Serb," "Sloven," "Montenegrin," and "Macedonian," and there was also the choice of "undecided," meant for people of mixed parentage or those who felt themselves to be "Yugoslav" and did not want to identify with the listed ethnic groups. There was a blank line for any nationality not listed. "Bosnian" nationality was not listed; it did not yet exist. (It would slowly appear more than twenty years later.) Bosnia was, at the time, a Republic based on a geographic region, as is Appalachia in the U.S. or Lombardy in Italy. None of the choices of nationality suited me. I wanted to discuss my nationality with my family and a few close friends, and consider their advice and opinions. I took the question of nationality very seriously. I felt that my nationality should be Jewish, but some of my friends offered the notion that no such thing as Jewish nationality existed. There was an Israeli nationality, they said, but I protested. I was never in Israel, and I did not speak Hebrew. I undertook a thorough analysis of the meaning of the word "nationality." For most people, the question of their nationality was easy enough to answer. The majority of people are born in a country where their ancestors have lived for generations. However, in every country, there are some people, certainly a minority, who have been born from parents whose country of origin was different, or whose ancestors came from somewhere else, and thus their nationality appears different from the local population. The best examples I knew were the Germans who lived in Yugoslavia for several generations. Most people considered them German, not Croat or Serb, and the majority of Germans themselves felt that they were Germans. There were other similar or more complicated cases. Such people first had to sound out their own feelings and decide: were they Germans or Croats? Then they had to deal with the fact that there might be a difference between how they felt about themselves, and how most of other people in the country felt about them. There was also a third question: what did the law of the country where one lived say about one's nationality? I gathered that the most important factor in assessing nationality was the objective reality imposed by the society in which one lived, including the laws at the time. The laws of a country, I noticed, could change abruptly. I made a further effort to study the true meaning of such words as "nation," "tribe," "nationality," "ethnicity," "race," "origin," "citizenship," and the like, and I used examples from recent history. Jews living in diaspora in Europe, no matter the country, and despite relatively recent laws of emancipation, were still mostly considered an alien minority. In debates with many friends, it was not generally agreed that the Jews even fulfilled the definition of a nation, because for the past two thousand years in diaspora, they did not have a common land, a state, or a territory they owned, where they "belonged". Some people argued that only a people living in a common land for at least a century, sharing a common history, culture, and language, and numbering at least one hundred thousand, often with a common religion, might be called a nation. Except for a common land, the Jews had all the other characteristics of a nation: a common history, language (Yiddish, Hebrew, or Ladino), culture, tradition, and religion, just like the Spanish, the French, Germans, Italians, or the Japanese. It was clear that the Jews had always had enough of distinct cultural characteristics to define them as a nation, and historically, two thousand years ago, they did have a land of their own, Judea, from which the Roman Empire expelled them into diaspora. Their number after the Holocaust was still well over ten million.

In my case, since both my parents were ethnic Jews, my nationality had to be Jewish, regardless of the fact that I was baptized and had never practiced the Jewish religion. What gave me a deeper sense of belonging to the Jewish nation was not just my parental origins, but the cognizance that I acquired from my ancestors a certain sensibility, a way of thinking, a certain type of humor, a distinct way of formulating a thought, a certain manner of grasping a situation, or a viewpoint from which to observe the issues around me. My mind had a culture with a distinct flavor, and this culture was recognizable by other people, at least those familiar with it. That culture has a parallel in all other nations, whether it is the Italians, French, Irish, English, Germans, Japanese, or Russians, etc.—all have their own distinct characteristics, humor, and cultural flavor. It is the delightful variety in each nation that makes the world so beautiful and enjoyable. My favorite Latin proverb was "varietas delectat" (variety delights), and I especially applied it to the differences in people's folklore and cultural inheritance.

There was yet another question to be dealt with. Having been born in Yugoslavia, in the then-province of Croatia, was I also a Croat? My father thought and felt that he was a Croat. Except for some of my close friends and a few people who were exceptionally broad-minded, most Croats did not consider me one of them. The majority of Croats considered me a Jew, and this was clearly meant in an ethnic sense. Does one have to accept what the majority of other people think, or does one have the right to claim a nationality of one's own choice? This question exposed a conflict that needed to be explored. If a person was born of ethnic Jewish parents but did not practice the Jewish religion, was he still a Jew? If the same person became a religious Hindu or Muslim, was he still a Jew? My answer to both of the last two questions was "yes"; that person was still an ethnic Jew. Religious persuasion and practice did not determine and could not change the ethnicity of a person. My life experience up to that point had taught me that my father was considered by Croats to be a Jew, even though he felt himself to be a Croat. It was clear that when it came to ethnicity or nationality, we were not what we aspired to be, but what the society around us decided. If the majority of people thought of me as a Jew, they were right. I had no Croat blood in my veins, and I concluded that my nationality was Jewish. I became one of a handful of people in Yugoslavia whose ID card indicated a Jewish nationality. In the next few years, I ran into a few other individuals of Jewish nationality; I was not alone.

In Europe, even today, being a Jew does not have a mere religious connotation. A Jew who became a Catholic convert in Europe is still considered a Jew. In the U.S., being Jewish is treated as a religious affiliation. In that respect, the U.S. is unique. In my discussions with many of our Jewish-American friends, they adamantly claim that they were Jews only by religion, but otherwise, they were Americans. This is possible because being of American nationality means that one belongs to a nation that was forged by fusion from many different nationalities. For that former national origin, we in the U.S. use the word "ethnic." In twentieth century Europe, thousands of assimilated Jews believed they were Germans or French or Hungarian by nationality, especially the ones who had converted to Christian religion and changed their names to become more native. Their delusion was cruelly unmasked when they were dragged into Nazi concentration camps and murdered because of their Jewish ethnic origin. A sad but perfect illustration of this point was made in the movie Sunshine, *about a Hungarian Jewish family that changed its name and religion. Members of its third generation were nevertheless persecuted and killed because they were considered Jews. A pure national or ethnic origin is often doubtful, for if one looks far enough back into history, an enormous number of people are actually of mixed origin. This is particularly true of Jews who spent two thousand years in diaspora. From a scientific and genetic point of view, every person in this world has about twenty thousand ancestors, and there is a good chance that in the distant past, some of my ancestors came from different tribes or nations of central and eastern parts of Europe.*

Finally, I want to say what my first choice now, today, would be. Although it may sound unrealistic, I would like to be just a person, a human, an individual; my own "conflict of being" would be immediately resolved. Imagining myself as a mere member of the human race gave me the comforting sense of carrying forward a genetic mosaic derived from many tribes, nations, and civilizations, including those that have been lost.

In reality, however, I know that by birth and my most recently acquired genes, I am a Jew, and this is what most people correctly consider me. My primary nationality is Jewish, and I believe that Jews were a nation long before the state of Israel was declared in 1948, but for many years now, I have also felt being American. This is my other nationality. There is no conflict: dual nationality is possible, and it is even permissible by law. I feel American for the simple reason that this land, where I have lived for most of my life, this America, is my home. It is my only home. Most Americans accept me and treat me as one of them. From the beginning of my stay, they made me feel welcome. I love and appreciate this land and its people, who gave me a chance to belong here. My feeling of being American is fortified by the awareness that most Americans or their ancestors were immigrants. Furthermore, I lived and worked for a significant amount of time in France, Germany, and Italy, and from those experiences, I am fully cognizant that in Europe, an immigrant might stay and live for over fifty years, and the majority of native citizens will still consider him an alien. In most European societies, Jews are considered aliens even if they were born locally. This is confirmed by many examples in literature or from other individuals' experiences, including Uncle Bernard in France. Such is not the case in the U.S. First-generation immigrants are accepted as Americans. It is the American way, and it is unique. A child born in the U.S. is considered of American nationality, regardless of the parents' origin or ethnicity.

LITTLE MEMORIES FROM THE FIFTIES

About seven years after the war, in 1952, the government in Yugoslavia recognized that the communist economy was not working. It was a complete failure. The government slowly promulgated new regulations and reforms that gradually led to the return of a freer economy. Factory workers were allowed to determine and to some degree to guide the production at their work places. Price regulations for agricultural products were lifted, and the forced purchase of agricultural products from farm collectives was discontinued. The city markets opened up, one could again buy dairy, produce, and meat from peasants in the open market, and suddenly, there appeared in the stores imported items that could be bought without personal coupons. For a steep price, everyone could buy rice, coffee, chocolate, bananas, oranges, and other items previously restricted to "special stores" meant only for the top communists. The communist regime realized that an economy based strictly on Marxist theories was unsustainable and led to economic bankruptcy. However, the relaxation of communist rules went only halfway. Many restrictions were left in place. *The result was that fifteen years later, around 1967, the Yugoslav economy had become so moribund that the government was compelled to lift the Iron Curtain and allow masses of unemployed people to go abroad. By 1969, one million Yugoslav workers were employed in Western Europe to support their families at home.*

To get the best and freshest meat, produce, and dairy at the newly opened market, Aunt Ester used to get up early in the morning. She needed very little sleep. Once a week, she woke me at 5:30 a.m., and we left the apartment by six a.m. The market was in the center of the city, about twenty minutes away on foot, and I accompanied Aunt Ester with four empty wicker baskets. Each of us would then carry two full baskets home. Butter and farmer's cheese in those days were sold in lumps of about a half to one pound, offered by the peasants on a large vine leaf, lying on the open bench with all the other farm products. The customer was allowed to break off with a fingertip a small piece and taste it to make sure it was not rancid. If it tasted fresh, one would bargain for the price, based on weight and the total number of items purchased. The milk still had to be boiled at home, for it was not pasteurized. The sour cream was in earthen crocks, and it was tasted by having a few thick drops poured onto the back of the hand, or by dipping a finger into it and licking it. Aunt Ester was very picky, and she knew where and how to find the best meat and dairy. We would fill our baskets and go home, partly by streetcar, and part of the way on foot. Upon arriving home, the food had to be repackaged into separate rations to be deposited in our recently obtained refrigerator (the old icebox had finally fallen apart). Some of the rations were frozen, to be used a few days later, and others were just refrigerated.

On one such occasion, upon slicing a very large lump of butter into two halves, Aunt Ester let out a loud shriek and started cussing the woman who sold it to her. There was a large baking potato smack in the middle of the butter. We quickly took the sliced lump of butter and potato back to the market. We were anxious to see whether the woman was still there; she was. Aunt Ester stood in front of the woman's bench, looked at her, and said, "Here!" and smashed the butter and the potato on the bench. She started yelling and berating the woman in the loudest possible way, to get everyone's attention. Aunt Ester demanded her money back, or she would call the police. The money was returned, including the streetcar fare for both of us. Aunt Ester then bought two smaller lumps of butter from another peasant, and the incident was over.

In the summer of 1952, I had an experience with lost luggage that was way ahead of present day problems with the airlines. Summer was the time for vacations on the Adriatic Coast, and our group of boys in high school arranged to spend a month's vacation in a boys' camp on the remote and desolate island of Ugljan, far from any town or village. The only large inhabited facility on the island was a psychiatric institution for chronically ill. Ivica and I decided to share one suitcase. The trip involved an overnight train ride to the city of Rijeka, a boat ride to Zadar, and a small boat transfer to Ugljan. As we left the train in Rijeka, our suitcase could not be found. We spent our vacation in the clothes we had on our backs.

The camp was simple, with tents for up to six people. Most of the time we were on the beach, and I wore a borrowed long T-shirt to conceal the fact that I had no swimsuit underneath. Luckily, we were in an all-boys camp. During that vacation, I helped a local photographer develop pictures of the campers, and so I even earned some money and a few free crossings into the city of Zadar. On the way back to Zagreb, our suitcase was waiting in the "lost & found" at the railroad station in Rijeka.

The school year of 1952/53 was not very exciting. I could not wait to enter the university. That year I had to decide on my course study at the university. Despite my great interest and love for physics, I decided to be practical and enter the school of medicine. Who in the West would need a physicist educated in Yugoslavia? Physicians were in great demand in most parts of the world. A medical doctor seemed the only sensible profession if I wanted some day to leave the country and find employment. My choice of profession still presented an issue: the sight of blood usually made me nauseous, but I would just have to overcome that problem.

In 1952, Michael graduated medical school and left home to work in Gospić, a town in mountainous central Croatia. Several months later, he had to look for another job. He took very good care of a patient, the young son of a local butcher. The butcher came to thank him and in gratitude handed him an envelope with money, as was the local custom. Michael declined to take it.

The butcher was offended: "What? My money is not good enough for you?" and he beat him up. There were witnesses, and the whole town heard about it. After such an episode, the young doctor had to leave town. He found a new job in a town in southeast Bosnia, near the border of Monte-Negro. There he soon met and married a teacher who happened to be the illegitimate daughter of the chief of the Secret Service of Yugoslavia. So we acquired into our family a communist. They had a little daughter, Vesna, and the following year they all came for a visit to Zagreb.

I remember the visit very well. The young family arrived with all their clothing packed in a large burlap sack. In their little corner of Bosnia suitcases were not in use. The communist teacher was on vacation, so she lay most of the day on the couch in the family room, chain smoked cigarettes, and drank multiple cups of strong Turkish coffee. Aunt Ester kept serving coffee and emptying the ashtrays. The young woman had no interest in going out and seeing anything of cultural value in Zagreb. Aunt Ester was not pleased with her daughter-in-law, but she very much loved and enjoyed little Vesna, her first granddaughter.

With Michael out of the house, Aunt Ester found a university student to move into our little maid's room. Nicola was from Hercegovina. He was a friendly, polite, and pleasant young man. He said that his father was killed in the war, but we never asked whether he died as a civilian victim of Nazi terror, or fighting as a Četnik or a Partisan, or perhaps of natural causes. Aunt Ester sometimes invited Nicola for a big Sunday lunch. Each summer, Nicola's mother sent us a large box of fresh apricots from their orchard. The sublet room brought us a little income, but the rental mainly served to fill the quota of people required to live in our apartment. If the government found that an apartment had less people than the allotted quota, they would assign a person to move in with us. That person would surely be a good communist, and we would not be able to speak freely in our own apartment.

At that time, I developed a liking for jazz and American music. For several years, we were able to listen to the short wave radio that transmitted news and music from the U.S. through a powerful substation in Tangier. The American songs and jazz were delightful. We would listen to the radio, write down the tunes, and then try to arrange them for piano and instruments. I joined a small student orchestra that played American dance music. At the time, I did not speak English, and I thought that the American radio station I was listening to was "Boys of America." It was not until about ten years later, in the U.S., when I realized that all along I had been listening to the "Voice of America."

Around 1952, we saw the movie *A Young Man with a Horn* with Kirk Douglas and Doris Day, and my friend Ivica and I both fell in love with the sound of the horn. Ivica bought a horn and started practicing, and I borrowed one from the music school, made the horn my primary instrument, and switched the piano to the secondary place. For a while, I had fun playing the trumpet. I knew I would never become a pianist because I was just not good enough for that, and I did not like mediocrity.

There was a memorable event in 1953 connected with the NATO decision to return the city of Trieste to Italy, and give the surrounding countryside to

Yugoslavia. The Communist Party immediately ordered protests in all major cities of Yugoslavia. "Spontaneous" demonstrations were well organized. Our school classes were interrupted, and we were ordered to assemble on the street in front of the school. Class by class, with a professor at the head of each class, we were told to march in the direction of the U.S. consulate, which was then in the center of the city. As our march proceeded past the second street corner, I jumped into the nearest apartment entry hallway and waited for the marchers to pass. When the coast was clear, I went home. The next day on the radio and in the newspapers, it was reported that the "spontaneous demonstrators" not only demanded that the Italian city of Trieste be given to Yugoslavia, but they also threw stones, broke windows, and thoroughly destroyed and plundered the U.S. Information Service offices (USIS) on the ground floor of the U.S. consulate. *Today, the American Embassy in Croatia sits far from the center of the city, in the middle of a barren field, all by itself, like a fortress, strategically close to the airport, and far from any tall buildings.*

In the late spring of 1953, we had the traditional class graduation trip. The trip had to be politically meaningful, and so the class went through areas where the Partisans won battles against the Nazis and Ustaše. The two-week outing was named "The Trip along the Peoples' Victory Trail." Our professors were smart enough to make also a few stops in nice places outside the required trail. We went first to the historic city of Sarajevo and then to the beautiful resort city of Dubrovnik, and finally trough the wilds of Montenegro, which was both a historic battleground and also quite rugged and beautiful. *In the last stage of the break-up of Yugoslavia, Montenegro became an independent country of about a half-million people. Its separation from Serbia was accomplished by a peaceful democratic election, despite the fact that thirty percent of the population was Serbian.*

My final year in high school was 1953/54. I had stopped going to the swim club and decided to try other sports. I tried field hockey a few times, but it seemed dangerous, with frequent injuries. Adjacent to the Jewish Community Club was the former Jewish Maccabees Sport Club, which had become the peoples' club for Greek-Roman wrestling. I joined it for several months, and though it offered a sport I did not enjoy, it kept me in good shape. In school, my grades were straight A's, and I did not have to worry about qualifying to enter the medical school. Students with straight A grades had to take only the written parts of the baccalaureate exam, mainly the essays in languages and math.

In the late spring of 1954, the long awaited moment arrived. I received my "Maturity Certificate" (baccalaureate diploma). The class pictures were taken in front of the school. Having finally achieved what I longed for during those last two years in school, I was suddenly overcome by a curious feeling of emptiness, the feeling one gets upon parting from a good, old friend.

In 1954, in the summer after high school graduation, the Jewish Community in Zagreb organized a vacation camp for all Jewish youth in Yugoslavia. All together, about fifty-five people signed up. I was asked to help with camp preparations, and I gladly accepted. The two other persons helping to organize the camp were older university students. The site chosen for the camp was on the island of Cres in the Northern Adriatic, where a very large house with twenty rooms could be rented for the equivalent of one dollar per month. The island of Cres used to belong to Italy, and had a predominantly Italian population before the end of the Second World War. After the war, the Italians opted to leave for Italy, and the city of Cres, formerly a town with 11,000 inhabitants, became a ghost town, with a few hundred people living in it. The Yugoslav government owned many empty homes that were available for rent. Our team of three was responsible for receiving and setting up cots, other furniture, and the kitchen equipment, which came by boat from Rijeka. This was both work and fun. One of the three of us spent most of his time in the nearby port of Rijeka, receiving and transferring supplies from the train to the ship. The second team member was Eliezar W., a third-year medical student at the University of Zagreb. He and I stayed in Cres to prepare the rented house for the campers. In the course of two weeks, we cleaned the house and set up the furniture and kitchen utilities. We began to understand each other better and better. We had no radio or any outside entertainment, and at night, we had many long conversations, interrupted only by an occasional scorpion slowly crawling on the ceiling over our heads. After disposing of that menace with a broom, we continued our conversation into the wee hours of the night. During those two weeks, we became close friends and were gradually able to open up to one another. Eliezar told me the story of his life, and it is worth telling it here.

He was originally from Vojvodina, a rich part of northern Serbia. During the war, Eliezar lost his parents and most of his family in the Nazi concentration camps. He was in Auschwitz with his older brother, and in the final days, just before liberation by the Soviet troops, the Nazis shot at prisoners indiscriminately. His brother was killed and fell upon him. Eliezar was alive, lying helplessly in a heap of dead and dying people. He was so starved and weakened that he could no longer move. Within hours, the Russian army liberated the camp and took care of the few survivors. Eliezar was like a skeleton, weighing only about sixty-six pounds. The Soviet Russian nurses transported him to a hospital, and it took three months before he recovered sufficiently to be able to walk and be released.

In 1945, when Eliezar was released from the hospital, he was seventeen years old. By 1947, he had finished the accelerated high school and started attending medical school in Zagreb. In 1948, when Tito broke up with Stalin, and the Yugoslav communists went their own way, Eliezar felt loyal to his Soviet Russian liberators, and he openly spoke against the split with "our big brother," the Soviet Union. Along with several thousand other communists who similarly spoke their minds in favor of the Soviets, he was arrested and sent to Goli Otok (Naked Island), a desolate, small, dry, and rocky island in the northern Adriatic, devoid of vegetation, but endowed with plenty of rocks, boulders, and stones. The inmates there broke boulders and rocks with chisels and sledgehammers, and they were made to build primitive stone dwellings and stone walls. Twice a day, they were re-educated about the "right way of communism." The lectures were accompanied by occasional beatings.

Eliezar was lucky to have been a first-year medical student. Once a month, he was taken on a boat to the port of Rijeka to help collect and bring medical and other supplies for the camp. Those trips, he explained, helped him retain his sanity. After three and a half years of brainwashing, beatings, and cleaving and carrying stones, Eliezar was released. He came back to medical school in Zagreb, but within several months, he was arrested again. He was sent back to Goli Otok for a second time. What Eliezar missed was that by the time he was released in 1951, Tito had made up with the Soviet Union, and so the "big brother" was again our friend. Eliezar, though, fresh from the gulag brainwashing lessons, this time spoke against the big brother. That second arrest lasted only several months, and when he was released, Eliezar finally realized that freedom of speech under communists meant that one could talk freely and without risk of being arrested as long as one stuck to the theme of weather or the anatomy of a dissected frog.

The Communist Party of Yugoslavia had an iron grip on the power in the country. It had within its ranks at most only ten percent of the population, but in a totalitarian state, ten percent of people holding all the power can easily intimidate, rule, and control the remaining ninety percent of the population.

When summer camp started, there was lots of fun. I met many young people from different parts of Yugoslavia, and among them, I found a girlfriend who was sixteen, very pretty, and pleasant. She was from Zagreb and appeared more mature than her age. It was love at first sight. However, I learned a new lesson: even with a pleasant person, incessant banter gets to be boring, notwithstanding balmy summer nights under the stars. The camp lasted a whole month, and we soon ran out of subjects on which we could have an intelligent conversation. I had more fun talking to Eliezar or some of the other people in the camp. That summer, I fully understood what was meant by "beauty of the mind," and I felt ever more mature.

AT THE UNIVERSITY

In the fall of 1954, I was accepted to the Medical School of the University of Zagreb, a six-year program leading to an MD degree. From then on, I concentrated all my efforts on becoming a physician, which left little time for sports and socializing, and no time at all for practicing or playing music. In the first year of medical school we had a class of 650 students, but more than a half were eliminated by the end of the academic year. This was achieved by high exam standards coupled with a rule stating that during the first two years of study, students who failed to pass all required exams by the time of matriculation into the next academic year would be dropped from the program. Thus, in our second year of study, the class had only about 300 students, and in the beginning of the third year, our class was reduced to only about 200 students. Those would eventually graduate and become physicians.

The harsh rule of elimination was introduced deliberately to remove from the ranks of physicians those students who showed a mediocre performance. There was fierce competition to pass the exams and get high grades. The school, with its basic science buildings and the dean's office, was located in the hilly upper part of the city, in massive old buildings built at the turn of the century by the Austro-Hungarian Empire. Some of the older professors were trained in Vienna, Austria, and they were rigid and highly demanding.

The medical school system at the University of Zagreb was unique. The first two years of study were similar to a pre-med college or the six-year medical school programs in the U.S. There was applied physics, chemistry and biochemistry, biology with genetics, and human anatomy in the first year, and in the second year there was human anatomy, histology, and physiology. The remainder of the study program was similar to any four-year medical school, with the usual clinical subjects; however, unlike in the U.S., this also included study and exams in all clinical sub-specialties. The curriculum was geared to produce "country doctors" (family physicians) who could competently attend to most medical needs and rarely have to rely on the help of specialists. Most specialists were present only at the universities in a few larger cities. The pre-med program had three semesters of anatomy. The dissection of a human cadaver, seeing blood, and touching tissue presented for me a special ordeal.

The dissection room was an enormous hall supported by heavy concrete columns, with endless rows of dissection tables, each with cadavers that were previously soaked in tubs of formaldehyde for months. Four students were assigned to each cadaver, and by the end of the first year, we had to complete the dissection, demonstrating all individual nerves, blood vessels, muscles, tendons, ligaments, and bones and removing all connective and fatty tissue between them. Finally, the internal organs were taken out and dissected to show their anatomic particulars. The skull and rib cage were opened with a handsaw.

It took a while before I overcame the nausea from the visual impressions and smell. In those days, students did all dissections with bare hands, without gloves. Luckily, I had enough dexterity to use the scalpel and forceps without having to touch human tissue with my bare fingers. Others were not so fastidious, and their instrument handles and hands would be contaminated with grease and formaldehyde. Every now and then, some of it would accidentally get on my skin, usually due to a careless move I made. No matter how much I washed my hands with soap and water, they retained a light smell of formaldehyde. I learned never to use hot water for hand washing: the hot water opened the pores and drove the formaldehyde and its odor deeper into the skin. Regardless of how cold it was in the winter months, I used only cold water for washing.

In the first academic year, we had to pass three major exams: one at the end of the first semester and two at the end of the second semester. The exams were given during a period of six weeks at the end of each semester, and at the end of summer again for a four-week period, just before matriculation into the next academic year. I decided to take all of the exams in the first few days of the spring exam period, and not leave any exam to the final period before the start of the next year. That way, I would have a free summer without pressure and the worry of having to pass the last exam only days before matriculation into the next year, or face elimination from the school. In that first year, I studied with an old friend and classmate from junior high, Dean K., the son of my pre-war pediatrician, the one who treated my injured wrist. Dean's parents, Dean, and an older sister spent the war in refuge with the Partisans. In the course of the war, his father served as pediatrician, but much more often as a general surgeon, orthopedist, and general practitioner. Because of the war, his father remained ill much of the time and often could not work for months. Dean and his family lived in their large, comfortable, pre-war apartment, and to break the monotony of long hours of study, we often played chess. That year, we played about 200 games of chess and meticulously kept our score. Unfortunately, Dean did not pass the required exams on time and had to quit the medical school at the end of the first year. I was left feeling guilty for all those chess games; we should have studied more and played less. Dean eventually worked for a Yugoslav travel agency, and several years later, he left Yugoslavia to settle in Caracas, Venezuela.

During the first year of medical school, there was a sad event: my best friend Ivica's father suddenly died during surgery. It was hard on Ivica, but he took it as well as one could. He had sensed for a long time that his father's illness was advanced and that he would not live very much longer. I had a hard time finding the courage to face his mother afterwards. Expressing condolences was difficult. The clichés one had to say on such occasions were superfluous. They all sounded so mechanical and phony. Of course, we were all sorry, but why did we have to repeat it? I was embarrassed. The whole proceeding made me blush and feel uncomfortable. When one feels sorry very strongly, it is hard to talk about it. Standing before Ivica's mother, I became tongue tied and was barely able to mumble a few incomprehensible words. I had no courage to look her in the eyes.

In that first year of medical school, I developed a habit that I kept throughout all six years of the program: in the afternoon before the day of the exam, I stopped reviewing, and in the early evening, I went with a friend to see a movie. I wanted to relax and have a good night's sleep before the exam. This method worked for me.

I passed all my exams by the end of the spring semester, and in the summer of 1955, I was free to rest and relax. After speaking to my classmate Ivan U., the two of us decided to repeat most of our high school class graduation trip, which due to his mother's illness he had missed. We rented a tent and made the itinerary: instead of going to flea-infested Sarajevo, we spent two weeks on the island of Hvar, off the port of Split, in the warm Dalmatian part of the Adriatic. Camping in a pine forest near a beautiful beach, we met many friends from Zagreb and had lots of fun. Special fun was found in the evenings, when we attended the town dance on the main square, in front of an outdoor café and restaurant.

Among other friends on the island was Leila T., a classmate of ours, who was spending the summer vacation with her parents. There was also a well-known soccer player from Zagreb, who was Leila's date. Her parents were dead set against this relationship, and they forbade her to see him. Ivan or I would take Leila to the dance floor, and in the far corner, hand her over to her date. At the end of the dance, we escorted her back to the table where her parents sat. In the daytime, while everyone was on the beach, the two lovers used to borrow our tent under a shady tree, and we did not mind, as long as they left it tidy.

After fourteen days, tanned and recharged, we continued our trip through Dubrovnik, stopping for a few days in Herceg-Novi, in the beautiful bay of Kotor, the only fjord in the Adriatic. In a small tent camp, we met some university students from Belgrade, and again we had a good time. There we had a little incident: when I wanted to photograph a beautiful sculpture, a memorial to a Partisan fallen hero, Ivan started to cry. It was then, after so many years of friendship, that he first told me that he used to have an older brother. At the end of the war in 1945, his brother decided to withdraw from Croatia with the Ustaše. He never came back, and there never was any news about his whereabouts.

Ivan was upset that I wanted to photograph the statue of a Partisan hero. Apparently, it was certain that the Partisans had killed his brother. I had to remind him what happened in 1941 and 1942 to my parents, other members of my family, and most Jews in Croatia. Ivan was unaware that during the war, the Ustaše killed hundreds of thousands of Serbs and tens of thousands of Jews and Roma, and he had a hard time absorbing what I told him. I thought, could it be that he lived all those years entirely sheltered from the truth? For a very long time, the two of us sat on a low stone wall in silence, looking at the sea below us without really seeing it. We never touched on the subject again.

We proceeded to travel through Montenegro, stayed a few days in a tent camp on the beach near the port of Bar, then took the narrow-gauge train, the oldest rail in all of the Balkan to the interior, and finally reached the beautiful, rugged 10,000-foot mountain of Durmitor. We decided to sleep in a hut I knew from the previous visit, high up on the shore of the Crno Jezero (Black Lake). It was the beginning of August, but at night, it got so cold that we had to put on all the clothing we had with us, wrap our tent around ourselves, and sleep on the floor of the hut. In the morning, we woke at dawn, frozen and hungry, and walked down to the nearest peasant house to get warm milk and something to eat. It was one of those mountain homes made of stone and logs. It had one large room with an enormous, low, platform-like, square bed, apparently for the entire family of three generations. There was a large open fireplace used for heating and cooking, with a large pot hanging on a hook, a smoldering fire underneath, and a chimney leading to an opening in the peak of the roof. A low partition separated the space for goats and sheep from the people. Two medium-sized shaggy dogs slept on the bed with the people. The air in the room was smoky, but it was warm. We received fresh, warm goat's milk in a crock that was on the outside sticky with dirt. We gratefully accepted it and did not worry about the hygiene of the container. We offered a small amount of money, and it was taken as a fair exchange. On parting, the head of the house wished us God's help, and we returned to him the same greeting.

We hitchhiked through the rest of the mountains and canyons of Montenegro in the back of trucks, traveling on narrow dirt roads that curved around the edges of enormous ravines. It was a frightening, bone-jarring ride. The trucks took the curves with too much speed, and we were occasionally thrown from one side of the truck bed to the other. Along and across the rivers Piva and Tara, we enjoyed some of the most spectacular scenery in Yugoslavia. Finally, we reached the town of Pljevlja, where many people spoke a language we did not understand and half the newspapers appeared to be Turkish.

The town was in a valley surrounded on all sides by barren hills and mountains. Looking around, we noticed in the city center a church steeple and an even taller minaret. On the surrounding slopes, we saw long columns of people coming in single file down the winding paths. The people streamed down the mountains from several directions, as if long snakes were converging on the town. We thought there was a festivity or a holiday. We were exhausted and did not dare to pitch the tent anywhere in town. We decided to splurge and rent a room in the only hotel in town. To be precise, we rented a "room to share", that is, only a half of one room, with one single bed assigned to us. The other bed in the room was already rented to someone else. The bathrooms were outside in the hallway, and everyone shared them. Ivan registered at the hotel with his ID card, and I had to sneak into the room later and illicitly share the single bed with him in a "head to toe" fashion.

It was mid-afternoon, and we sat on the terrace in front of the hotel to have some simple food. A man joined us at our table and ordered a carafe of local red wine that was thick and dark like ink. He was local and spoke Serbo-Croatian with the sharp accent of that region. He struck up a conversation, first asking where we were from. He appeared friendly and invited us to drink with him, asking the waiter for two more glasses. One does not decline an offer to drink with someone in those parts; it might be taken as a personal offense. We accepted the offer and thanked him. Then we drank. Another liter (full quart) was ordered, and then another one. After three carafes of wine, as dusk started settling over the hills, our host bid us good-bye and left the table, staggering but obviously content. We were happy, too, and relieved that he finally left. When we tried to get up, we realized we were quite drunk. We decided to sit for a while longer outside in the cool, fresh air. Ivan was the first to get up; he had to go to the bathroom. He staggered away, and I had to wait for him and follow later. It got dark, and the fresh air on the terrace felt good. After a long time, Ivan emerged on the terrace and sat next to me. What took so long?

Ivan spent some time throwing up and washing in the bathroom. He also visited our room and found that the other tenant was already in his bed and snoring. It was my turn to go to the bathroom. When I got up, I could walk in an almost straight line, but when I entered the warm, stuffy hotel corridor, I suddenly felt sick. Halfway down the hallway, I heaved and started vomiting, leaving a dark red trail all the way to the bathroom. I, too, spent some time washing with cold water. When I made it to our room, I plopped down next to Ivan like a log and fell asleep in an instant. When we woke in the morning, the sun was already high, and the other tenant was gone. Our heads felt like drums. We took a little tea for breakfast and prepared to go to the railroad station and get tickets for the final leg of our trip. Our destination was Belgrade, the capital of Yugoslavia, where neither of us had been before. The people we met in the tent camp in Herceg-Novi had invited us to stay with them, or at least to visit them. We boarded a narrow gauge train called "Ćiro" that arrived already chockfull of people, and during the entire trip of twenty hours, we had to stand, packed in like sardines. The train slowly chugged through the mountains of central Serbia, stopping frequently in small towns along the way. At dawn of the next morning we arrived in Belgrade.

Ivan went to stay with a distant relative, and I stayed with Cousin Luisa and David Weiner and their family in the adjacent town of Zemun. I had a chance to talk with Luisa and David, and for the first time, they treated me as an adult. They were members of the Communist Party, and David was a well-paid manager of a large, governmental import-export firm. For his service during the war, he also received a very high pension. Luisa never heard from her father, Uncle Ernest, but I knew only that both Uncle Ernest and Felix lived and worked together in Milan, Italy.

One night, we talked for a long time, and David told me that during the past several years, he and Luisa had lived through some difficult times. First, in 1947, while still in the Army, David was having a haircut in the army barbershop, and he overheard another officer cursing the Jews with ugly anti-Semitic expletives. David was so incensed that he got up and punched the officer in the face. David was an amateur boxer, and he bloodied the officer's face and knocked him to the ground. However, that other officer had a higher rank than David, and consequently,

David was demoted and transferred to a small town. The other officer was only reprimanded. Then, in 1948, during the split between Tito and Stalin, David's younger brother said something wrong and was arrested, and taken to the Goli Otok to be "re-educated."

During the next several months, David said, he slept with a loaded handgun on his night table. After four and a half years of fighting in the woods with the Partisans, and being several times wounded in battle and losing an eye, David said, he was not going to allow anyone to arrest him and take him to do forced labor on some barren island; he would rather shoot the arresting officers and then kill himself. However, nothing ever happened to David, and when he was demobilized, he received a high pension and a well paid managerial position with the government.

For several days, Ivan and I explored Belgrade, a city larger and clearly more cosmopolitan than Zagreb. We had an excellent lunch at the home of the students we met in Herceg-Novi. The people of Belgrade struck me as open, friendly and outgoing. We in Zagreb were usually more reserved. Finally, I parted with Luisa and David, and with Ivan boarded the train to Zagreb. We had a great trip and a good vacation, but we both longed for home. We were glad to have weathered our trip without any incident, and we started making plans for our next year in medical school.

In the second year of medical school, we had to pass three major exams: one after the first semester, and two after the second semester. I again decided to take all exams as early as possible to get another full summer's rest. The subjects were much harder than in the first academic year, especially anatomy and physiology. This time, I studied by myself because I found that my learning was most satisfactory when I was alone, though reviewing with another person had its advantages. I discovered that when it came to studying, especially memorizing, I was the visual type. If I could see a picture or write something down, the image of the written words remained in my memory like a picture. I took exhaustive notes during lectures and made drawings or sketches, and all this remained in my memory. If I only heard the spoken words, I could not remember them for long. I remembered very well the faces of people I met, but had trouble remembering their names unless I saw them written down. During that second year of medical school, based on my grades from the first year's exams, I earned the position of teacher's assistant in chemistry. This brought me a modest income for the next five years. Along with the TA position, I gained access to the professor of chemistry, Dr. Pinter. He encouraged me to do a little research in the lab and asked me to do electrophoresis of milk on long strips of paper to separate various proteins, a novel method at that time. The procedure took a full day before the results could be analyzed. *Several years later, in the U.S., I found that the electrophoresis had been much refined and had become a standard method for quick measurement of proteins in blood and urine.* In this first research project of mine, I did not make any significant findings, but I learned research methodology and a few useful laboratory tricks. I noticed that the professor was reading English medical literature and other books, and one day, Dr. Pinter gave me my first lesson in the English language.

"English," he said, "is really two separate languages: one spoken and one written." He understood everything written, he explained, but spoken English he could neither understand nor speak.

All exams at the medical school were oral, and they were usually given in a small classroom with a chalkboard. One stood in front of the professor, and there was regularly an audience of ten to twenty students who came to listen in to get acquainted with how the exam was done. The exams were usually given in the morning, and a maximum of three students would be admitted, one by one. Many of the old professors were stern and rigid, some were sexist, and some were outright cruel, interrupting the student with sub-questions or negative comments, and finally advising the student to "come back and try again in a month."

One had a nasty habit of telling a student to draw a horizontal line across the chalkboard. When the student stopped at the edge of the board, he ordered the student to continue the chalk line across the wall and then across the classroom door. Then he ordered him or her to open the door and continue the line on the outside. In this manner, the student was told that he or she failed the exam and should leave. Such rudeness did not sit well with the communist administration, and by the time I entered the university, the most obnoxious professors had been tamed, and upon intervention by the Communist Party, several had been expelled from the faculty.

I took the anatomy exam on the first day of the exam period, and I had the bad luck to be assigned the much-feared chairman of the department, an old, crusty prof educated in Vienna. My exam lasted a solid hour, a small part of it being practical. Even today, I can still remember every question. For the practical part, I had to dissect and demonstrate all five branches of the facial nerve on a cadaver, and it went well. The oral part also went smoothly, except for one long, awful moment. When the prof asked me about the spleen, I described all I knew about its anatomy, but he gave me a long look and said, "Is that all you know?"

I stood still for a few seconds reaching to the bottom of my memory to finally remember the one anatomic detail that I obviously had omitted. Finally, the prof asked me a tricky question: "Which muscle is responsible for humans being able to walk erect and move their legs forward?" I paused deliberately, as if I had to think very hard, but I knew that it was none of the logical muscles on the front side of the thigh. It was one deep inside the abdomen, along the lumbar spine and inside the upper pelvis, a muscle that reaches only the uppermost end of the thigh bone and is not visible anywhere on the body surface.

"Iliopsoas," I answered.

The old prof was satisfied. The exam was over, and for the next few days, I walked around with the usual empty feeling of relief coupled with exhaustion. In late spring, at the end of the second semester, I passed the other two exams, and thus I was assured admittance into the third academic year of the medical school.

I could relax, for I knew that in a few years I would graduate with an MD degree. As a bonus, I had the summer of 1956 free.

My social life during the first two years at the university was not too active. I still dated the young girl I met at summer camp in 1954, but intellectually we were a mismatch, and this relationship was going nowhere. By the end of 1955, we broke up. In the evenings, I used to stop by at the medical students' club, where I could pick up a good game of chess or meet interesting students from other schools at the university. I started dating girls from the university, especially those from the school of languages, who seemed peculiarly attracted to the medical club. I also often met with old friends and high school classmates, either at one of their apartments, or if the weather was nice, on the corner of the main city square. That was where all young people, especially university students, habitually met every night around 7:30 p.m., walking slowly back and forth along one side of the square and checking who else was there. This 'promenade' style of meeting other young people is common in most cities of southern Europe, and the street or place where it is practiced is known as "corso."

"Shall we meet at the corso?" needed no designation of time. It was always between seven and nine p.m., and it was practiced even in rain, unless there was a real downpour.

During practical labs and between lectures at the medical school, I met many new colleagues and made at least one good new friend. There were so many people in our first-year class that I never got to know all of them. During the second year of school, I began to know quite a few, and among them, two faces stood out. One was a fellow whose face had such a striking similarity to Pierre Mendes-France, the premier of France, that he could easily have played his double. Mendes-France was a Jew who in France, of all places, advocated drinking more milk than wine. What surprised me most was the family name of the student with the Mendes-France likeness: it was a typical Slavic-Croatian name ending with -ić. One day after class, I happened to walk towards the city center with this fellow, and we started talking. He was from Rijeka, the northern Adriatic port that for generations belonged to Italy. I asked him whether any of his relatives were Jewish, and he confirmed it right away. He explained that his grandfather had changed their family name to sound Croatian, and during the war, they had no trouble, especially since Rijeka (then Fiume) was under Italy, and Italians did not poke into people's origins three generations back.

The other interesting face belonged to a girl, another face in which I recognized Jewish features. She was always well dressed, wore shoes with high heels, and kept her hair in perfect order. She appeared reserved. Her face was oval with large, asymmetrical, almond-shaped brown eyes. She had black wavy hair and a small nose with a distinctly curved profile. I noticed that an older student frequently joined her in her walks to and from school, and it was obvious that they dated. Eventually, we were introduced at a lab session, and I found out that Iva G. indeed was Jewish. She had lost her parents and nearly her entire family in the war, and she was being supported by a single surviving aunt who lived in Bosnia.

At The University

During practical lab sessions, we frequently talked the way that many medical students did: about any subject other than medicine, but particularly about literature and music and art. Gradually, we became good friends. Iva was funny and spirited and had a knack for practical jokes. We enjoyed each other's company. I discovered for the first time that one could be good friends with a girl without love or sex. Her steady boyfriend was a handsome senior dental medical student. He, too, was reserved, and I did not know much about him, except that he would soon graduate. At the time, I had no clue that after his graduation, Iva's boyfriend would immediately become a teacher on the faculty of the dental school, an indication that he was a well-connected member of the Communist Party. Iva and I maintained our friendship, never straying into political discussion, and we never discussed her boyfriend.

Iva had attended an all-girl high school in the upper town of Zagreb, and here is an episode from her school, which she told me at the time. The Serbo-Croatian language course required that students each year write at least one essay, and the professor would choose the theme. The essay time that year came shortly after a significant national holiday, a day that celebrated and commemorated the final victory of the Partisans over the Nazis and Ustaše, called the "Day of Liberation" of Yugoslavia. Each year on that holiday, our national hero and beloved leader, Marshall Tito, gave a speech that could be heard on the radio and was printed verbatim in all newspapers. Not surprisingly, the theme assigned for the school essay was "the significance of our Day of Liberation," just what Marshall Tito was talking about in his great speech.

To save time, Iva had a quirky idea: she took Tito's speech from the newspaper and copied most of it word for word into her high school essay. Tito was an intelligent man with many talents, but in the language department, he was a complete failure. He was a naturally poor speaker, and his grammar and syntax were completely askew. After all, he spent many years abroad, mostly in Russia, where he left another wife and family, and besides, Tito's mother was Slovenian, so his command of Serbo-Croatian was not the best. Iva's language professor apparently neither heard nor read Tito's speech in the newspaper, and he gave Iva a failing grade on the essay. Iva went to the class leader and pointed out that her grade should be at least passing. She admitted being in a squeeze with time, and verbatim copying most of Tito's speech. How could it be graded with an F? Since the unpleasant incident needed to be resolved as quickly and quietly as possible, the class leader sternly reprimanded Iva, and the hapless professor corrected her grade to a passing level. To everyone's benefit, the little episode was forgotten.

At the end of my second year in medical school, I had a little incident regarding a subject that was neither medical nor important. During the first two years at the university, all students were obligated to take courses in pre-military education, and we had to pass an exam at the end of each academic year. I had thoroughly ignored the pre-military course and lectures, and I took and passed the first-year exam without doing any reading. In the second year of medical school, I failed the pre-military exam and then had to study the little manual. That was the only exam I ever failed in medical school, but for that particular failure, I felt rather proud. The pre-military education course, however, did get me into trouble. As a requirement to pass the course, we were taken to a shooting range and given an army rifle, a Mauser used in the Second World War, to shoot five bullets into a target at 110 yards (100 meters) and another five bullets to shoot at 220 yards (200 meters). The rifle had a distance adjustment, but no magnifier, and the bull's eye at 220 yards appeared as a mere black dot. I had a steady hand and good eye, and somehow all of my ten bullets went into the bull's eye. I had the best result in our class. The military officer came afterwards to congratulate me and asked if I was a member of a rifle club. When I told him that I never practiced shooting before, he did not believe me. I told him that I had imagined the target was the head of an enemy soldier.

"What soldier?" he inquired, and I blurted out a silly joke: "An Egyptian."

This was a bad thing to say, even if in jest. For that little jest, I was nearly expelled from medical school. However, because of my past, and perhaps because the communists who had a say in the matter possessed a sense of humor, I was severely reprimanded and my deepest apology was accepted.

This happened in 1956, the year of the bloody Hungarian Revolution and the time of the Suez Canal crisis. In Budapest, the Soviet Russians fired tank canons into civilian protesters, and human blood flowed in the street gutters, while the West did not react. It was also the year that Egypt seized the privately-built Suez Canal, but the U.S. ordered the British and French navies to lay off and told Israel to withdraw from the Sinai Peninsula. So it was that Suez Canal was taken over by Egypt, and afterward for some years, the canal remained non-functional: tankers had to go around the Horn of Africa to bring oil from the Persian Gulf. This was still a time when the U.S. gave orders and other countries followed without fuss. My Egyptian joke was only a reaction to what was happening in the world, but it was in bad taste, and it was certainly a stupid and dangerous thing to say. Our beloved Marshall Tito had a great friendship going with Nasser of Egypt (and with U Nu of Burma), and Tito had a taste for travel and luxury, including sailing his yacht up the Nile.

In the summer of 1956, I did some photography work to earn money, and then took a two-week vacation on the mid-Adriatic coast in Zadar. With a group of classmates and other students, I stayed in a local school dorm, and we all enjoyed visiting the beaches and exploring the town. Zadar was an interesting small city. It had a beautiful medieval church and a picturesque harbor. It also had an inordinate number of buildings left in ruins and overgrown by weeds since the end of the Second World War. The reason for such neglect was that communist authorities considered Zadar a "reactionary city." For centuries, it belonged to Italy and had the status of a free port, with its citizens enjoying freedom from customs duties. The citizenry was half Italian and half Croat, and before the war, all the people were relatively affluent. Under communist rule, most of the population opted to leave for Italy, and the remaining Croats did not like the new communist regime. Naturally, the government refused to make any effort to rebuild the city.

At The University

The third year of medical school was the easiest and most uneventful as far as the courses were concerned. There was only one exam to pass at the end of the academic year: microbiology. Most of the time was taken up by attending lectures and practical labs in pathology, pharmacology, and various clinical subjects. I had plenty of free time and was able to do some photography and again earn a little money. Our class had a certain number of Communist Party members and some who were members of the Secret Service, and most of my friends quickly learned to recognize them. The communists had frequent Party meetings for which they stayed in the classrooms in the evenings after classes. Among other things, the communists were also distinguished by their attire. They wore suits and ties. This dress code was new: the communists were for years critical of capitalists who wore suits and ties. Ten years after the war, the communists acquired a taste for dressing up. Having been told for so many years that we were all supposed to be "comrades," the rest of us wore open shirts and casual clothing. To counter the communists' suits and ties, I used to wear to class just a black turtleneck and a pair of black corduroy pants. After all, we were supposed to be a society of proletarians.

The well-dressed Communist Party members at the university actively solicited the students to pledge for volunteer work during the summer school recess. The pledge meant that one had to spend a whole month doing physical work at a construction site. That particular year, the program was to build "the Highway of Brotherhood and Unity," a highway that would connect Croatia with Serbia. When approached, I said that my body weight was too low for physical work, and I declined to make a pledge. Some students caved in out of fear, or because they wanted to gain favors from the communists. They either needed a place in a subsidized dorm, or they wanted a small government stipend to help with the cost of living, but most of those who pledged and worked with the communists were planning for their careers. They wanted to have a "brighter future." By ingratiating themselves to the communists, those students hoped to be considered for membership in the Communist Party. That goal would serve them after graduation to obtain a residency training position in a desirable specialty or at least a job in Zagreb, rather than being sent to work as country doctors in a remote provincial town or village.

My steadfast refusal to pledge for volunteer work and my attitude towards the communists earned me the worst possible record in the files of the Communist Party. Based on that record, each student received a letter of recommendation upon graduation, which was mandatory for employment. The letter was called a "personal characteristic," and it was issued by the office of the Communist Party. Eventually, I got a hold of a copy of that letter. I was described as a "negative element," an enemy of the people's movement, uncooperative with the communist cause, and the worst of accusations—I was a son of a capitalist merchant. The letter gratuitously added that I was a "good student," implying a C grade average, a lie—my grades were straight A. I could not care less, for I knew I would not spend the rest of my life in the communist paradise. It occurred to me that someday, translated into English, this nasty letter of recommendation would represent a very positive document, for I was declared to be against all that the communists stood for. In Yugoslavia, with that kind of recommendation, I would never get a job in Zagreb, nor would I ever be allowed to enter residency training in a specialty. I could only end up as a country doctor in some remote corner of the Balkan.

Once again, I passed the one required exam for the third academic year in the spring, so that in the summer of 1957, I had ample free time. But first I had to complete an obligatory clinical internship in public health, which was scheduled for the entire month of June. The public health internship was done in teams of four medical students with one faculty physician who was the team leader. Our destination was Lipik, a small town in northern Croatia. I teamed up with Ivan U., and the other two students were Reza T. and Fred Z., a happy couple. The leader of the team, Dr. R., was a surgeon, and he brought along his wife, who was a pediatrician. Our team had to visit various facilities and villages to learn and record the sanitary conditions and other aspects of public health. The area was rural, with some of the best agricultural land in Croatia, along with some forested areas. There was no major industrial plant in the region.

During a visit to a small graphite mine, only the three males on our team were allowed to descend into the mineshaft. Reza was excused on the account of a miners' superstition: "A woman's presence in the mine brings bad luck," we were told. We received miners' shirts and pants to put over our underwear and spare our good outer clothing. We each also received a helmet with a small light. The mine was only about 350 feet deep, and we had to descend vertically, using twelve-foot ladders, each ending on a little wooden landing platform. The rungs of the ladders were about twenty inches apart, and they were wet, muddy, and slippery. I felt like I was stepping into a void without any footing under me. Ivan went first, I followed him, and Fred was last. My light stopped working, but I could see sufficiently from the light coming from Ivan's and Fred's lamps. As we descended, the mud from Fred's boots fell on my helmet, neck, and shoulders. Reaching down with my foot and feeling for the next rung, I sometimes stepped on Ivan's helmet, which was closer than the next rung of the ladder. Ivan yelled and cursed. We finally reached the bottom of the vertical shaft, and there was a little space where we rested. Then we advanced on all fours along a narrow, low horizontal tunnel supported by multiple, heavy, wooden crossbeams. Ivan and Fred were tall, and every now and then, I heard a thud and a curse. As they tried to lift their heads to see ahead, their helmets bumped into a crossbeam. After a few screams and curses, we reached the end of the tunnel and met with the team of working miners. The air in the shaft was hot and heavy, stale and stifling. There was no visible source of ventilation. The working conditions were appalling. The shaft walls were moist; at least there was no dust. Graphite ore is a black, thick, greasy mud, and it was dug with shovels and then carried in large metal pails to a small elevator platform with no sidewalls. We stayed only long enough to observe the work and make mental notes. We could not wait to get out of the mineshaft. As we reached the space by the first ladder, we rested a while before climbing to the surface. I noticed that the elevator platform was pulled up by a steel rope through an adjacent second vertical shaft. There was a sign indicating that workers were not allowed to use the elevator; it was to be used only for the ore. This time, I chose to climb up last. As Fred and Ivan started moving up the first ladder, greasy mud started falling in my face and on my shoulders. I looked at the elevator platform. All I needed to do was take off a pail of ore and step in its place. It was done in two seconds, and all I had to do was to push a red button on the side of the elevator. Within the next minute, I effortlessly came to the surface. No one on top seemed to notice. Ivan and Fred finally came up panting. Reza had a good laugh when she saw us. With greasy black mud smeared all over our faces, we looked worse than chimney sweeps. Afterwards, the three of us showered for half an hour, but the black mud seemed embedded in our skin pores. We carried the black blotches and spots for days. Writing a sanitary report about the mine conditions was no fun: we had to maneuver between the naked truth and the politically acceptable. Our team leader, Dr. R., was clearly a member of the Communist Party. We peons represented the reactionaries, since no member of our team ever pledged to volunteer in public works.

One day, we visited a logging operation. It was unremarkable except for the fact that workers' lunch was a minor spectacle. The loggers' cook made a beef stew with large chunks of beef and mutton cooked on site in a giant cauldron over an open fire. The amount of food a logger could eat seemed unbelievable. In addition, some of the loggers showed off by swallowing whole chunks of meat without chewing, washing it down with local beer. It was a performance worthy of a freak circus act. After the show, it was easy to come up with a public health report. We had to be a little inventive, but we could certainly state that the heavy workers had an abundance of nutritious food.

On another day, we visited a remote village that could be reached only by a footpath through the forest, either on horseback or by walking. We chose to make it a nice long hike, and it took two and a half hours one way. We arrived shortly before noon and met the village mayor, who invited us to lunch in his house. There we sat on chairs around a large wooden table. A huge loaf of brown country bread and a knife were passed around, and each of us cut his own slice of bread. A large platter with half of a dried raw ham on the bone was put in the middle of the table, and we each had a turn cutting off a piece of ham. A bottle of plum brandy was passed around the table, going from mouth to mouth.

In the meantime, I noticed a subtle movement on the ham: a few little worms were slowly wiggling between the meat and the bone. Ivan did not see them right away, but I caught his looks when he saw the brandy bottle with its filthy brown neck approaching. I watched with interest when his turn came to drink and he had to bring the bottle to his mouth. He leaned the bottleneck on his chin and tried to drink without touching it to his lips. So did I, but half the brandy went down my neck all the way to my underpants. Then Ivan noticed a lone worm inching across the bone in the ham. We lost our hunger, but took a few bites of the bread. We had walked all morning and needed some sustenance. Besides, it was clear that our host gave us his best. The homes in that remote village had neither electricity nor running water. There was no plumbing, either, and of course, there were no toilets. Instead, there were latrines with deep pits hidden behind bushes adjacent to the barn. The villagers obtained their drinking water from an open well in the ground, and right next to the well was a tiny pond where the animals drank and the women did their laundry the old-fashioned way, by swinging each piece through the air and hitting it hard against the stones at the edge of the water. The pond was the source of a little creek that wound through the fields and disappeared in the adjacent woods. After visiting the water well, our team was asked to see a woman who was very ill.

We were shown to a house. There, in a small room with closed windows, was an elderly woman lying in bed. A blanket covered her. A swarm of flies covered her emaciated face and bare arms. When we entered, a young girl got off a chair, picked up a tree branch from the floor, and started fanning the woman. The flies took off like a black cloud. The patient was moaning and did not answer any questions. Dr. R. uncovered her and found a large, ulcerated, and infected wound on one of her breasts. After a brief examination, he concluded that the woman had terminal breast cancer and nothing could be done. After our long trek home, it was not easy to make a public health report that would show reality without being offensive to the authorities.

During that month, we also visited several well-developed, rich villages that had electricity, nice homes with attached outhouses, and deep wells with healthy drinking water. Most houses had little gardens with vegetables and flowers around them, and many had an adjacent orchard with fruit trees. On such days, we enjoyed making our public health reports as much as we enjoyed eating locally supplied tasty meals and fresh fruit. After the first two weeks of the public health internship, we took the train back to Zagreb for a weekend of city recreation. Our public health program also required that we visit a sizable local institution for chronic mental patients. This was the most frightening experience of the summer, and every member of our group shared the fear. As we were escorted through the wards of the hospital, we took mental notes of the prison-like gates and enclosures, and various conditions and situations in which we saw the patients. The staff introduced us to a "king," an "emperor," Napoleon, with an arm resting over his belly, and several other notable personalities. They all appeared peaceful and friendly. "Caruso" sang for us, and we clapped. Empress Maria Theresa was all graciousness. Then we were taken outside to inspect the large backyard and garden surrounded by a two-story wall. The nurses waited for us at the door of the building.

It was summer, and the patients milled about or sat freely in the garden. Some had taken off their clothes and walked around naked. All of a sudden, several huge, muscular men approached us with threatening facial expressions. That is when we got scared. We felt like leaving as fast as possible, but we had to walk slowly and make believe that we belonged there. After a few tense, close encounters, we left the garden and returned to the building without suffering harm. When we finally left through the front door of the building, we all shared an audible sigh of relief.

Our final visit of the month was to a nearby spa that touted its waters as having the power to improve or restore women's fertility. An old physician ran it, and after our formal visit to the facility, he invited our whole team for a nice supper. We were in a rich region, and there was plenty of good food and wine. As our internship was ending, and the wine was flowing, we were all in a very good mood. During that supper, even our team leaders, Dr. and Mrs. R., appeared to thaw. At one point, Dr. R. asked our good host what ingredients made the spa water enhance the women's fertility. The doctor hesitated for a moment. The water had many minerals and complex chemical compounds, he said, and he was not sure which one component and in what way the spa water worked, but the good results certainly spoke for themselves. The proof, he said, was that many women got pregnant as soon as they returned home to their husbands. In any case, he added with a smirk, whatever may be that active ingredient in the water, around the spa were many young local lads who were polite and always willing to help the guests in any way they could. By then, we all were a bit tipsy. On parting, we thanked our host for a great evening. The following day, we completed our final public health report, and the summer internship was over.

At home, two notable events occurred in 1956/57. First, Nicola, the student residing in our maid's room graduated and moved back home. About the same time, my friend and medical classmate Iva was actively searching for a single room to sublet. I introduced her to Aunt Ester, and soon Iva replaced Nicola and moved into our little maid's room. Aunt Ester did not allow house visits, and Iva's boyfriend never came to our home. Iva and I often met at home in the evening, and we sat in her room where she read poetry that we both liked, especially Yesenin and Bodelaire. She had a pleasant alto voice, read Russian poems in the original language, and after a long day of studying medical subjects, we just wanted to relax and have a good time outside of medicine. Aunt Ester looked at our friendship with a different eye and clearly disapproved of it. No matter how much I tried to assure her that Iva was engaged and we were just good friends, Aunt Ester could not accept or comprehend it. I ignored her pointed comments and innuendos, but this misunderstanding would eventually culminate in a significant change of my path to graduation.

The second event occurred in the spring of 1957: my first cousin Luisa, her husband, and two sons moved to Zagreb. Being "well connected," they were given a large duplex apartment in a modern building, and I occasionally visited them. However, because they were members of the Communist Party, I never wanted to get too close to them. Since the age of fifteen, Luisa had had no connection with her father, Uncle Ernest, and I felt that she was suffering from this separation. During one of my visits, I said I would try to get in touch with my uncles in Italy, and then to connect Luisa with her father. From old friends of our family, I obtained my uncles' address in Milan, Italy, and wrote a letter addressed to both Uncle Felix and Ernest expressing my wish to see them. Within a short time, I received a reply signed by both of them, inviting me for a visit. Passports and exit visas were extremely difficult to obtain; we were still behind the Iron Curtain. On my application for the passport, I stated that I had not seen my uncles in Italy for over ten years.

Within several weeks, to my surprise, I received a passport with the required exit visa. Perhaps Luisa and David helped me obtain the passport and visa, but I never asked them, nor did I want to find out about it. Anyway, the government's rationale for issuing a visa was that a medical student would not permanently leave Yugoslavia but would rather return to complete his education.

PART III

A TASTE OF THE FREE WORLD

A PRIZE

Having obtained the passport, I promptly started looking for a student summer job in the West. The Alliance Française in Zagreb offered student jobs in France. Along with students from other countries in Europe, I was to help harvesting wine grapes in the Beaujolais region, just north of Lyon. I had never studied French, but this did not bother me in the least: some of the students would surely speak German. Immediately after returning from the public health internship, I started preparing for the trip. It did not take a long time. All I needed was a duffel bag with a few pieces of clothing, a toothbrush, and a razor with a few blades, and I was ready to go. Off I went by train, and I was feverish at the thought that for the first time, I was to leave Yugoslavia and travel to a free country in the West.

My first stop was Milan, and with my duffel bag over the shoulder, I walked over three kilometers (two miles) from the rail station, past the Duomo, all the way to my uncles' apartment in Via Ausonio. It was very exciting for all three of us to be together after so many years. Uncle Felix and Ernest remembered me only as a small child. They last saw me when I was six years old. It was a pleasant, short visit, and after a few days, early one morning, I left for France. I would visit them again at the end of summer, on my way back to Zagreb. From Milan, I continued by train through Switzerland, towards France. On the train, I kept my face glued to the window, imbibing the beautiful Alpine views, scenery I knew only from pictures in the books. In the late morning, when the train stopped in Geneva, I decided to get off and see the city. I intended to continue my trip to Lyon on a later train the same afternoon.

It was my first short stay in Switzerland, and I was excited. I walked through the old city and the university quarter, and there I met a group of local students who were very friendly. I got by very well, speaking German. One student offered to give me a tour of the old city. As usual during the summer, the student dorms were mostly empty, and this fellow invited me to stay overnight in his dorm and see more of the city, including the nightlife. I accepted, and we had an interesting evening. When I told him openly about the life in Yugoslavia, he asked whether I was interested in staying in Geneva and continuing my medical studies there. It was apparently possible to obtain asylum and even to receive a small stipend to attend the university, but I did not find it acceptable. Many of my courses would have to be repeated, I would have to learn French, and all that would prolong my study by an additional two years. The next day, in the late morning, I went to the station to board the train for France. A Swiss border official checked my passport and started yelling at me in French, which I did not understand. I answered in German, which for some reason enraged the official even more. It turned out that I had only a one-day transit visa for Switzerland, and therefore had no right to spend a night there. I broke the Swiss law. I was about to leave, so what more could

I do? The border official finally calmed down, and after I apologized and promised that it would not happen again, he let me board the train. At least I learned a few things about Switzerland:
1) Passport control in Geneva was right inside the train station.
2) French Swiss did not like to hear or speak German.
3) The Swiss were sensitive about the limits of their transit visas.
4) Swiss officials become reasonable when they see that nothing is to be gained by following rigid rules.

In Lyon, I went from the train station to the nearby bus terminal, where I took the bus to a little village near the chateau where I had a job. From the village, I still had to walk about two miles to the chateau, which was actually a large mansion with several adjacent farm buildings. The farm was in the midst of gentle rolling hills with vineyards as far as the eye could see.

The region was well known on account of its proximity to Clochemerle, a village used by Gabriel Chevalier in his famous novel by the same name, in which he intimately described the life of people in rural France during the twenties. I had a translation of the novel *Clochemerle* at home, and I loved it. I had read and re-read it more than once. The student workers at the chateau were from France and other countries of Western Europe.

We were housed in a side building in several rooms with cots. The facilities were simple and adequate, and so was the food. The work was hard. We got up at dawn, had a simple breakfast of coffee, bread, butter, jam, and cheese, and then were off on a small truck into the vineyards. The grapes were picked into large metal pails, which were carried and emptied into a larger vat at the end of each row of vines. The wooden vat had two shoulder straps, and when it was full, the vat had to be carried on one's back to the road where the farm truck was parked. At noon, we were taken to the farm for a good lunch that included a bottle of ordinary red wine for each of us. There was a one-hour rest, and then we were taken back to the vineyards till dusk. That year, 1957, was one of the worst years for vineyards in the Beaujolais region. Following excessive rain and regional hailstorms in early summer, the grapes were relatively small and sparse. Even during my stay, the weather was not good: it often drizzled and rained while we were harvesting, so that the ground was muddy and slippery. At the end of the day, everyone was dirty and tired, and during work, there was relatively little social contact between the students. I arrived there in mid-July, and the harvest finished early, about mid-August. The student work in the area was done, and even though I earned barely more than the cost of my travel, I was glad it was over. Picking wine grapes in bad weather was no picnic. On one weekend, I did visit Clochemerle. Thirty years later, it appeared very different from the description by Chevalier.

My next stop was Avignon, where I was to visit Uncle Stanislav's brother Uncle Bernard and his family. Uncle Stanislav had written to Uncle Bernard that I would be arriving sometime in summer, and I sent Uncle Bernard a card a few days before departing from Lyon. When I arrived in Avignon, it was not hard to find Uncle Bernard's address. He had not changed much except for a few more gray hairs and a more portly body. His wife was a little heavier too, and their new baby, Jeanne-Marie, who I never saw before, was by then eight years old. Their son Ben was at work; he was a postal clerk in Paris. Sara was fully grown, but I recognized her right away. She was nineteen and preparing to repeat the baccalaureate, a particularly hard exam in France. Sara showed me around the city, and we even went to see a movie. I had ample time before I had to go home, so I asked Uncle Bernard if there was any student work in Provence. He told me without hesitation that there were no student jobs anywhere in that region. He did not need to ask anyone; he knew. During my visit at Uncle Bernard's, I noticed that all three meals his wife served were small, as if they were rationed or on a restrictive diet—a tiny piece of meat, one slice of bread, a little vegetable, or salad, and a little cheese for desert. Perhaps it was for health reasons: Uncle Bernard was a bit portly, and his wife and Sara also appeared well rounded. Sara clearly did not like her stepmother, and when we were alone, she explained to me in German that her stepmother was saving money from the weekly household allowance and stuffing it into her separate savings account. I thought she was considerably younger than Uncle Bernard, and maybe that was the reason she needed the extra savings.

On the third day of my visit, as soon as Uncle Bernard returned home from work, he came to me and with a kindly smile handed me a surprise present. It was in an envelope. I thanked him and said that he really need not have given me anything, and I was grateful for his kind hospitality. When I opened the envelope, I discovered that my gift was a bus ticket from Avignon to Nice. Uncle Bernard pointed out that the ticket was dated and stamped as valid for the next morning. From Nice, he said, I could easily get myself a train ticket to Milan. In this way, I was given to understand that after three days, my visit was over. Of course, I also thanked his wife and Sara. I had the impression that Uncle Bernard's wife was not too pleased with my presence and wanted me to leave as soon as possible. Perhaps I was disturbing Sara's studies for the baccalaureate exam.

I left early next morning. Sitting on the bus going through Provence, I saw through the window that the table-grape harvest season was in full swing. The weather was beautiful, and in the vineyards along the road, I saw rows and rows of grape pickers filling shallow wooden boxes with golden yellow table grapes. The area was flat and had ample fertile soil along both sides of the river Durance, which ran for a while along the road we traveled. What a miser my uncle was, I thought. There was plenty of student work in the region, if one were only to ask, but now it was too late. I was on a moving bus. I hoped to return to work in that area the following summer. Picking table grapes in sunny weather appeared much nicer and easier than dealing with the wine grapes, and it might be more fun.

On the way along the French and Italian Riviera, I sat on the train and enjoyed the scenery. The rocky coast and occasional beaches were beautiful, and I thought I would have to come back another time for a better look. Again I spent a few days with my uncles in Milan. Uncle Felix and Uncle Ernest worked long hours in their office, which was just a block from their apartment. Their spacious apartment was on the main floor of a modern apartment building, not far from the center of the city. It was furnished in a tasteful, though old-fashioned style, with heavy mahogany furniture, embellished with sixteenth and seventeenth century original oil paintings, and about half a dozen antique clocks. Uncle Felix was obviously a connoisseur of art and a collector of antique clocks. Uncle Ernest had diabetes and had to inject himself daily with insulin. He sometimes cheated and ate sweets, which he obviously liked. On the table in the dining room, there was always a small bowl filled with Amarettini di Saronno, and it was then that I first tasted them and developed a liking for them. Uncle Felix and Uncle Ernest would bring home from the deli and grocery good meats or vegetables, and I tried to be helpful in preparing the meals. For the first time, I was introduced to fennel as a vegetable, and for dessert, I discovered the bacci. Uncle Felix tried to eat only kosher food, but he was not very successful. Uncle Ernest was Catholic, and he ate everything.

On this second visit, I stayed a little longer, since I had enough time, and we had the opportunity to talk more than during my short first visit. When my uncles were at work, I felt idle and asked if I could be of any help while exploring the city of Milan. They sent me on several small errands—to the bank, to collect something they were due, or simply to act as a messenger. My Italian language skills were practically non-existent: I relied on my rudimentary knowledge of Latin, to which Italian is very close. On Sunday, we all rested. I felt in our conversation a certain tension, and I knew that it was because of the old dispute between Uncle Ernest and Uncle Stanislav. Although that awkward subject hung over our heads during my visit, we never touched on it. Uncle Ernest did not wish to talk about his daughter Luisa. Nor did my uncles ever ask if I needed any help from them. We said our good-byes cordially, and we all declared that I should come back to visit them again and spend more time with them, so we could get to know each other a little better. In a certain sense, we were strangers, but I yearned to get closer to them, and I also wished that Uncle Ernest would get together with his daughter Luisa, but that subject could not be touched.

On the way home, I stopped in Trieste. Uncle Stanislav gave me an address to visit with a friend of his. The friend expected me, put me up for the night, and the next day I was loaded with wares ordered by Uncle Stanislav, items that were hard to find in Yugoslavia. I took with me as much as I could, being careful not to arouse suspicion in the Yugoslav customs officials. In my pockets, I carried folded ladies' underwear and bras, and on my body I wore, one over the other, three ladies' corsets. Into the lining of a new raincoat were sown many pairs of ladies' nylon stockings and a few light ladies' undergarments. In my duffel bag, I carried packs of talcum powder, black tea, coffee, and many other useful and scarce items. I passed the border without a problem, relieved that my first trip abroad ended without any setback. Some of the items I brought home were for our use, and others served to make a little profit and defray the cost of my trip.

The fourth academic year of school awaited me with the largest and hardest exam of the entire medical school curriculum: pathology. Studying for it, I soon forgot all the exciting sights and impressions from my first trip abroad. The pathology exam had to be taken after five semesters of courses and labs, and the exam itself took two full days: first a morning for autopsy dissection and an afternoon for diagnosis of multiple microscopic slides. There was a second morning for discussing the gross findings in formalin-preserved tissues kept in large glass jars, and on the second afternoon, I had to answer multiple questions in an oral exam. I passed the exam without a hitch, and as usual, felt relieved but completely drained afterwards.

At that time, I was still occasionally visiting the Jewish Community Youth Club. On one such occasion, I was invited to join a newly formed Jewish Community Choir, which would hopefully travel and give performances in the West. The prospect of more traveling abroad and visiting various countries in the West was always alluring. Living behind the Iron Curtain, one never had enough of such opportunities. Members of the choir would get exit visas without any problem, and so I decided to sign up and become a member. Having passed the pathology exam, I could devote some time to choir practice, which was usually held in the evenings. It was announced that in the spring of 1958, the choir would go on a tour to Paris and visit the World Expo in Brussels. Choir rehearsals consequently increased from the usual bi-weekly to four or five evenings per week. The conductor, Mr. D., was an experienced and capable musician who conducted other large choirs. For our tour, he borrowed a few professional, highly qualified, soloists from a large national choir. Suddenly, there was an influx of many new choir members from the Jewish Community. Some were students, and some were middle-aged people who liked the idea of being able to travel abroad. Some of the new members could not sing too well, but they were qualified by their membership in the Communist Party. The tour was scheduled for the second half of May 1958, and everyone got more and more excited. Choir members had to contribute money towards the cost of travel, but some could not afford it. The Jewish community offered to help out, and in probing those who claimed to need financial help, it turned out that some of the applicants were actually not so needy. The issues were aired at an open meeting of the choir, and in the course of discussion, one got to know the personalities of the choir members much better. I certainly gained an insight to the human condition: several needy persons were too embarrassed to ask for financial help, whereas a few relatively well off individuals vigorously argued that they needed it. Mediating financial issues with such people was no fun, but a fair decision was reached in the end, and only those who needed help received it, even if they did not apply for it. The well off were left to foot their own bill, and suddenly they could afford it.

The last two weeks before the trip, the choir began to practice every evening. When the day of the trip arrived, everybody had the same problem: how to smuggle out a few extra dollars (which we were forbidden even to possess), to have sufficient pocket money. Each of us managed in his own way. The customs officials who boarded the train before the last stop at the Yugoslav border found some dollars in the possession of our borrowed (and well-paid) soprano soloist. She was arrested on the spot and taken off the train. There was great excitement, because much of our tour program hinged on this soloist. Our conductor, Mr. D., himself a member of Communist Party, immediately sent a telegram to Zagreb to pull strings to release her. He succeeded, and she was put on the next train to Paris. Several anxious hours passed before the hapless soprano caught up with us in Paris.

After crossing into Italy, the first train stop was in Trieste. For most of the people in the choir, it was their first time outside of Yugoslavia. At the Trieste rail station, we bought several bottles of Coca-Cola and had fun observing people tasting it for the first time. One girl took too large a gulp, started choking on the sudden release of fizz, and the brown liquid squirted out of her nose. We all had a good laugh. In Paris, we were housed in a building two blocks off Champs Élisée, in the center of the city. Such a good location would be very expensive, but we were put into an older building that was in the midst of renovation, with scaffolding on the outside and provisory wooden barriers all along the inside staircase. We had at our disposal several large rooms with multiple cots, and some cots were in a large foyer. Our concert was scheduled at the well-known La Sale Pleyel, in a walking distance from our housing. We had two days of rest and practice rehearsals before the concert. We also had some free time to explore Paris, and this was most exciting. On this first visit to Paris, I was more interested in walking around and seeing parts of the city, famous buildings, and churches than the Louvre or other museums. We went around in small groups and savored what we could. Everyone was excited, and in the evening after choir rehearsal, when we came to our residence and the lights were turned off, people just kept talking between the cots. No one felt like sleeping.

On our second evening, I opened the piano in the corner of the large foyer and started playing. I had not played since entering medical school, but Paris somehow put me in the mood, and I played some of my favorite Chopin waltzes. In the large space behind me, someone was dancing with a ballet motion. When I stopped playing, Dobrana L. encouraged me to continue. She was, she said, in a mood to dance. I was surprised, because she and I usually had very little contact. In the past, on a few occasions, we expressed quite different opinions, and we did not seem to get along too well. This time, we both were in a good mood, and so I played on and she danced for a while longer. Later that night, in the darkness of the foyer, we exchanged a few pleasant words, she lying on her cot and I crouching beside her before returning to my room to go to sleep.

A Prize

Our concert the following night went without a glitch, and it appeared to be quite a success. The applause at the end was loud and long lasting. We all recognized that our conductor's talent, patience, and charming personality brought our choir to such a high level of performance. Of course, the borrowed soloists had helped a great deal. Our repertoire was not easy. Aside from various Yugoslav and Israeli folk songs, we also performed several classic French songs, the slaves' chorus from Verdi's opera *Nabucco*, and Handel's *Messiah*.

Our tour continued to Metz, where we were housed in large dorms in an old fortress-like building that at one time must have served as either barracks or a monastery. I shared the dorm room with Stanko P., and in the afternoon after we settled in, he asked me if I would like to taste a little cake that his grandmother baked for him. Out of a tin, he took a couple of solid Danish cakes, gave one to me, and started eating one himself. The cake tasted very good. When I took the second bite, I felt something hard inside the cake, and out came a small cellophane envelope containing a neatly folded twenty-dollar bill. Stanko laughed as he pulled another bill from his cake. That was some way to smuggle out the dollars. After the choir practice, some of us went for a walk to explore Metz in the evening. We broke into small groups and wandered around under the ancient arcades, admiring the low arches and thick supporting columns. It turned dark and it was a balmy night. The narrow streets of the old town grew quiet. I found myself walking with Dobrana and her best friend in the choir, Moira A. We started discussing all sort of topics, from literature to music, and walked around for over an hour. Dobrana had a bold and refreshing view on many subjects, while Moira appeared more reticent. We all enjoyed the evening and slowly returned to our residence. When I finally settled to go to sleep, I decided to talk with Dobrana again, whenever there was another chance. Was it possible that Dobrana felt the same way? I would have to find out.

The following night, our concert in Metz again went very well, and the next morning we continued to Brussels, Belgium. There we were housed in a building with dorm-like rooms, located a bit away from the center of the city. During our free time, we visited the splendid old central square in the city and of course saw the famous statue of Manneken Pis. We all received tickets to visit the World Expo, and that is where we spent most of our free time. This was a new experience, not to be compared with anything I had seen before. In a large area on the outskirts of Brussels, each nation built a pavilion to showcase the achievements of their industry and arts. In the center was the famous Atomium. It was a futuristic building resembling the shape of an atom and built as a symbol expressly for this exposition. Our concert in Brussels was again successful, and the following day we were taken by bus to the city of Liege, where we gave a second concert. Everything good ends, and the next morning, our tour was over. We had to pack and board an overnight train from Brussels to Milan. In Milan, we stayed just long enough to catch the next train for our return to Yugoslavia.

During that train trip, Dobrana and I sat together and spent a lot of time talking. We talked incessantly, slowly discovering that we had been quite mistaken about one another: many of our views and interests coincided. We each possessed a very different personality, but this fact now seemed to elicit mutual attraction and interest. The train trip was very long, and as we got tired and started to fall asleep, my head rested on Dobrana's shoulder, and just before being immersed in sweet slumber, I felt her incredibly soft, silky hair brush against my face. In the middle of the night, when I woke up, my head was cradled in her arms, and her face was resting on my shoulder. She felt warm and cuddly. At the time, I was not dating anyone, and I wanted to date her. Her eyes were wide open and so were mine. In the semi-darkness of the train compartment we looked each other deeply into the eyes, a moment that seemed to last very long. Our mouths came slowly closer, and we kissed, very long. Again, and again we repeated it. We did not care if someone saw us. When they did, we became "the news" of the trip.

After arriving home, we started seeing each other every evening after our school activities. We talked for hours and got to know each other better. Dobrana was attending the school of engineering. We both studied during the day, but the evenings were reserved for being together. I would walk her to her home, which was far out, nearly an hour from the center of the city. My friends teased me for walking so far, but I did not mind. Over time, Dobrana and I opened up to one another more and more, daring to touch even on politics, which was among young people usually taboo. Our views differed very little: we both disliked communism, but Dobrana had at least some admiration for Marshall Tito, whereas I was cynical and felt that any communist sailing around on his yacht and having castles, mansions, and foreign bank accounts was a hypocrite. Dobrana was right: with Tito's brand of communism, Yugoslavia was relatively better off than people in other communist countries of Eastern Europe, which suffered under the Soviet brand of communism.

Tito's demise and the bankruptcy of the communist economy would eventually open the door to nationalist hate mongering among various Yugoslav ethnic groups, with the most aggressive radical elements in each province taking the lead and staging the bloody break-up of Yugoslavia, while moderate reasonable people in all parts of the country were simply mowed over.

Despite being younger, Dobrana's feeling and taste in art, especially painting and sculpture, was far more refined than mine was, and in those areas, I had much to learn from her. Her understanding of literature was also better than mine, though I had been exposed to no less reading of the good classics. I had a stronger sense for socioeconomic events, and my musical background was broader. In areas where I was harsh and rough, she was sweet and mellow. On issues where I saw only "black and white," she helped me find a middle ground. We complemented each other and learned from each other. I could bare myself to her like to no one before, and Dobrana soon felt closer to me than my dear cousin Oliver did. She was the first person who could make me mellow. The impenetrable inner shell of my mind, that part of me that remained firmly closed to any other person, gradually opened to Dobrana. To her, I could reveal my most personal feelings: my anger at the injustice and cruelty of people in our society, both present and in the recent past. We were able to discuss anything, from social conditions to private issues about our parents (in my case, my uncle and aunt), the problems associated with generational gap.

My days and weeks with Dobrana passed very fast. At some point, I realized that what I thought would never happen to me, was happening. I was in love with Dobrana, and the more I got to know her, the more it felt as if a very old dream of mine was becoming real. Her looks and her mind, her warmth and liveliness, her sensitivity and decency, all drew me towards her like a magnet. And so, at a time when I least expected it, luck finally did shine upon me. I discovered the best imaginable person, one who I wanted as a life companion and a true, understanding friend, wife, and mother of our children. She was the ideal person that I used to dream about, but seeing the harsh reality of life, did not dare hope for. I felt I'd received the prize of my life.

I trusted Dobrana implicitly, and the moment had come that I had to reveal to her that I had made a vow to my dead parents that I would fulfill the wish they had: to leave Yugoslavia and move to the land they once wanted to go. Dobrana was a single child. She was born like myself, by Caesarian section and had no other siblings. Would she come with me and leave her parents behind? There was still some time before my graduation from medical school, but I was anxious to know her feelings. One day, I summoned the courage to come out with it and pose the question. I wanted her to give it sufficient thought, perhaps talk to her parents or a close friend. She made the decision on her own, and the answer was positive. I was greatly relieved. I could not bear the thought of backing out of my vow to leave Yugoslavia.

Dobrana, 1959

THE FAMILY ONE MAY NOT CHOOSE

For the summer of 1958, I again arranged through the French Institute (Alliance Française) to go to work in France, this time harvesting table grapes in Provence. Naturally, I would stop for a visit with my uncles in Milan. In the early summer of 1958, our choir made a short trip for a concert in Sarajevo, Bosnia, and by then, Dobrana and I were inseparable. With heavy hearts, but optimism for the future, we talked about the coming weeks of separation, which Dobrana would spend with her parents at the seashore in her father's native Istria. We would write and stay in touch.

The farm I was going to in Provence was in Les Vigneres, a small village in the rich agricultural area along the river Durance, close to Avignon and near some of the most beautiful small towns in the region. I stayed with my uncles in Italy only a few days, promising to remain longer on my return trip at the end of September. The views along the coast of the Italian and French Riviera were so alluring that I had an urge to get off the train. In Marseille, I changed to a train for Avignon, and from there to a local bus for Les Vigneres. The farm was easy to find, though it was two miles from the bus stop in the village center. I arrived at dusk, walking, quite exhausted. Already present at the farm were six friendly Italian students from Padova. This time, I came to France armed with a French text for foreigners by Mauger, with the intent to seriously study French. Since I spent most of my time with the six Italians, I ended up learning much more Italian than French. Italian was easier to learn, especially because the Italian students offered a lot of fun. Still, I did learn sufficient French to get by. Three more students from the Yugoslav Republic of Slovenia arrived a few days later, but they mostly kept to themselves.

While the previous year in the Beaujolais region, I only saw farm managers, this time I lived closely with a French family, the owners of the farm. Our cots were in a tall attic space on top of the house. Lunch and dinner were served in a country kitchen, where we all sat with the boss and his wife at a wooden table. It was there that I had my first experience with hearty, homemade French food, including the shock of a completely rare, bloody beef steak, straight from the kitchen grill. I felt sick and asked the boss's wife to grill it a little longer. She mumbled something I did not understand, probably what a fool I was, and put my meat back on the grill for another half a minute. Soon I would learn to eat rare meat and enjoy it, too. I was again introduced to drinking red wine with every meal. There was a yard full of chickens and a huge cage of pheasants. Once a week we ate a pheasant, which was far tastier than chicken. The boss also gathered all sorts of wild mushrooms from the woods, another delight I had never tasted.

I continued to learn about French culture and customs. In the past, I learned from reading translations of French literature, which I loved. I knew a lot about the spirit and culture of the Gallic people from their literature, but now I gleaned a few more tidbits from real life. The boss's wife was originally from Paris. One day, she told me that if each morning one were to use in one's coffee just one less cube of sugar, after thirty years, one would save many thousands of francs. She kept her own separate bank account, which she regularly augmented by saving from the weekly allowances the husband gave her for keeping the household. On another occasion, she explained that one takes a warm water bath only once a week, and that, too, saved a lot of money over the years. Such wise saving techniques, I was told, were common in France, and that is why France had become such a rich country. (That is why one can often smell a French person from yards away, I thought). Though I came from a poor country, I felt that this sort of thriftiness was a cultural trait; people were simply brought up that way. France was not a rich country because people used a little less sugar each morning or less hot water every week. The math of such savings did not add up to becoming a rich country. I remembered Uncle Bernard's wife with her tiny food portions and separate bank account. Three hundred years ago, Moliére must have met plenty of characters who inspired him to create the character of *Harpagon*. This detail of French culture seemed to have deep roots.

The owner of the farm, his wife, and little son had comfortable living quarters with running water and a modern bathroom and toilet. We students had an outhouse, and we showered in an outdoor enclosure sheltered from the wind by a wooden wall and a heavy burlap curtain. After picking and occasionally eating grapes all day, one would be sticky with grape juice in the evening. The shower water for the student workers was drawn from a roof reservoir that was heated by the sun. The reservoir was not large, and we tried to speed up the showering, or else the last guy would draw only cold water.

Picking table grapes of Chaselas and Grand Vert variety was easy. We advanced along the vineyard in parallel rows that allowed us to chat incessantly, all the while cutting and arranging the grapes in shallow wooden boxes. The students from Padova made sure my Italian skills improved by the day. They let their beards grow, and for the first time, so did I. One of the Italians had his father's car, a large old Fiat, and in the evenings, he packed all seven of us in it to go to the village center. There we sat at the outdoor tables of a bistro, and I was introduced to the refreshing local drink *pastis*. In the village center, there were always lots of students from other farms, who came from every possible country in Western Europe; a few were even from Poland. I learned that it was better to work on a larger farm, and next time, I figured I wanted to be closer to the village center. On Sundays, we students would visit Avignon, Cavaillon, or Arles, which were all close by.

After a few weeks of work, one of the Italian students said he felt weak; he was obviously sick. I looked at him. His eyes and skin were yellow. He had jaundice. His belly was swollen and painful, and he clearly had something wrong with his liver. He was taken to Avignon, and immediately left by train for home. Later, he wrote that he had hepatitis. We all hoped it was just too much wine, and not anything else.

In early September, the remaining five Italian students departed, but not before they taught me to sing all the funny Italian student songs. The grape harvest was finished, and the boss asked the three Slovenes and me to remove the vines from an old vineyard that was to be converted into an orchard. This was hard work. The ax bounced off the tough vine, and it took three or four hard strokes before a vine came down. I was getting tired and falling visibly behind the three Slovenes, who could knock down the vine with a single stroke of the ax. During lunch, the boss commented on my slow work, but his wife asked him to have patience. It took me nearly a whole day before I learned that each vine had a supple area about an inch below the soil surface, and there one could easily cut it with a single stroke. I also noticed that because of the steady wind, the mistral blowing always from the north and bending the vines in the opposite direction, the roots of the vines pointed to the north. The three Slovenes obviously knew the trick, but as friendly as they were, they would not tell me. We removed the vines in about six days, and then the three Slovenes departed. There were still some more table grapes to be picked in the boss's father's vineyard, so I remained to work for another week.

This time, I earned enough money to afford a week's vacation in Paris. I went to a youth hostel that in 1958 cost exactly one dollar per night. It was located at the last subway stop in the northwest suburbs, but I did not mind. Most of the people in the hostel were students, and many were from Senegal. It was interesting to be with people from Africa. They were friendly and gentle, and they all spoke French very well. This time, I really explored most of Paris on foot. My lunch I usually purchased at Les Halles, the huge open market that has long since been removed from the center of Paris. I went to see the Louvre. Despite my poor experience with Uncle Bernard the previous year in Avignon, I promised Uncle Stanislav I'd visit his brother. Uncle Bernard by then had moved to Lille, and one morning on a Sunday, I took the train from Paris and came to Uncle Bernard's apartment in Lille. He was home, but his wife and the younger daughter were at her mother's house in Antibes on the Riviera. Sara was home, but she was busy, locked in her room studying all day with a boyfriend. Lille was a relatively unattractive gray, industrial city, and it drizzled all the time. Uncle Bernard took me to a flea market and bought a few yards of heavy, rough cloth, a gift for Uncle Stanislav, who needed a new winter coat. Uncle Bernard wanted me to visit on a Sunday when the stores were not open, so he could get something cheap at the flea market. I felt bad at having to take such a miserly gift to Uncle Stanislav. I returned to Paris on the afternoon train, thinking of how I wasted the day.

After a full week in Paris, I took the train to Milan, again through Switzerland. This time, I decided to get off and briefly visit Lausanne, which had no border police to bother me. I explored the city on foot, bought my first electric shaver, and used it to trim off my beard. I found a free ride on a charter bus over Simplon Pass, and returned to Milan the same evening. My uncles were pleasantly surprised at my speaking some Italian. In the evenings, I relaxed with them, but during the day, they were very busy, and I had fun further exploring Milan. With a part of my earnings, I bought a small, portable American-made transistor radio, then a novelty in Yugoslavia. With its short wave band, I could listen to most western stations. I visited the Jewish Community Center in Milan and arranged for our choir to visit and give a concert the following spring. On the way from Milan to Trieste, I stopped for several hours in Venice, enough to go through the city and visit the famous La Biennale Exhibit. In Trieste, I again stayed overnight and loaded up with articles that were in demand in Zagreb. At home, I reconnected with Dobrana, to whom I had sent some letters and postcards from the trip.

The ninth-semester courses had already begun, and my friends had been signing my name on the attendance sheets while I was absent. The school year 1958-59 had a single large exam covering two subjects: internal medicine and pharmacology. The exam could be taken in the spring at the end of the tenth semester, and I decided to take it as soon as possible. The fifth year of medical school again required hard studying. Ivan U. persuaded me to study for the exam with him. A decent text of pharmacology did not exist, and he had excellent and thorough lecture notes. In turn, I persuaded him to join me for work in France the following summer of 1959, and he agreed. He would enjoy it, for he had taken French lessons at the Alliance Française for several years. Between the regular classes and practical clinical labs, we studied many long hours towards the exam.

During the winter break, between the ninth and tenth semesters, I again went to visit my uncles in Italy. I arrived on a Friday, and they were not home. There was a message with the concierge to take a local train to Como, then the boat that stops in the village of Carate-Urio. There was a quarter-mile walk on a narrow road, partly cut into mountain cliffs, to reach their villa from the cay. The villa was set on a steep mountainside with a large terraced garden that was criss-crossed by several paths and steps. Adjacent the entrance gate was a garage cut into the cliff like a dead-end tunnel. The path from the gate zigzagged up in several hairpin turns to end at the ground floor terrace. The villa had three floors and multiple rooms overlooking the lake and surrounding mountains. The garden behind the house continued steeply upward with more hairpin turns. It had palm and citrus trees, mimosas, and flowers even in February. This was amazing, when the city of Milan, in the valley to the south, had still snow on the ground. My uncles explained that the lake area was sheltered from the cold north winds by the high mountains, and it was tempered by the relatively warm lake. In hot summers, the lake area was the coolest spot in Italy, and in winter, it was relatively warm. The garden was Uncle Felix's pride, and a professional gardener tended it. In the upper part of the garden, was a tiny swimming pool.

At the villa, we had enough time to talk, and the issue of the dispute between Uncle Stanislav and Uncle Ernest about the missing gold coins finally came up. Uncle Ernest flatly accused Uncle Stanislav of having stolen his gold coins, which represented all his savings at a time when he was in dire need. Living in Trieste, Italy with his two stepsons, he said, he struggled to survive. He made soap and sold it from door to door while his older stepson Boris had bone cancer and needed hospitalization, Uncle Ernest lamented. (I knew that Boris had died of bone cancer. He always had a "lucky bump" on his ankle that exempted him from military service during the war.) Uncle Ernest continued spewing offensive remarks against Uncle Stanislav and his "Galician and Romanian origin".

His tirade hurt me. I, too, was half-Galician. I had known of the dispute between Uncle Stanislav and Uncle Ernest, but hearing the accusation made so plainly was shocking. I did not want to start an argument and waited till Uncle Ernest finished what he had to say. He finally asked where my loyalty was. Now was the time to answer and counter his accusations. The question of my loyalty, I felt, should never have been raised. I took no sides, but felt close to all of them, and I loved them all, even if for a long time I was not near the uncles in Milan.

Before I had a chance to continue, Uncle Ernest interrupted and let me know that he would need a lot of time before he could really trust me as a family member, because I grew up in Uncle Stanislav's house and was under his bad influence. On the inside, I was boiling over, but I was old enough to keep my cool. I preferred to answer Uncle Ernest when I had enough time to think of what to say. Uncle Felix did not say much, but he seemed to nod and go along with Uncle Ernest.

The open mistrust of my uncles offended me, but my love for Uncle Stanislav was undiminished, regardless of the vile accusation. I had a different idea as to who took Uncle Ernest's money. My uncles in Italy were my closest remaining family, and it was sad that they were questioning my trust and loyalty, issues that they created and perceived by themselves. I reminded them that Uncle Stanislav was the one who unselfishly took care of Oliver and me for all those years. It appeared to me, I said, as if Uncle Ernest cared more about his lost money than about me.

I pointed out that in 1946, Mrs. T., Ernest's friend and former mistress was a widow with two little sons and no known source of income, and yet, in 1948 she was able to take her teenage sons and leave Yugoslavia. How could Uncle Ernest be so sure that Mrs. T. hadn't felt the need to keep his gold coins in addition to his gift of jewelry? Yes, Uncle Stanislav had four children to feed, but Uncle Stanislav had a good business, which a year after the war was thriving. No one expected that two years later his business would be nationalized. No one could tell for sure who took Uncle Ernest's gold coins. The more we talked, the deeper grew the chasm between my uncles and me. Uncle Ernest kept accusing Uncle Stanislav, and I kept saying that the issue was irrelevant, and in any case, it could not be resolved with certainty.

To compound the problem, Uncle Ernest had wild mood swings from one extreme to another. Some days he was sweet and tender, and other times he was quite brusque and offensive. At the time, I did not realize that his mood swings had to do with his diabetes, that is, the level of his glucose. My rift with Uncle Ernest grew worse because of what he said to me when he got all excited. On one occasion, Uncle Ernest told me that he regarded me as "fifty-one percent Galician, with only the name of a Meier." During another of his bad moods, he told me that he would make sure that all his possessions were given to charity, rather than to his daughter Luisa or me. His steadfast refusal to contact his only daughter was vexing. I knew that Luisa ran away from home at the age of fifteen, but who knows why? Uncle Ernest said he never wanted to see her again. I told him she had a nice family and two sons, and that after all these years, it was time for him to forget the past and make up with her.

The ugly comment Uncle Ernest expressed about Aunt Ester's (and by inference, my mother's!) "Galician origin" was most offensive, for he expressed utter disdain and prejudice against people from Galicia. "Galicians are all thieves," he said.

Later, when I thought about his comments calmly, I suddenly felt quite content. Being half a "high-class" Hungarian Jew, and half a "low-class" Galician Jew, I could only have a good laugh about it. It was a pleasure to be of mixed background; one is completely free of any notion to look down upon someone else. I found it ludicrous that a Jew from Hungary considered himself a "higher class" than Jews from Galicia or Romania. That any Jew should be afflicted with prejudice was disgusting. After all, the Jews were, for the last twenty centuries, treated as a subhuman breed, a lower race. It was abominable that after all the discrimination and persecution the Jews had suffered, any one of them should still have his mind polluted by prejudice against others.

When I had a chance to be alone with Uncle Felix, I asked how he felt about the issue. He said, the fact that Uncle Stanislav had an apparently prosperous business with good income was not a proof of his innocence, but he admitted that one could not be sure Mrs. T. was faultless, either. I knew Uncle Stanislav, I said, and I knew he would never take something that did not belong to him. Uncle Felix then told me that he did not know Uncle Stanislav so well, but he did know Aunt Ester. The truth might never be known, he added. Since for all these years he had lived and worked with Ernest, Felix didn't want to cross his brother or have a dispute with him. That was understandable, but not very satisfying.

Uncle Felix then asked if I would ever consider staying with him and Uncle Ernest and working with them to eventually take over their business. I will never know whether that question was just a test, or was it for real. I told him that my intent was to become a physician, and I would not want to work in any other profession. I also thought that working next to Uncle Ernest would be no fun, but that I kept to myself. Uncle Felix then told me that after the war, when Uncle Stanislav salvaged all the furniture from Grandpa Meier's house, there was a very valuable old, Dutch oil painting, titled *Falstaff*, which Felix left in grandpa's house. Years ago, Uncle Felix said, he wrote to Uncle Stanislav asking him to return to him the painting, but Uncle Stanislav never answered his letters. I was not aware that Uncle Stanislav ever received any letter from Uncle Felix, but it occurred to me that as Aunt Ester had a dislike for both Ernest and Felix, if she ever got hold of a letter from Uncle Felix, she might have read it and then thrown it away.

The Family One May Not Choose

As for that painting, I knew it very well. It hung in our family room, a typical small Dutch portrait of a merry man with a big belly, a red bulbous nose, and smiling eyes holding a goblet of red wine in his right hand. I had no clue that it belonged to Uncle Felix, or that it was valuable. I was pained over it, but decided not to get involved or to mention it to Uncle Stanislav. Anyway, Uncle Stanislav during the war personally arranged to smuggle Uncle Felix to safety over the border into Italy. How could he now bother about one painting, no matter how valuable it was? Uncle Felix also told me that he had my grandfather's gold pocket watch, and that he would someday pass it on to me... On two points, we agreed: first, Uncle Ernest's material loss had nothing to do with me. I was eleven years old at the time, and second, it was best not to discuss this divisive issue again. Finally, Uncle Felix pointed out that he had no influence on what Uncle Ernest believed. No matter how much I would have liked to know the truth, I had to put this whole issue out of my mind.

From talking with my uncles, I understood that their business in Milan was quite lucrative. They owned five separate corporations. Their oldest business was the manufacture of generic detergents and soaps, which they packaged under different labels for other companies. They owned an olive oil business, buying up whole crops of olives in the south of Italy and later selling the refined oil product under a generic name. They had a chemical business based on a secure self-contract to be the sole importer in Italy for an ore from the Belgian Congo that was crucial for the production of safety glass, used in large windowpanes. They owned a franchise for small tobacco and news stores and kiosks over a large part of Milan, and finally, there was a real estate division involved in selling and buying condos, land, and homes in the Milan region, including the villa in Carate-Urio on Lake Como, which they kept for their own use. My uncles appeared well off, and I could not understand why they kept ruminating about material losses that happened so many years ago. I looked around: I was on the shore of beautiful Lake Como, and what was I doing? Instead of enjoying the beauty of the area and having a good time with my uncles, I was having miserable discussions with estranged relatives, leading to a deepening rift between us. I was not the only one who had problems with Uncle Ernest. His stepson Željko also had a hard time getting along with him. Uncle Felix told me that several years earlier, Željko left for Australia to start a new life, and I understood that he wanted to get away from Uncle Ernest.

Upon our return from Lake Como to Milan, my uncles were busy in their office, and when we saw each other in the evenings, we did not discuss their lost fortune. In the meantime, I finalized the engagement for a concert by our choir in Milan for March 1959. The choir management had also secured an engagement for two days later in Florence, and I looked forward to a small choir tour of northern Italy. I left for Zagreb feeling sad: there was an insurmountable rift between my uncles and myself. What bothered and disgusted me most was that our rift was caused by money. Having lost my father, I longed to have a closer relationship with his brothers, but they treated me as if I were a stranger, or worse, an agent from my mother's side of the family, which they accused of theft. I felt hurt and rejected, but I did not want to believe it. I parted from my uncles with mixed feelings.

Our one-week choir tour was at the end of March 1959, and during that trip, Dobrana and I again enjoyed a lot of time together. We visited the magnificent Duomo Cathedral and other sites in Milan, and I went to greet my uncles very briefly. In Florence, we had some free time to see the city and loved it. We thought Florence was the most beautiful city we had ever seen. Our concerts in Milan and Florence were well received, and the week in Italy ended too fast. We were back in Zagreb to study for our exams.

At the end of May 1959 was the fifth anniversary of my high school graduation, and our class organized a gathering with supper at a restaurant on the northern outskirts of Zagreb, in a village past the last tram station under the Sljeme mountain. Along with a simple meal and some wine, our classmates updated on one another and we all had a good time. Returning home with the last nightly tram around one a.m., Ivan suddenly said he had something very important to tell me. He had withdrawn his application for the early term of the exam at the end of the current semester, and consequently he would stay in Zagreb to study over the summer and could not join me to work in France. Ivan explained that he felt he could not adequately prepare himself for the exam by the beginning of June. It was a shock. The term for withdrawing the exam application had passed several weeks earlier, but obviously, Ivan did it without telling me anything until this very moment. He said he was "too embarrassed" to talk about it earlier. This late, a mere two weeks before the exam, the rules did not allow me to withdraw my application. Thus, I was committed to take the exam in the first week of June. It would be impossible to continue studying and reviewing for the exam together.

Ivan was kind enough to lend me all his lecture notes till my exam, and from the next morning, I would continue to study and review by myself. The whole episode left me feeling betrayed, and thereafter, my friendship with Ivan cooled off. I also realized that our friendship was uneven. I was completely open and trusting, while Ivan held back and never opened up to me nearly as much.

I passed the exam well and slowly started preparing for my trip to France. The French Institute that year no longer offered arrangements for student jobs, and I decided to go to Provence and find a job on my own. I took a couple of weeks to relax and spent as much time as possible with Dobrana. The coming summer would again bring us weeks of separation. As for my uncles in Milan, we exchanged a few letters that only reflected our mutual estrangement. I would still visit them again, for I did not want to give up hope that our relationship might improve. I grew up believing that "blood is not water," and that family ties remain strong. In that department I still had lots to learn.

That summer, Michael had separated from his wife in Bosnia and escaped to Italy. He stayed in Rome with the family R., the parents of Gogo, and our relatives by marriage. Michael intended to seek work in Ethiopia, where there was a need for physicians. Uncle Stanislav asked if on my way to France I could detour to Rome and take certain items to Michael. I did not mind; Rome would be a beautiful city to visit. This time, aside from carrying some of Michael's personal belongings, I had to obtain an official, stamped, and sealed transcript of his medical studies from the dean's office at the university. Uncle Stanislav gave me an envelope containing 100,000 dinars (at the time worth about $100) which in Yugoslavia was a small fortune, with instructions to go to the dean's office and hand it to the secretary to insure that the transcript was done, and at that, promptly. This would be a novel experience. Though I knew that envelopes "under the table" were commonplace if one needed something from a public official, I did not know how this was done. Uncle Stanislav said, "Just do it! You will find a way."

It was said that money opened doors. I knew that if one needed an operation and did not want to wait three years, an envelope to the surgeon and one to the hospital administrator would do.

One afternoon, just before the dean's office was to close, I waited in the hallway and studied the bulletin board till the secretary came out and locked the office door. Then I started walking on the same path with her and engaged her in small talk about the weather and such. After ten minutes, we were in town, and she stopped at the nearest tram station. I stopped, too, and then I gathered the courage to tell her that my older cousin Michael needed a transcript of his school records. She remembered him very well. Her tram was approaching the station, and our conversation suddenly came to a standstill. I knew I had to act. But how? When she started walking towards the tram door, I summoned the courage to pull the envelope from the inside pocket of my jacket and hand it to her. She slipped it into her handbag without looking at me and without a word, and then we both said, "Till later." She stepped onto the tram, and I walked away, trying to recover from the shock. It felt like losing my virginity with an experienced woman.

A few days later, I had Michael's medical school transcript in my hands. I traveled to Rome carrying three heavy suitcases with Michael's belongings. I also had to carry all sorts of food that Aunt Ester thought would not be available in Italy. Michael met me at the train station, and we took a tram and a bus to reach the large apartment that belonged to Gogo's parents. Of course, Aunt Ester loaded me with ample presents for the hosts. I spent a happy week in Rome as their guest and managed to see most of the city. Gogo worked in a real estate agency in the center of the city, and his wife Barica (Karel's sister) worked as a private secretary to an Italian movie actress. Gogo gave me a ride into the center of the city early each morning when he went to work. From there I explored on foot all day, and in the evening, I returned to Gogo's office for a ride home. One morning, as we came out of the apartment, Gogo's Fiat, which was parked on the street in front of the house, was sitting very low. Moving closer, we realized that all four wheels and tires had been stolen during the night.

The high-rise apartment's balcony overlooked the ancient walls of Rome, and right outside of the walls was one of the notorious shantytown neighborhoods. It looked just like the one shown in *Miracle in Milan*—all cardboard and corrugated steel, with a forest of TV antennas sticking up from the shanties. Gogo's car wheels must have come in handy for someone down there. That day, we took a bus and a tram to get downtown. Gogo bought new wheels with special locks on them.

On this first visit to Rome, I remembered all the lessons from its glorious history. There was an incredible mixture of beautiful renaissance buildings and monuments from antiquity. Some of the marble statues from antiquity were better preserved than those from the Renaissance. What was left of the Roman Forum, the Coliseum, and the Baths of Caracala was far more impressive than I could ever imagine from reading and seeing the pictures in the books. The baths were so grand that the Opera of Rome gave regular, open-air performances in their space (the original wooden roofs had long disappeared).

After a great week, I left Rome full of impressions. From the train, I got a glimpse of the leaning tower in Pisa, and as the train rumbled along the beautiful Ligurian coast, through Genova, and along the already-familiar profile of the Italian and French Riviera, my thoughts slowly shifted to France. I had a touch of anxiety. This time I had to find a job all by myself. I hoped that it should not be too difficult to find a job in the same area of Provence I was familiar with from the previous year. I arrived in Avignon, slept over in a youth hostel, and early the next morning went to the bus terminal. There I met an Italian student, Silvano Scodari, who was waiting for the bus with the same purpose: looking for a summer job in the area. I persuaded him to take the bus to Les Vigneres and come with me. Silvano was from southern Italy, from Naples, and he looked unusual for a southern Italian. He was over six feet tall with light brown hair and blue-green eyes. A prominent hooknose was the only southern Italian sign in his appearance. He told me that his family actually came from Sicily, and that possibly some of his ancestors were of Norman origin. He was friendly and soft-spoken, and while working side by side for the next three months, we became good friends. We arrived a little too early for the grape harvest, but that way I could better choose my job location before the other students arrived, and there were always many odd jobs one could do on a farm.

In Les Vigneres, we went to the largest farm, the one belonging to the well-known family De Lafargue, which owed several chateaus and properties in various parts of France. They had a real chateau, a mansion in which they lived, with adjacent side buildings for workers, acres of vineyards and various fruit orchards, and a small, private, winemaking cellar. The owner, a man in his early sixties, was home and he interviewed us. Silvano did not speak French, but luckily, the owner spoke fluent German. We were immediately hired to do some odd jobs for a few days under the leadership of the farm foreman, who lived with his family in one of the side-houses. The other students were to arrive in a few days, and so our first job was to tidy up and clean the student quarters, which had a dining hall with a fireplace on the ground floor. The cots were laid out in the loft above, and being the first there, we chose the nicest location by the window.

When the students arrived, there were twenty-four in all, and they came from all possible locations. Half were French, and this was good: my French language skills could improve. The others were from Ireland, England, Holland, Belgium, and even from West Berlin. The extended family of the owner lived in the mansion with two grandchildren—a girl of three years and an infant for whom the family had a German babysitter.

After speaking to the owner, I learned that he was a veteran of the First World War and a titled count. He owned a big convertible jalopy that he proudly presented as the first twelve-cylinder convertible Packard imported to France. The car was still in moving condition, but the body was in poor shape, and it was used only for local trips to the market and for transporting small farm loads. The owner's son was there visiting from Paris. He worked in the French movie industry as a stage designer and drove a sleek British sport car. A few years later, I noticed his name on several French movies.

Picking table grapes was done with a pair of scissors, and the grapes had to be nicely arranged in shallow, rectangular wooden boxes, with the riper, better-looking, golden yellow ones on top. Any grape that was brown or shriveled had to be snipped off. I made sure that all my boxes looked good, and this was noticed by the foreman and later the owner. As a reward, the owner took me along when the grapes were being delivered to the point of sale and collection in the nearby town of Cavaillon. I would make a last check that all box surfaces had only healthy looking grapes. They fetched a better price. At the farm, we all had bicycles at our disposal to go to the village center in the evenings. Those who had too much wine with dinner had to walk. On Sundays, we made bicycle excursions as far as Arles, Avignon, and other small towns. The food was served three times a day in the dining hall, and it was good, hearty food with one whole bottle of ordinary red wine per day for each of us.

The workday started at 6:30 a.m.; we took a half-hour breakfast break at 7:30 a.m. and a two-hour lunch break at noon. The afternoon work started at two p.m. and went on till six p.m. The mornings were cool and dewy, and in the hour before breakfast, we got all wet working among the vines. As usual, the weather was sunny and dry and the northerly wind, the mistral, blew most of the time. I became friendly with two students from Paris, and soon realized that they were a "couple". They were intelligent and friendly and taught me much French. One of them occasionally had a fainting spell; he allegedly had some kind of congenital heart condition.

After a few weeks of work, with the money earned and with the help of the owner, I bought an inexpensive, used moped with a 49 cc engine. Thereafter each week, I went with a few other students to various, more distant places: Tarascon, Marseilles, Pont du Gard, La Fontaine de la Vaucluse, l'Isle sur la Sorgue,

Les Saintes-Maries de la Mer, etc. This was my longest and best summer in France. When the harvest was finished, the students left. The young German babysitter left with one of the students from West Berlin. Silvano and I remained a little longer to help in the wine cellar, where a "small amount" of wine was made for family consumption. De Lafargue, we thought, must have a huge family. One more job remained: the removal of old vines from an old vineyard, and this time, it was the giant Silvano who was falling behind on the job. He was frustrated seeing me, as short as I was, getting ahead and leisurely knocking off each vine with a single stroke of my ax.

Silvano stopped to rest, sweat dripping from his forehead, out of breath, then mumbled, "Tu, ma che sei, Ercole?" (You, what are you, Hercules?) After letting him struggle and curse the rubbery vines for about five minutes, I started laughing and explained to him the trick. When I asked the owner why we were removing the vines, he said that vineyards involved too much labor, and he was gradually replacing them with fruit orchards, which required less care and work, and were much less susceptible to the vagaries of weather. This trend was spreading throughout France, so that most of the ordinary wine consumed in France had to be blended with imported wine from Italy, Spain, and Morocco. At the end of our stay, I resold the moped, again with the kind help of the owner. A few days later, our work was finished, and early on a crisp morning in mid-October, the owner took us to a corner of Route 6, then the main road between Paris and Nice. When Silvano and I parted, we stood on opposite sides of the road. Silvano wanted to hitchhike to Paris, and I to Nice. He was picked up first, and my turn came five minutes later.

My driver was an art dealer from Paris, traveling in a large American station wagon loaded with paintings in the back. He was bored driving alone and glad to have company. He was going to Nice, and he asked if I minded making a little detour with a stop at Vauvenargues, near Aix en Provence. If I could go all the way to Nice, of course I did not mind. In my knapsack, I had some good apples and pears from the farm orchards, and I shared them with him. Vauvenargues, it turned out, was a castle owned by Picasso, and the dealer was to leave some of Picasso's paintings to be repaired by the artist. We did not stay long. Picasso had left the day before to stay at one of his studios in Vallauris near Cannes. This, too, was conveniently on the way to Nice. The art dealer had another little detour to make; he wanted to visit his daughter, who was in school in a little town near Toulon. I came gladly along. We next stopped in Vallauris, where Picasso was working on his plates and pottery, and there the dealer left the paintings for repair.

In the late afternoon, we arrived in Nice, and I was dropped off at the train station. I decided to explore the city and then try to hitchhike all the way into Italy. After reaching the road along the city beach, I found that there was no hitchhiking in that area, because that road, called the "lower corniche," was served by a regular trolleybus. I enjoyed the close views of the Riviera and ended up walking on foot along the road from Nice to Monte Carlo. The coastal area was so beautiful

The Family One May Not Choose

that I just walked on without noticing the distance or time. My duffel bag on my shoulder, I walked about seven miles. I reached the center of Monte-Carlo late in the evening. The cars parked along the streets at night were in those days mostly not locked, and I picked a large sedan and went to sleep on the back seat.

At dawn, I woke and went to a nearby water fountain to wash my face and drink some water. Then I fetched a bottle of milk for breakfast, walked around Monte Carlo to see it in the early morning sunshine, and finally took a trolleybus to the border town of Menton, where I hoped to pick up a ride into Italy. It worked: at the border gas station, I found a driver willing to take me all the way to Genova. It was one of the scariest rides I ever had. At the time, there was no highway along the coast, only a nice two-way road. The driver took the curves along the coast of the Italian Riviera with the greatest speed he could. All the way, I clutched at the right roof handle of the car. I learned about good Italian drivers first hand. In Genova, with my head still spinning from the car ride, I took the train to Milan.

The visit with my uncles was short. I had to hurry home; I was late for my next semester. While I tried to avoid any disagreeable discussion, Uncle Ernest at one point coolly said that I was coming to visit them only because they were wealthy. This was the limit, but I did not want to start an argument. I was again hurt and disappointed. Later, alone with Uncle Felix, I told him that under the circumstances—especially after Uncle Ernest's comments—I would not visit them anymore. Uncle Felix was always calm and gentle, and I still felt attached to him. He and I agreed that I could call him if I was in town. Uncle Felix asked me not to write him, for he did not want to have a problem with Ernest. I left Milan, and after the usual stop in Trieste, I returned to Zagreb to be with Dobrana and attend the sixth (and last) year of medical school.

At home, I had enough time to think about my relationship with Uncle Ernest and Uncle Felix. "Blood is not water," I thought, but it is not a glue, either. A family seemed to be like music: most people liked it and found it pleasing and beautiful, but some just couldn't hear the music. I thought of my dear cousin Oliver. He, too, had become estranged from me. Both of my uncles in Milan did not like my defending and being loyal to Uncle Stanislav. I wanted the satisfaction of having the last word with Uncle Ernest, but without any argument or quarrel. I sat down and wrote a short letter addressed only to Uncle Ernest. In a plain, blunt manner, I let him know that family ties, and not his personal wealth, motivated my visits, that his attitude towards me, and the rest of my family, was abominable, and that consequently I did not wish to see him again. I knew Uncle Felix would see the letter, and he would have to understand how I felt. I never saw Uncle Ernest again.

That fall, I was aggravated by Aunt Ester's constant insinuations about my relationship with Iva G., who lived in our apartment. I was annoyed and reached a point that I did not wish to put up with it any longer. Within days, I decided to move out and live on my own. In no time, I found a sublet room in a large apartment. When I told Uncle Stanislav that I had decided to move out, he wanted to talk to me in private, and we went for a long walk through a city park. He wondered if my moving out was influenced by my visits with the uncles in Milan. Without going into detail, I explained that my relationship with Uncle Ernest and Felix was not good, and I was moving out because I wanted to be free of Aunt Ester's constant surveillance and comments. He was sad, and so was I, but he said he understood my reason. On that occasion, I finally dared to ask Uncle Stanislav why he put up with Aunt Ester's constant ranting. Was he not bothered by it? Could he not ask her to tone it down? We were sitting on a bench in a little garden with a fishpond, and Uncle Stanislav was quiet, obviously thinking about my question. After a while, he said he knew Aunt Ester very well. She had changed during the war when they lived in constant fear, waking up at night, full of anxiety and listening if someone was ringing the doorbell, worrying about their two teenage children. After the war, he said, Aunt Ester's nerves were shot; everything upset her, and she started running her "bulletins". He learned to accept her as she was, and over time, he learned not to be upset by her behavior, for he knew that she could not help it. Above all, he said, he loved her, and for the sake of peace, he let her vent her frustrations in her own way. That is why he did not like to interfere or confront her.

I did notice that after Aunt Ester vented sufficiently, she usually calmed down. There would be peace in the house, at least until her next frustration. During the war, he continued, in the most difficult moments, she always encouraged him and gave him strength. Then he reminded me, "in every family, it is the woman who holds three pillars of the house." I have heard that saying before, but till then, I never understood its deeper meaning. We stopped talking, each absorbed in our own thoughts. Uncle Stanislav was right. I thought of my two uncles in Italy. They had no one to hold the three pillars of their house. It occurred to me that if Uncle Ernest's wife was alive, he would not be able to treat his daughter Luisa so harshly, nor would his stepson Željko have gone away to Australia. Every now and then, the tiny little red fish in the pond sparkled in the late afternoon sun. Uncle Stanislav taught me something worth remembering. We got up, exited the quiet little Japanese garden, and started walking home.

Living on my own meant hardship, sharing a large room with three other students, studying in libraries and coffee shops, doing my own laundry, eating slop in various student cafeterias, and ultimately delay my graduation from medical school. Nevertheless, I was happy to be free and feel independent. A large part of my strength and confidence came from the support I received from Dobrana. Soon I found a better sublet, a small maid's room off the kitchen in the apartment of a colleague at the medical school. His mother was a widow and needed the money, and I had enough savings to last me well into the next summer.

THE GERMANS

I had two more exams to pass before graduating medical school, and I needed to go abroad one more time before graduation in order to earn and save some money for the time when we finally left Yugoslavia. My target was Germany, where factory workers were in great demand and earnings were relatively high. Due to its phenomenal growth and economic success after the war, Germany was considered the economic "miracle country" of Europe. *After being left in ruins, with most of its factories destroyed by the war or dismantled and hauled away by French and British allies, Germany was rehabilitated by the U.S. Marshall Plan. The real basis of the economic miracle was that Germany started its recovery with new and most modern factory equipment.*

Aside from the chance of good earnings, there was another, deeper reason I was keen on visiting Germany. I was curious to see for myself the people and the country that hatched the Nazi movement. I wanted to experience firsthand whether most Germans were "monstrous evil Nazis," as they were still being portrayed in Yugoslavia fifteen years after the war ended. My curiosity drove me towards where the evil of Nazism originated. I wanted to see and get to know the German people. Knowing of my desire to work in Germany, Ivica's mother arranged that I receive a job offer in Reutlingen, a small industrial city in the state of Würtemberg. Depending on conditions, I could work for several months. The factory made metal parts for different equipment, and it offered a very good hourly wage, with bonuses if one produced above the production norm. Dobrana would spend part of her summer vacation at her best friend's house in Dalmatia. We promised each other that it was our last long separation. We would write to each other, and on my way back from Germany, meet in Venice, Italy.

After an overnight train trip, I arrived from Zagreb to Reutlingen. As instructed, I called the factory executive, Mr. Ernest I., by phone, and he picked me up from the train station. Although I had not spoken much German for many years, the language came back to me without difficulty. One can hardly forget his mother tongue. Mr. I. took me by car to a sublet room in the house of a retired teacher in the nearby town of Pfullingen, and the following day, Sunday, I was invited to lunch at his house. I rested, explored Pfullingen, located the streetcar that would take me to work, and the following day, with a small bouquet of flowers in hand, I easily found my way to Mr. I.'s house. He introduced me to his wife Ursel, and his mother, Oma I.. They received me very warmly, and did everything to make me feel comfortable, though I felt shy and remained reticent. I had to explain my knowledge of German. That was easy—my parents were born, raised, and schooled in the old Austrian-Hungarian Empire. At one point, I overheard Mrs. I. comment to her husband about how small my hands were and wonder how I would be able to work with the heavy press machines in the factory.

I was instructed to report for work at the factory on Monday at eight a.m. and to first register at the office. The registration had one unexpected moment: I was asked to declare my religion. Apparently, in Germany, every worker must pay a tax for maintaining religious institutions, just like social security and medical insurance, and in an instant, I reverted to Catholicism. I thought that in Germany it was more practical to be Catholic. After my registration was complete, a foreman introduced himself and gave me instructions about the work. From there, everything proceeded smoothly. I was taken to the factory floor, about the size of an acre, with dozens of press machines evenly spread throughout. I was assigned a press machine and shown how to make a metal piece, one at a time. The piece would eventually become a spring, and it could be used in a variety of equipment and cars. The foreman showed me a box of oily metal pieces and demonstrated what I needed to do. He put one metal piece into the mold of the press machine, and then put both hands on the handles on each side of the machine, and pushed down. The machine tool came down with a heavy "thump" sound and immediately lifted up, leaving the metal piece molded into a new shape. The foreman took it out of the mold and threw it into a box containing finished parts. I made a few pieces slowly while the foreman watched, and then he said, "So, weiter machen…" (so there, continue working).

Before leaving, he instructed me to call him if anything went wrong, or to report to him when all the parts were done. A machine counter registered the number of pieces I made in an hour and the total for the day. One could take a few short breaks, there was a one-hour lunch break, with the lunch taken in the workers' self-service cafeteria, and there were locker rooms with showers to use in the late afternoon after work. About half the workers were German, and the other half were foreign, mostly from Greece. I got along with the workers very well, though the Greeks' German language skills were limited. As a newcomer, I had to explain my knowledge of German, and again I said that my parents were originally from Austria. During short breaks and in the cafeteria, I meshed with the workers and soon got to know most of them by first name. The work was not difficult. I had no trouble reaching the required production norms. Soon I was able to work so fast that I made a hundred percent more pieces than the norm required. My earnings doubled. Saturday was only half a workday; the afternoon was free.

I had relatively little contact with the retired couple in the house where I had the sublet room. I went on walks to explore the town, and while I was at it found that summers in Germany were quite rainy. I had to buy a raincoat and an umbrella. On my walks, I wandered into the cemetery in Pfullingen and noticed not a single Jewish gravestone. I wondered if no Jews ever lived there, or if they had a separate cemetery.

On Sunday after my first week at work, I was again invited to lunch at the house of Mr. I., with a warning not to bring flowers or anything else. I began to feel more at ease. The little white lie about being a Catholic did not bother me; after all, I was baptized and as a child, I had been a practicing Catholic.

The Germans

Family I. lived in an old house in the upper part of town with a view of the adjacent hills and mountains.

My first impression was that they appeared to be nice people, but I knew nothing about them or their past. They had no children. Mrs. I. no longer worked. She took care of the house and her elderly mother-in-law, who could hardly walk due to severe arthritis. It turned out that Mrs. I.'s father was killed in the First World War, and she never knew him. In the afternoon, after lunch, Mr. and Mrs. I. invited me to join them for a walk up in the Schwäbische Alb, the mountain ridge that was about 2500 feet high, extending for miles in an east to west direction, overlooking Reutlingen and other small towns in the area. We went up by car, parked, and soon we were hiking along a shady path that offered views of the picturesque towns in the valleys below.

Walking and talking gave us opportunity to get to know each other a little better. My German was rusty, but it improved by the hour. I told them I found the work in the factory relatively easy, and I was warned not to discuss with other workers my salary, or how much I was able to produce above the required minimum hourly norm. The workers would resent me, Mr. I. explained, and fear that the management might raise the norms. However, management was well aware that the norms were set relatively low, and much more could be produced per hour, if needed. The management, he explained, did not want the workers to burn out. I was going to work for only a few months, Mr. I. said, and the workers were supposed to remain there for a good number of years, even decades. I understood. Many years later, this experience would serve me when I was managing a lab with over fifty technicians who occasionally slacked off on the job. I wanted them to stay and keep their jobs for as long as possible, but above all, I wanted them to work carefully and avoid making mistakes. It all came back to the old Latin proverb, "Festina lente!" (Make haste slowly!)

The following Sunday, I was invited for lunch with Mr. and Mrs. N., the family that owned the factory. They lived in a new villa on a hill in a newer, exclusive part of town, and it took me some time to walk up to their house from the tram station. Mr. N. shook my hand limply, and during lunch, he sat, ate his food, and hardly spoke at all. His lively wife did all the talking. She was short and plump and had a face that reminded me of my Aunt Ester. She had that same, rounded nose profile, but she was blond and blue-eyed.

At lunch, I met their two sons, Siegfried and Holger. Siegfried was about one year younger than I was, and Holger was about three years younger. With them, I could relax. We had a good time. The younger son, Holger, resembled his mother, and Siegfried looked more like his father. After lunch, the two brothers invited me to join them for a walk along the Schwäbische Alb. Before I left, Mrs. N. wanted me to take a small gift, a souvenir from the visit to their home, and she gave me three fancy bottle corks, each fitted with a semiprecious stone mounted on the cork with a silver stem. (I did not know what to do with such a fancy gift, but I kept the corks for all these years.)

In the afternoon, the two brothers took me to see the little castle Lichtenstein perched up on the Alb right above Pfullingen. While we were walking along a path in the adjacent woods, a huge bear appeared, slowly advancing toward us. With Siegfried and Holger standing behind me, I was left facing the bear. I froze for a moment, and the bear stood up on his hind legs and observed me. After a long second, I realized that it was only a man dressed in a bearskin. The two brothers had great fun seeing my reaction and laughing. In the course of the summer, they took me out several more times, once to a concert of Bach's music in the old Protestant church of Reutlingen.

My work in the factory became more comfortable each week. I bought a pair of inexpensive leather gloves, and increased my speed of slipping the pieces of metal into the press mold and taking them out when the cam lifted. Every several days, I got a different metal spring to produce. Some weeks I produced on average 150 to 200 percent above the required hourly norm. Sometimes I got a job that required production of only a few hundred pieces, and then my work speed would drop significantly and barely meet the norm. Each new item took several hours of adjustment before I could reach a high speed.

In my leisure, I started reading. The book that interested me at the time was *The New Class* by Milovan Djilas, a book forbidden in Yugoslavia but readily available in Germany. [24] Though he used to be one of the closest companions of Marshal Tito, Djilas was critical of the way communism was practiced and distorted, and he was put in jail for several years. He wrote the book in jail, exposing the failure of communism in Yugoslavia, and the book was smuggled out of jail and published in the West. Communist or other autocratic governments do not always appreciate the unpleasant truth. People in Yugoslavia hardly dared whisper about Djilas or his book.

On subsequent Sundays, the I. family took me on outings to show me different parts of Würtemberg, which abounded with beautiful baroque churches, libraries, and several castles. Once, we went all the way to Karlsruhe for lunch at their relatives' house. We spent a lot of time talking, and after a few months, I felt more comfortable with them. The Nazi period in Germany was taboo. No one I met would speak about it, and I never broached the subject, either. All books from the Nazi period were forbidden, especially the infamous *Mein Kampf* by Hitler, the one I really wanted to read. One day, as we were walking along the Alb, I asked Ernest if he could somehow find me this forbidden book. I was curious to read what Hitler wrote many years before the Second World War even started. The book was illegal and hard to obtain, Ernest said, but he knew someone who had it buried in his garden, and he would try to get it for me.

For the next several weeks, I spent my evenings reading *Mein Kampf.* [9] Hitler's plan to destroy the Jews, to expand Germany by taking lands from the countries to the east of Germany, and eventually to starve the Ukrainians to death and take over their fertile lands was clearly laid out. The plan was so outlandish that most people who read the book at the time felt that Hitler was crazy and would never go through with it. After I returned the book, Ernest and Ursel slowly started talking about the prewar time. They told me that living under the Nazi regime was a horror. After the Nazi takeover in 1933, people became aware that relatives in mental hospitals were disappearing at an accelerated rate. They all suddenly "died." It became obvious that mental patients were being killed by the order of the authorities, to create a pure Aryan race, free of mental illness. People noticed, Ernest told me, that those who spoke against Nazi authorities or were known communists were arrested without due process of law, harshly interrogated, and mistreated at the prisons. Very few were ever released alive. Most communists were sent to concentration camps, and after a while, their relatives were notified that they died. Several years later, around 1936, authorities started a more active persecution of Jews. The process was gradual, and for a long time, people were told that Jews needed to be "resettled in the eastern regions of Europe," in Poland, which was invaded in 1939. The systematic killing of Jews, Ursel told me, became widely known in Germany only later, during the war. By that time, the Allies were heavily bombing Germany, and the Jews were blamed for the war and all the hardships the German civilian population had to endure. At that point, most ordinary Germans were starving and cared only for their own survival.

Ernest said he was conscripted to serve in the army. Consequent to his previous business experience, he was made into a supply officer and sent to Africa to serve under General Rommel. In 1943, when the U.S. invaded Africa, he was taken prisoner and spent five years as a POW in the U.S. before he was released and returned to Germany. Ten years of Ernest and Ursel's lives were ruined by the Nazi war, and they never had children. Ernest had a brother in Ulm, but their relationship was strained. His brother managed to stay in Germany and sit out the war at home, enjoying his family and children. I had a feeling that Ernest's brother was a member of the Nazi Party, though Ernest never said so. After the war, his brother had a good job and was better off than Ernest was. Thousands of Nazis obtained or kept good jobs after the war, and nobody bothered them. It was an open secret, Ernest said, but people just kept quiet about it, and no one discussed their past. It appeared that during the first fifteen years after the war, the new generation of children was growing up knowing nothing about the Nazi period in the lives of their parents, and their history books had a void for that period.

On one of our Sunday walks, on the path over the hilly ridge above Tübingen, I decided to open up to Ernest and Ursel. I told them about my Jewish origin and what happened to my parents and family. They were astounded. Then Ernest and Ursel revealed to me a few other facts. They told me that Mrs. N., the factory owner, came from an old Jewish family. During the Nazi period, Mrs. N. was covered by the Aryan Right obtained through her husband who served during the war as a German officer in the area of the Baltic (Lithuania), and that ever since he returned from the war he had suffered from depression. *Years later, after having seen the Holocaust Museum in Washington, I began to suspect that Mr. N. very likely was cognizant of or had witnessed the atrocities and massacres of Jews by German troops with the aid of collaborating Lithuanian militia.[1] German records and photographs of those atrocities are present in the museum. Seeing mass murder could throw any normal person into a state of depression, especially one who wore the German military uniform and knew his wife was Jewish.*

The I. family was clearly against the Nazis, and I found that they were not alone. There were many such German families. It all resonated with what I remembered reading in the German literature from the Nazi period. There was the novel *Brothers Oppenheim* by Lion Feuchtwanger, a German writer who escaped from the Nazi regime to California. He described Germany in the same terms as did Mr. I. *Love thy Neighbor,* by Erich M. Remarque, another refugee writer from Nazi Germany dealt with a similar theme. I began to see Germans and Germany in a different light. By 1960, West Germany had laws that clearly condemned Nazi or anti-Semitic ideology, more so than any other country in Europe. Any Nazi bias was condemned and punishable by law. In reparation, Germany subsidized the state of Israel with millions of dollars each year. Although many old Nazis were still in Germany, they generally kept quiet. A very high percentage of Germans had joined the Nazi Party in the thirties, particularly people in the professions. The perverted Nazi laws were upheld by a high percentage of judges who joined the Nazi Party. Forty percent of physicians in Hitler's Germany were members of the Nazi Party. Most ordinary Germans in those days were supportive of the Nazi government for one simple reason: for the first time after the First World War, they had jobs, earned a living, and were able to regain their dignity. Most would find out the full scope of what the Nazis were really up to only years later. Those were the sad facts of the German past, but things were turning different in 1960. After what I saw and heard during those months of working and talking to people in West Germany, my view of Germans became more balanced. Germans in 1960 were just people, humans with strengths and failings, similar to any other people. They still would not talk about the Nazi period, but it was clear that they understood that something was terribly wrong in their past. They needed more time to come to terms with it. Certainly, the bulk of Germans in 1960 were not Nazis, contrary to the way they were being described by communists in Yugoslavia. Based on my own observations, the doubts, misgivings, and suspicions I carried in Yugoslavia were slowly removed, and by the time I left Germany, I had a more positive and realistic picture of the country.

Regarding the evil that happened in the thirties and forties in Germany, I began to understand its roots. Honest people with families and small children to worry about were intimidated and silenced by the Nazis. Knowing that in Yugoslavia, a mere ten percent of communists controlled the rest of the population, I understood the problems of ordinary Germans under the Nazis and Hitler's dictatorship. I could not hold a grudge against the Germans of today, for I understood that one couldn't blame a whole nation for crimes committed by a group of their members who were criminals and represented a minority of German people, even if that minority was sizable. The bitter feelings about the events in my childhood began to heal. In that regard, I felt a great relief, I could accept the past as it was, and while I never wanted to forget that past, I did not feel any resentment towards the people of the present. I would, of course, remain on guard if anyone gave me the slightest hint of a Nazi attitude. I knew that in most European countries involved in the war, thousands of people lived in denial, former active Nazi collaborators who felt that they "did not do anything wrong."

France had plenty of Nazi collaborators, but to heal itself, France had a taboo against talking about it. The documentary film made by Marcel Ophüls in 1969, The Sorrow and the Pity, which showed the scope of French collaboration with the Nazis under the Vichy government, was for many years banned from being shown in France. After all, despite the bravery of the French resistance, it appears that at least half of the French people either sympathized with or was on the side of Hitler and the Nazis. During the Second World War, France provided seven thousand volunteer soldiers to fight side by side with Nazi SS troops on the Eastern Front. It took France forty years before it finally brought to trial a few of top Nazi collaborators who, together with the Vichy government, committed crimes against humanity by rounding up Jews, including small children, to be sent to Nazi extermination camps. Till then, the criminals were not only living free, but were even admitted into high government positions. Of course, a few months before liberation of France, many of the Nazi collaborators became great patriots, conveniently joining the French resistance movement, and were thus exculpated from the sins of their collaboration.

Germany is today the only country that has fully accepted and officially condemned its sad history during Nazi rule. Observers may notice that countries that were occupied by Nazis, or were independent but openly collaborated with them, now, sixty years later still have not come to accept the truth of their collaboration or to admit the crimes committed by their past leaders and citizens. The full scope of crimes committed during the Second World War continues to be denied and covered up by revision of local history.

Dominated by this revisionist spirit, many politicians in those countries continue to fan ethnic, national, and religious intolerance and overt hatred against other people—those of different ethnicity, nationality, or religion. Xenophobia is promoted by politicians under the banner of nationalism and patriotism, to deflect the blame for their own failings. One may only hope that someday a new generation will bring about a change, and the revisionists' fabrications will be replaced by the truth.

* * *

In December of 1960, I started preparing for my return from Germany to Zagreb. I left all my savings in a bank in Reutlingen and entrusted Ernest I. to look after my bank account. I had a Swiss transit visa good for two days before passing into Italy, and I planned to spend a night in Zurich to finally meet my relatives, family Eisner, of whom my uncles in Milan had previously told me. Stefan Eisner was my father's first cousin. When he moved from Vienna to Switzerland, he converted to Christian religion. In Switzerland, he had a business manufacturing insulation and other materials for transfer of high voltage electricity, and his firm was listed on the Swiss stock exchange. In December, I parted with Ernest and Ursel I., and they saw me off on a train to Switzerland. In Zurich, Uncle Eisner invited me to meet him and his wife at their apartment in the evening after supper. They received me cordially, and we spoke for about an hour. They were excited because their little daughter Kathy had just a day before returned home after a long stay in the hospital. She was recovering from a severe burn injury for which she would need more corrective surgery in the future. *Her case was later described in a Swiss textbook of pediatrics as the first instance where a patient's life was saved after suffering a burn on over eighty percent of the skin.* Their son was serving his tour in the Swiss army, and I never met him. We parted and I promised to stay in touch. The next day, I explored Zurich, bought a watch as a present for Dobrana, and boarded the train for Milan. In Milan, I briefly called Uncle Felix and told him about my meeting with his cousin in Zurich. My thoughts were already elsewhere. I was to meet Dobrana in Venice, and we would stay there for a few days.

TOGETHER

From Milan, I took a train to Venice, found a room in a small hotel, and then went to the station to wait for Dobrana's train. When we met after such a long time, it was sheer bliss and joy. Holding hands, we walked all over Venice and imbibed its beauty. It was off-season, and there were no crowds. Some streets were flooded, and we had to walk on elevated wooden planks from one bridge to the next. We did not mind. We wanted to get engaged in Venice, and we stayed for three days. At a little goldsmith's store, we had our rings custom made in our own simple design, and they were ready the next afternoon. We stood on a small square near a little fountain, and there exchanged our rings. We were engaged. We needed no ceremony or witnesses. For the next several weeks, we both developed a habit, every now and then, of happily looking at our ring, touching it, turning it a few times around the finger, and smiling.

After three happy days in Venice, we went to Trieste and stayed another two days. While drinking tea in the evening at the hotel, I said something that made Dobrana laugh so hard that the tea came out of her nose and mouth and onto her skirt. We laughed even harder. The next morning, we explored the city and nearby Miramare Castle. Finally, we went shopping for some items we needed, mostly clothing. For the first time in my life, I bought myself a new, complete suit, with matching pants and jacket made just for me. It was black and elegant, and I needed it for medical school graduation. In the clothing store, the owner asked me my name, and I jokingly told him that my name was so bad that he could hardly pronounce it. The merchant then said that if I thought my name was bad, his own name was even worse. This was a subtle way to signal that we were both Jewish and had "funny names." The merchant's last name was indeed "worse" than mine: Israel. Meier, after all, could be Austrian, Swiss, or German.

When Dobrana and I returned to Zagreb, our friends noticed the rings on our hands, and the news was out. An older acquaintance of mine, a goldsmith in Zagreb, Žarko T. engraved our names inside our engagement rings: my name in Dobrana's ring, and "Dobrana" in mine. We decided to eventually retain the same rings as our wedding rings.

We continued to study for our exams at the university. Within a week of my return I passed the combined exam in public health and legal medicine. We celebrated New Year's Eve at a party with many of our friends, who by then knew about our engagement. In the spring of 1961, I had one more exam before graduation: surgery with orthopedics, combined with ear, nose, and throat, and ophthalmology, and that required nearly three months of serious preparation.

In the meantime, we started making plans to leave the country. Obtaining an exit visa in my passport while I was still a student was relatively easy, but once I graduated and had my diploma, it would become another matter. There was a regulation that people of Jewish origin were allowed to leave the country if they wanted to emigrate to Israel, but such emigration was exclusive of any another destination. To go to Israel, one had to first obtain an official document, the Release from Citizenship, and that is what I applied for. We thought it might be better if Dobrana applied separately, before we got married.

I obtained the Release from Citizenship in about two months, in April 1961. Dobrana's release was not ready, and when she inquired, she was given an appointment to appear at the office of the Secret Service in Zagreb. Her appointment turned out to be a nasty, provocative interrogation into why she wanted to leave the country. Did she not like living in Yugoslavia? Was there something wrong with Yugoslavia? Since she had a Croat last name, why would she want to go to Israel? Well, her mother was Jewish. After half an hour of interrogation, Dobrana was told to come back in a month. Her interrogations continued from month to month on a regular basis, and each time, they were more unpleasant. It was an ordeal, and her Release from Citizenship was not forthcoming.

In the middle of March 1961, I passed my last exam, and my medical school graduation would take place at the end of the month at the dean's office building of the University of Zagreb. Instead of six, it took me nearly seven years to graduate. During that time, I spent a total of twelve months in Western Europe, but the delay of my graduation was well worth it. Dobrana and I decided to declare our marriage on the day of my graduation. We announced it to Dobrana's parents and all of our close friends, and explained that, at the moment, we did not want to have a large wedding ceremony. Since I was starting to work as an intern on April 1, 1962, we actually had no time to schedule and arrange a formal civil marriage. We also did not want to disturb Dobrana's application for the Release from Citizenship, and decided to postpone the official civil marriage. We did not care much for ceremonies, and what mattered was that in our hearts we felt married.

My placement for rotating internship was in a provincial town in northern Croatia, between the rivers Sava and Drava. That meant a long commute from Zagreb by train. On our declared wedding day, Dobrana moved in with me, at an address much closer to her school. My landlady did not mind, since I would be away for the whole week and would come home only on Saturday afternoon, to leave again for work early on Monday morning. I gave the landlady a raise in rent. My intern's monthly salary was the equivalent of $20, minus a small deduction for the housing at the hospital. Life in Yugoslavia was cheap, and it was not worth much more. My earnings were commensurate.

Working for the first time in a provincial hospital was a novel experience. The level of medicine practiced there was a whole step or two lower than at the university clinics in Zagreb. There were no funds for decent equipment, medications, or personnel. Some peasants in the area still delivered their babies at home attended by women who were midwives by acclamation and had no credentials other than "experience". My first rotation was in surgery, where I had to assist the chief surgeon in all surgical procedures. His hands were completely raw with partly missing skin. He bled under the gloves while he operated. I noticed that the chief of surgery often acted as if he was under the influence of alcohol. I was told that he had to take a drink before surgery to alleviate the pain in his hands. His skin injuries came from radiation. In his younger days, he used to set broken bones directly under the x-rays, until he noticed his skin falling apart. Orthopedics as a specialty existed in those days only at the university clinic. Under the head surgeon's supervision, I was allowed to do small surgical procedures, including repair of a hernia, removal of an appendix, or repair of traumatic wounds, while he "assisted" and supervised me. During surgical rotation, I sometimes also had to act as an anesthetist. The specialty of anesthesiology also existed only at the university clinics in Zagreb. Giving anesthesia was a frightening experience because it was done by simply dripping ether from a little bottle onto a gauze mask covering the patient's face. I had to watch not to breathe too much of the fumes myself. I was never sure whether there was too little or too much ether in the patient's facemask. Every now and then, I had to check the patient's pulse or remove the facemask for a moment to observe the condition of his or her pupils. At the end of the three months of surgical rotation, I was happy I had not put anybody to sleep for good.

My next rotation was in internal medicine. My duties also included covering the emergency room, and there I had an experience for which the medical school did not prepare me. From time to time, a patient would show up, the likes of whom I never heard of during the years of my medical education. The patient would claim, "Everything is hurting. My whole life is hurting." There was an "ouch" wherever I touched. I never figured out what was wrong with those people. The attending physician on emergency duty showed me how to treat this illness, which he quietly called "hysterics." When he was sure that there was substantially nothing else wrong with the patient, he administered a small amount of calcium intravenously, and this had an immediate and miraculous effect. The pain would be wiped out within seconds of calcium entering the circulation.

The patient would say, "I feel very hot. There is heat in my head," and then quietly sit in the chair. After a few minutes, the patient would get up and demand to go home, apparently cured of the "hurt in the whole life." Anyway, the number of beds in the hospital was insufficient to admit all these patients. Aside from seeing regular patients in internal medicine, I also had another task. In a separate hospital unit for patients with active TB, I had to do daily microscopic checks of sputum for TB bacilli. I did not like it, but it was part of my job.

In the meantime, Dobrana arranged for our official civil marriage at the regional city office in Zagreb. In the middle of the summer, I took off a long weekend, including a Friday, for our marriage. We still did not want, nor could we afford, a big, private wedding ceremony. Two of Dobrana's best friends agreed to be our witnesses. On the morning of our wedding, the toilet in our apartment got plugged up, and I promised the landlady I'd fix it. It was a difficult case, and I had to spend more time than I planned. Dobrana went ahead to hold our spot in the marriage queue in front of the city office, and I arrived for the wedding a few minutes late. We patiently listened to the obligatory speech from the communist official urging us to support our people's government, which was making it possible to enjoy a happy family life. Our two witnesses signed, and finally we had the official certificate of marriage. Perhaps marrying a Jew would help Dobrana get her Release from Citizenship. So we hoped.

Our delayed official wedding, however, had a consequence that we did not foresee. All weddings were routinely listed in the local newspapers, and people who habitually read obituaries and wedding announcements did not miss ours. Dobrana's parents told us that some of their friends casually asked, "Did your daughter not get married already in March?"

"Oh, well, ah, yes. That is…" and they produced some explanation for the late news coverage. It was hard to answer such embarrassing questions. We apologized to Dobrana's parents, and they were very understanding.

Josip, a classmate and a friend from our high school days graduated from medical school and started his internship in the same hospital where I was working. He had a motor scooter and let me join him on our weekly commute. We immediately canceled our assigned in-hospital housing, and instead rented a furnished private room that we shared off the hospital premises. The price of the room rental was well worth it because we could avoid frequent calls on alternate nights when we were off duty and supposed to get some rest—the rented room had no telephone. However, as we soon found out, the room had flees. We had to sleep on DDT-powdered sheets and be careful not to carry any of the unwanted tenants home for the weekend.

My next rotation was in obstetrics and gynecology, and this was hard work. In obstetrics, every second night I was delivering babies, and in gynecology, it meant a whole day bending over and doing D&Cs (dilatation and curettage), as if the patients were coming in on a conveyor belt. The hospital had three sets of instruments for D&C: while one set was being used, the second set was being cleaned and sterilized in boiling water, and the third set was cooling off to be ready for the next patient. After two weeks on that service, I could do a D&C in less than five minutes, blindfolded. Unlike at the university clinics in Zagreb, D&Cs in small provincial hospitals were done without anesthesia. At best, the patient received, a few minutes before the procedure, a phenacetin pill as a preventive painkiller, and this was worth as much as a placebo. The local doctors called it "Hungarian anesthesia." The patients, though, were tough. They gritted their teeth, but kept still and did not cry or complain or fidget. Of course, they were told that if they made any sudden move during the surgery, there could be severe internal injury, so they did not dare budge till they were asked to move off the table onto a stretcher.

Medical practice in the backwaters of Yugoslavia was both primitive and brutal. And yet, there was at least one upside. The women who came to the hospital to deliver their babies were kept in the hospital for five full days after a normal delivery. In the course of hospitalization, the women were thoroughly instructed on how to take care of the baby and themselves when they arrived home. Their babies were also checked for any problems before they were released. After a D&C, we routinely kept a patient at least overnight, to check on the next morning rounds that there was no serious residual bleeding or sign of infection. Lack of hospital space compelled us often to put two patients head to toe in the same single bed. That was not a pretty picture, and today it may sound incredible.

Here an explanation is due: communist Yugoslavia, following the example of the Soviet Union, passed a law stating that every woman had the right to have an abortion in a government clinic. There was no fee involved. The purpose of the law was first to reduce the number of serious infections, perforated wombs, and occasional deaths from infection that used to occur when abortions were performed illegally, by unqualified persons. The other purpose of the abortion law was to help the communists reduce the number of children for which the government paid child support. In the first years after the communist revolution, the government issued generous child support, and there was a child born in many families nearly every year. After a while, with growing government deficits, child support was reduced progressively for every child after the first three, and was eliminated from the seventh child on. The restriction of child support, along with distribution of free condoms and the abortion law reduced the rate of childbirth quite effectively, at least in some parts of the country. These population measures had no effect in those parts of Yugoslavia where people did not fully understand the facts of life and contraception, or simply preferred to follow their own cultural tradition rather than governmental suggestions.

I often saw women come to the hospital "because of bleeding," but at the same time they also had a raging fever. In the backward villages of Yugoslavia, many peasant women were not aware of the abortion law. They still went to unqualified midwives, who started them bleeding by sticking a piece of wire or a carrot root into their womb. Along with starting the bleeding and a partial abortion, that primitive procedure usually caused an infection. A D&C done on an infected and softened uterus carried a high risk of perforation and serious complications, and in such cases, the procedure had to be done with a delicate hand. In the hospital, the D&C to stop the bleeding and complete the abortion was performed by a qualified physician in a clean medical setting, and the women were saved from further complications or death.

Meanwhile I remained in close contact with Ernest and Ursel I., and they wrote that they would like to spend a ten-day vacation camping on the Adriatic, and asked if I would consider coming along. I accepted and immediately obtained a two-week vacation for August 1961. About the same time, Dobrana was to leave on a tour of Israel with the choir. Mr. and Mrs. I. came equipped with a tent and three foldable sleeping cots, picked me up, and we continued towards the Adriatic. The first two nights we camped at Plitvice, a group of emerald green lakes in central Croatia. Multiple waterfalls and small streams connect the little lakes. The water is crystal clear, and hiking the trails along the lakes, we saw trunks of fallen trees lying at the bottom, all white with layers of encrusted calcium carbonate.

The region is rich in porous calcium rock formations. Many small rivers in the area disappear underground, and then reappear in another location. In that area was a dam built by the government to create an artificial lake that would produce electric energy. However, due to porosity of the terrain, the lake never completely filled up with water.

Our next stop was on the Adriatic beaches, where we had perfect weather. We stopped in Zadar, Šibenik, the nearby waterfalls of Krka, under which we went bathing, and finally Trogir and Split, with its famous palace of the Roman emperor Diocletian. South of Split we camped for several days on a bluff overlooking a beach. In Split, I contacted a friend whose family owned a small motor boat, and for a barter of some of Ernest's camping equipment, this friend took us on a day's boat trip to a small, uninhabited island. We took with us a cooking pot, a small bag of rice, and a jug of local red wine.

We swam in the limpid, clean blue ocean, and with a spear gun, we easily caught several fish around the reefs. A makeshift grill was made from the rocks on the beach, and a fire was started with pieces of driftwood. The rice needed no salt; it was cooked in the pot with clear seawater. Then we grilled the fish on the remaining embers. To quench our thirst, we drew water from a rain-collecting cistern on the island, and mixed it half-and-half with our red wine. This drink, locally called "bevanda," is taken instead of the bad tasting rainwater. For dessert, we ate delicious grapes that grew in the nearby vineyards. There was a code: one could pick all the grapes one could eat on the spot, but no grapes could be taken out of the vineyard. On our return trip, we camped one more time on the northern Adriatic, in the town of Novi Vinodol, and then I was dropped off in Zagreb. Ernest and Ursel proceeded to Austria and home.

Following weekend Dobrana returned from Israel, full of stories from her trip. The choir won the first prize at an international festival. Israel, she said, was pretty and green in contrast to the barren desert seen across the border. Israel was also a dangerous place, she said, and there were frightening moments when the bus driver, on a road along the border at night, demanded that everyone be quiet, turned off all the lights on the bus, and coasted quietly down a long hill in complete darkness. Everyone on the bus who remembered the Second World War and its blackouts understood that they were in a country at war.

In January 1962, I was supposed to rotate to the pediatric service, the easiest part of the internship, where one could get some rest. Instead, the hospital administrator informed me that I would continue on gynecology service for three more months. Referring to the rules of rotating internship, I tried to object to this change of schedule, but the administrator simply sent me a written order for my next job assignment. I did not like it and looked for another position. There were still enough places in the country that were less desirable and had unfilled internship positions. The closest one to Zagreb was in a small town in the mountainous, southern part of Croatia. The winters there were brutally cold, and the whole area was desolate and wild. Within a week, I had a new job to continue my internship as of January 2, 1962. At the same time, our landlady gave us notice, and we had to move out by the end of December. Dobrana had to find a new sublet room. This time, she found a spacious furnished room in a large apartment, where the single bathroom and kitchen had to be shared with eight other people. There was a strict schedule: the use of bathroom had time limits, and the use of the shower was restricted to twice a week. We did not cook and so we never found out how the single kitchen was shared.

What I best remember from my short remaining internship is that the hospital was small and there were mostly trauma patients seen in the emergency room. Practically all doctors on duty had families in Zagreb and commuted weekly so I had plenty of company on the long train rides. My rented room in town was unheated, and each evening when I came back from the hospital, the water in the washbasin was frozen solid. The steam from my breath was visible in the room. One night, when I got into my bed and covered myself with the freezing sheets, I experienced a bout of heart palpitation induced by the cold.

Dobrana's Release from Citizenship was still not approved, and at her last interrogation in December, she was told that it was "held up at the federal office in Belgrade." In January 1962, Dobrana made an appointment with the Secret Service office in Belgrade. She had a good friend in Belgrade who she knew from summer vacations in Istria, and she could stay at her apartment. The federal Secret Service office in Belgrade told Dobrana that her documents had been referred back to Zagreb. She returned home empty-handed and promptly requested another appointment with the Secret Service office in Zagreb.

PART IV

EXODUS

"WE ARE FREE"

In the beginning of February 1962, there was relatively little work in the hospital and I started planning for our escape to Italy in the spring. We would take a vacation to go hiking in the Slovenian Alps near the Italian border. My own Release from Citizenship was good for only one year, and if I did not use it and leave the country within that period, the document would expire. In that case, I would be called up for military service in Yugoslav army, which would be a complete waste of time.

One day, while I was waiting for the next patient in the emergency room, I was called to the hospital administration office to answer an urgent, long-distance phone call. Dobrana was calling from Zagreb, and she sounded very excited. She greeted me and only said, "It has come!"

I understood and asked, "By mail?"

She answered, "Yes, come home!"

The next morning, I resigned from my internship as of the end of the month. In the beginning of March, we were both in Zagreb and had our passports stamped with a Yugoslav exit visa "valid only for emigration to Israel," and we obtained a transit visa for Italy valid for three days. Supposedly, we were going to board the ship for Israel in Naples. We started to prepare for the trip and packed only a few essentials. To all our friends, we said only that I had a new job in Istria, and we were moving out of Zagreb. In that way, abruptly canceling our lease and taking a train toward Istria (and Trieste) would not arouse any suspicion as to where we were heading.

Then a classmate of mine, Vlada Z., heard that I was in Zagreb for a couple of weeks and asked if I would like to substitute for her husband for a week in a village where he worked in a government-assigned office as a country doctor. They wanted to go skiing in the Slovenian Alps, and they would leave at my disposal the entire house with a fully equipped medical office. This sounded interesting, and I agreed to be a country doctor for a week. The village was located in the fertile valley near River Sava, and when I arrived in the first days of March, the spring rains were on. The mud was up to my knees. The "taxi" from the station was a wagon with a horse and driver.

Vlada's house was warm and comfortable, and a maid made the fire each morning, cleaned the house and office, and prepared the meals. Office hours were not set; they were all day long, whenever someone appeared with a medical problem. With the mud all around, there was no place for me to go out of the house, anyway. The workload was mostly easy routine, but two patients that week were memorable. On one occasion, I was called to go to a peasant's house to help deliver a baby. A horse and wagon waited in front of the house. To walk to the wagon, I borrowed Vlada's husband's rubber boots. The boots were a little too large and after a careless step, my foot came out and stepped directly into the mud up to my knee. I limped back into the house to clean up before I could reach the horse-drawn wagon. After an hour's ride through the mud and potholes, I arrived at the peasant's house and went inside.

The expectant mother was about seventeen or eighteen years old, and it was her first baby. I asked the whole family to move out of the room while her mother prepared some hot water to wash my hands. The young woman was in a clean bed, and her mother had laid out fresh, clean linen. I was scared: what if the newborn was a stillborn, or if after delivery, the mother had severe bleeding, or if something worse happened? The people in the house did not look menacing, but they did not look friendly, either. Nature was on my side: a healthy baby was born without too much interference by me. There was one lesson that I learned very well from my professor of obstetrics: "During childbirth, keep your hands in your pockets as long as you can; just let Nature do the job!"

After delivery, I lingered around the house till I was sure that everything was well with the mother and the baby. I was happy to be taken back to the office without an incident.

The second interesting case that week was a matron of about fifty, brought to the office complaining of excruciating pain in her belly. She was moaning and howling with pain. She was obese, and her lower belly was bloated like a balloon and hard like a soccer ball. She had no complaint other than increasing pain for several days and denied any other trouble. It took me a while to examine her before I decided to check out her bladder. I found in the office cabinets an old glass catheter with a short rubber hose and a basin. When I passed the catheter, a powerful stream of urine came from the bladder and soon filled the basin. The urine overflowed and made a puddle the floor. The woman was relieved and kept giving long sighs of pleasure. Her balloon belly came down. Later, I heard the maid cursing while she was cleaning the office floor. The next day, the patient's family brought me a pair of live chickens. I had the maid put them in my friend's chicken coop. It rained all week, and I was happy to stay in the house, read some books from the shelves, and daydream about our imminent trip. At the end of the week, I took the "taxi" to the station and the train back to Zagreb. When my friend returned to Zagreb to pay me for the week's work, she said, there was a lot of rain in the Alps, too, and they could not do much skiing, but they had a good week of relaxation.

Dobrana and I had still a few days left in Zagreb. We went to say good-bye to Uncle Stanislav and Aunt Ester and told them we would stay in touch with them. Dobrana and I also went to see the Professor, and he wished us luck, and said he was happy to see us go into the Free World. Only to Dobrana's parents and the Professor did we reveal our true destination—all others we would notify after we were safely in Rome.

One day, we went to have a good lunch at a seafood restaurant that served lobsters. We had been conditioned to think that lobsters existed only in Yugoslavia, and that it was probably the last time we would be able to enjoy such a delicacy. The day of our departure was set for Monday, March 19, 1962. Only Dobrana's parents, my best friend Ivica, and one of Dobrana's best friends knew the date and time of our departure, and they came early that morning to see us off. The parting was difficult, especially with Dobrana's parents. We were excited and happy. The locomotive gave a few puffs, and the train started moving: we were off. I had in my pockets some of my own dollars, and an illegally high amount of Yugoslav dinars given to us by Dobrana's father. These monies had to be hidden somewhere on the train to avoid any risk to ourselves. Shortly after the train got under way, I got up and went to the toilet in our car. I looked around to hide the money. The edges of the paneling were frayed, torn, and bent from people trying to stuff their money behind it to hide it from the border patrol. That would not do. There had to be a better way. Above the sink was a round steel container of liquid soap. That might do. I unscrewed its top, put the bundle of money in a condom, tied a double knot to seal it, placed the condom into the soap container, and screwed the top back on. I pressed the button on top of the container, and the liquid soap streamed out, as it should. I used the toilet. By then, the train had stopped in Ljubljana, the capital of the province of Slovenia, and the border patrol came aboard to start checking people's documents and luggage while the train was on the way towards the last stop at the border. Somebody knocked hard on the door, trying to enter the bathroom. "Just one minute," I said as I washed my hands. When I opened the door, it was a man from the border patrol who wanted to go into the bathroom. I returned to my compartment where Dobrana anxiously awaited. We sat nervously, expecting the border patrol to check us out. There was a routine search of our luggage, and everything was found in order. The personal search also went fast, and it was not very thorough. After a long while, the train stopped at the border town and we saw the Yugoslav border controllers leave, escorting with them a few unfortunate passengers. The train started moving again. As it accelerated, we let a sigh of relief: within the next few minutes, we would cross the border into Italy. I went to the toilet to retrieve our money, discarded the soapy condom, and put the roll of cash in my pocket.

Within less than half an hour, we found ourselves in the train station of Trieste. We were free.

"We are free!" we kept saying to one another, and the thought only slowly penetrated into our heads. We had our suitcases with us, but the customs office was closed. That Monday was St. Joseph's Day, a holiday in Italy. It was a long weekend, and we were told we had to spend a night in Trieste before our luggage could be checked by customs. I begged the customs official in Italian, explaining that we were just poor students from Yugoslavia, and surely had nothing to report to customs. We both were non-smokers and carried no cigarettes, a big concern for Italian customs. The Italian official took pity on us and let us pass with our luggage, without any inspection. Our next train was an overnight express to Rome, and we had several hours before its departure. While Dobrana watched our luggage in the waiting room, I went into the city and exchanged our dollars and dinars for Italian lire at the nearest gas station. In the early evening, we boarded the train for Rome.

The next morning, our train pulled into the Roma Termini station around six a.m. We put our luggage in the station checkroom, and holding hands went walking through the streets of Rome. I knew the way very well; I remembered the city from my first visit in 1959. We both felt like singing, and we did. It was a warm spring morning with an intermittent drizzle. We did not mind the rain. We were overjoyed and not at all tired, despite the night spent sitting on the train. Walking and holding hands, every now and then, one of us would let out a happy yelp. We are in Rome! Finally free! From the station, we walked all the way down to the Tiber, across from St. Angelo's, and then back past the Pantheon towards the Forum. On the way, we stopped in a small pastry shop and had coffee, hot chocolate, and pastries for breakfast. We were giddy with happiness. From a street vendor we bought an umbrella. We kept walking till ten in the morning, not too early for making a phone call to a private home. When Mr. R. answered the phone, I explained our situation, and he immediately invited us to stay with them in the guest room, the same one Michael had used when he was living in their apartment. Our rent would be very reasonable. After all, we were family.

Our Italian transit visa was valid for only three days, and on the second day, we went to the Rome police headquarters to give up our Yugoslav passports and declare ourselves refugees from communism. Within a few days, we were each issued a white passport, the type designed for stateless persons. Our next step was to apply for immigration to US. I knew from Michael's example that the best way to get immigration assistance was to approach the Jewish agency HIAS (Hebrew Immigrant Aid Society). When Michael's attempt to find work in Ethiopia hit a snag, HIAS suggested he change his destination to the U.S. While all other Jewish agencies assisted refugees only if they wished to immigrate to Israel, HIAS was willing to assist with immigration into any country. We have been grateful to HIAS for its broad-minded approach, and for all these past years in the U.S., we have been members of and have continuously contributed to HIAS. (Curiously, HIAS was completely unknown to most of our American Jewish friends who we later met in the U.S.) We registered our refugee status at HIAS and were immediately offered a small monthly financial assistance, free medical and dental insurance, a small monthly ration of various staple foods, basic household items (pots and pans), and English courses at the HIAS offices. We accepted all but the financial aid, which we did not need. We contacted Ernest I. in Germany, and he immediately wired us the money from my savings account. I noticed that there was quite a bit more money than I left in the account, even counting the interest. When I inquired, Ernest wrote that "some monies were added" as gifts for my birthday and for our wedding. We were grateful. Our total savings were not very high, but we hoped we would not have to stay in Rome too long.

We immediately sent Dobrana's parents our address and explained our status as awaiting U.S. Immigration. I wrote to Uncle Stanislav and Aunt Ester and to my friend Ivica, explaining that our destination was the promised land of the twentieth century: the USA. Dobrana's mother wrote that she would like to come for a few days and visit us in Rome and Uncle Stanislav and Aunt Ester wanted to come and see us, too. Staying with family R. was pleasant. We went on daily explorations of Rome, and that was most enjoyable. It was like being on a honeymoon one year after we got married. We walked the streets of Rome with our hands locked and occasionally still let out a loud yelp of happiness. We visited the beautiful monuments, churches, and plazas and discovered many interesting little neighborhoods. We often took our lunches or snacks in a *rosticceria*, a deli serving delicious finger-food.

The English lessons at HIAS were slow and boring, and we did not like them. In the American Library, we bought a large Webster's English World Dictionary, and studied English at our own pace at home. We used the Eckersley textbook provided by HIAS and began to skip the HIAS lessons entirely. I thought it would be much easier to learn English on the spot in the U.S., anyway. Dobrana's mother came, and we took her to St. Peter's church and other sites in Rome, and made excursions to Lago Albano and the Tivoli Gardens outside the city. Then came Aunt Ester with Uncle Stanislav, and they gave Dobrana a belated wedding present. A few months in Rome passed very quickly, like in a dream. Gradually, we came down to earth, and started getting a little anxious about obtaining our immigration papers. Every now and then, reality would pop into our heads. How were we going to manage in the U.S.?

One day we noticed that Mr. R. was not well: he was losing weight and refusing food. He was constipated, and I helped him with enemas, but there was no result. I finally persuaded him to see a doctor, who immediately ordered him to go for x-rays. I was asked to pick up the x-rays and bring them to his doctor. He had cancer of the stomach.

Surgery was scheduled, and I donated a unit of blood. As a physician and relative, I was allowed to be present in surgery. When the surgeon took out the stomach with the tumor, he showed me that the tumor had completely obstructed the stomach, and that there was much more metastatic cancer left in the abdomen. Mr. R. recovered very well from surgery, gained weight, and was soon able to eat normally. The surgeon told him that he had at most about one year to live. Mr. R. did not want his wife to know the truth about his illness, and we all kept it from her.

"It was just a bad ulcer," we said. Mr. R. called his son Gogo, who was at the time working in Germany, and told him about his illness.

One day, Gogo's wife Barica (Karel's sister) came to Rome on business. She was leading a tour group to Italy, and stayed in Rome for several days. Barica did not get along with Mrs. R., and she cruelly told her that Mr. R. had cancer and very little time left to live. This was a very painful shock for all of us.

In July, the HIAS informed us that we needed to go to the American Embassy to be "examined" for immigration. Part of it was a medical examination with chest x-rays and lab tests at the American Hospital. In those days' people with active TB or syphilis, or membership in the Communist Party, were not allowed to immigrate to the U.S. Our medical tests and examinations passed without a glitch. The other part of our examination was an interrogation by an officer at the U.S. embassy to check whether we were free of the "communist infection." An official from HIAS was on hand to translate, if absolutely necessary. By then, we both knew about three hundred essential words of English, and we could understand some, if it was spoken slowly. At one point during the interrogation, I had to say that, yes, at the medical school I was a member of an organization, the Union of Student Youth, into which all medical students were automatically enrolled. The interrogating officer somehow misunderstood that I was a member of the Communist Party. Luckily, the alert HIAS official caught the error and made sure it was immediately corrected. Finally, the interrogator asked us to stand up and he said something about our hands. We did not fully understand him. He spoke with a strange accent, which a few years later we recognized as coming from the southern U.S. He repeated his statement in different words, and then we caught the familiar phrase heard in many American movies: "…hands up!" We were puzzled. Did we say or do something wrong?

Dobrana and I looked at one another, and then silently followed his instruction. We both rose to our feet and raised our hands, just like in a western movie. Suddenly, there was a massive explosion of laughter from the HIAS official and the American interrogator.

"No, no, no. Raise just your right hand!"

Aha! It finally dawned on us: we were being asked to swear that everything we said was true. We went home exhausted, needing a rest. For the next two weeks, we anxiously awaited the results of the embassy interrogation. The notice came in the mail: we would get an entry visa under a special law designed to admit refugees from communist countries. *The law was designed for refugees from Hungary after the 1956 uprising, when about one million Hungarians escaped to the West. The same law was thereafter applied to Cubans and all other people escaping communist countries.*

What remained was to arrange for our travel. HIAS wanted us to go to the U.S. by air, flying out of Paris. To fly to New York in one day seemed too sudden; we preferred to go by ship. To that end, we told HIAS officials that Dobrana had a dreadful fear, a real phobia from flying based on a previous unpleasant experience in Yugoslavia. No matter how hard "I tried," I could not persuade Dobrana to fly. HIAS gave in and agreed to put us on a ship. After all, we were paying for the trip ourselves, and the price was the same whether one flew or sailed—about $300 per person, very expensive for our means. About one week later, we were told to get ready for the trip. An American ship was sailing from Genova on August 12, 1962, and two vacant places were reserved for us. HIAS in the meantime lined up a job for me as a medical clerk in a New York hospital. Before I could become an intern in the U.S., I had to pass a medical equivalency test for graduates of foreign medical schools, but I would worry about that later.

Shortly before our departure, I took a train from Rome to Milan for a brief meeting with Uncle Felix, to say good-bye to him before leaving for the U.S.

We Are Free

We met briefly for lunch in a small restaurant near his office. As we parted, I thought we might never see each other again. However, four years later, in 1966, Dobrana and I vacationed in Europe and I called Uncle Felix in his office. We met for lunch in a small restaurant in Milan, and I introduced to him Dobrana. Uncle Felix was then about seventy years old, and afterwards Dobrana said to me, "Well, now I know how you will look when you get older."

During the next several years, Dobrana bore us four children, and for the next ten years, we did not travel to Europe. In 1974, Uncle Stanislav let me know that my uncles in Milan had died. Although he did not communicate with them directly, he heard the sad news from mutual friends in Zagreb. I felt bad. I should have sent my address to Uncle Felix after I came to the U.S. This thought bothered me so much that once, in the wee hours of the night (morning in Italy), I dialed my uncles' phone number in Milan. I still knew it by heart like a little singsong. After many rings of the phone, the Italian operator came on the line and told me that the phone number I dialed had been discontinued. So it was true, both of my uncles had died, and I would never see them again.

There is a little more to the story about my father's family. During the Easter school recess of 1989, I took our two younger children, Millie and Dora, for their first visit to Europe. Dobrana was working at IBM and had a tight program deadline, and our older two children were in college. To give the girls a good taste of Europe, we were to spend ten days in all four major language areas of Switzerland. After skiing for a couple of days in Saint Moritz, the onset of warm spring weather and sudden avalanches prevented us from driving to Lugano over a mountain pass within Switzerland. Since the passes were closed, I decided to get to Lugano by driving south through Italy, along the Lake Como. That way, I could show the girls my uncles' house, where I visited them many years before. As we stood on the road in front of the villa, Millie noticed that our last name was still on the doorbell next to the gate. I was puzzled. Did one of my uncles have a son I did not know about?

I rang the bell, and after a few moments, a middle-aged man stepped out on the terrace above the road and asked who I was looking for. When I inquired who the "Signor Meier" in the house was, he said it was Felix. I introduced myself, and the man excused himself for a few moments and went into the house. Soon he came out and politely said that Uncle Felix was not ready to receive a visit. It would be better, he said, to return in the early afternoon. He gave me the private number to call before coming. It was Easter Sunday, and I was quite shaken up. Fifteen years before, I had been told that both my uncles in Italy had died.

I took the girls for lunch in the nearby city of Como, and in the afternoon, we returned to the villa. As we climbed up the path to the terrace, there was Uncle Felix, dressed in a suit and sitting on a pillow in a large wicker armchair. Slowly, and with obvious strain, leaning on his two canes, he got up. He stood in front of me all stooped, and gave me a long, inquisitive look. Then, in that cozy little dialect of Zagreb, he said, "Izzyly, you have grown taller since I last saw you."

In a flash, I knew that though he had to be over ninety years old, he still had all his wits and humor. His spine was bent with age and arthritis, and indeed, he had become shorter than I. Uncle Felix introduced the middle-aged man as his adopted son, Vito Massaccio-Meier. I introduced Millie and Dora, and we all sat down to talk. We spoke Italian so that Vito could participate. Vito brought out some soft drinks, and the girls went to explore the garden above the villa.

My first question was about Uncle Ernest.

"Cancer," Uncle Felix said. So it was Ernest who died fifteen years ago. Felix told me that towards the end of his illness, Ernest asked his doctor to give him some extra insulin to end his suffering. After Uncle Ernest's death, Uncle Felix moved his apartment and business offices into their new building in another part of Milan, and there he got a new telephone number. I was happy to hear that before his death Uncle Ernest did make up with his only daughter, Luisa. Luisa and her son Živko afterwards frequently visited with Uncle Felix in the Como area, and Živko eventually found a wife in Valtellina. Uncle Ernest's stepson Željko stayed in Australia and never came back, not even for Ernest's funeral. Uncle Felix hired Vito to help him in business, and after several years of working together, they got along so well that Uncle Felix adopted him as a son. Vito would carry on with the business and take care of Uncle Felix in his old age. Vito had a good rapport with Uncle Felix, and they behaved just like two old friends. In the last several years, Uncle Felix had developed severe arthritis in the hips and had problems with his heart. He had arrhythmia for many years and had to have a pacemaker. When I met him in 1989, Uncle Felix was ninety-three years old, and he was on his third pacemaker. In the evening, the girls and I said good-bye to Uncle Felix and Vito, and I promised to stay in touch. The girls and I proceeded to Lugano.

The following summer, in 1990, Dobrana and I vacationed in Italy and arranged to visit Uncle Felix and Vito. On that occasion, we also met with Uncle Ernest's daughter, my cousin Luisa, and her husband David Weiner. My adopted cousin Vito was very congenial, and he and Dobrana prepared lunch for all of us. That is where Dobrana learned a new recipe for spaghetti, and we named it "Spaghetti Vito." Instead of butter or sauce, break an egg (or two) over the steaming spaghetti and mix quickly; the heat of the spaghetti will boil the eggs into a delicious sauce. Add grated, aged Parmiggiano Reggiano, and it is done. Delicious! Being a bachelor, Vito was a good cook.

Luisa and David told us sadly that their first son Krsto died at the age of forty. He had lung cancer. Their second son Živko was a professor at the University of Zagreb, married, and had two children. David also told us that he and Luisa had "never been real communists." Dobrana and I smiled and changed the subject. A member of the Communist Party with a plum job, the highest possible income, and the best possible housing was not a real communist? Perhaps in his heart he was not, but he enjoyed all the benefits of a communist. The communists were well prepared for the imminent break-up of Yugoslavia. To stay in power they forgot the communist slogans and started blowing the horn of nationalism.

In the evening, Dobrana and I parted with our rediscovered family and went to our hotel in Lugano. The following spring, in 1991, we had a phone call from Vito. Uncle Felix had quietly died at the age of ninety-five. I asked Vito to save me a good picture of Uncle Felix, for I had none. He promised he would. I was glad to know that Uncle Felix in his old age found someone he could trust as family. In summer of that year, we again traveled through northern Italy and arranged to briefly visit Vito in his apartment in Milan. He offered us some refreshments and we chatted for a while. He said he could not find a photograph of Uncle Felix. That was strange, but it did not matter. Before parting, we invited Vito to visit us in New York, and he said he would surely come, probably the next year. The following year, we were again vacationing in Italy and found that Vito had sold the villa on Lake Como, the two condominiums, and his entire corporate business in Milan. He moved away, leaving no address, and I never heard of him again. Was Vito afraid I might put forward a claim of inheritance? Uncle Felix never passed on to me grandpa's watch, which he once promised. Perhaps he changed his mind because he had not heard from me for so many years.

During my last visit with Uncle Felix, he was 94 years old, and he still remembered to talk about the "valuable" Dutch painting that Uncle Stanislav never returned to him. He told me that he even went about it through the courts and Italian embassy in London, U.K. He directed his demand to Uncle Stanislav's daughter Bluma while she lived in London. That last little detail, together with Vito's subsequent disappearance, provided me a very satisfactory closure to my relationship with Uncle Felix and Uncle Ernest. I was finally satisfied that the decision I made in my youth, to leave Uncle Ernest and Uncle Felix out of my life, was a good one. When Uncle Stanislav told me that both my uncles had died, I felt remorse that for so many years I never tried to contact them. I was lucky that Uncle Felix stayed alive, and I could meet him one more time, for then I knew that any remorse for having "abandoned" my uncles was unnecessary. In fact, remembering many examples in literature, from Balsac to Thomas Mann's *Buddenbrooks*, many families had rifts and feuds. Later in life, I heard stories from friends about their own family feuds, mostly caused by money, usually bad loans, or issues with inheritance. My family was not at all unique. My two lone uncles lived without a family around them. Their properties and money were all they had, and so they clung to what they had...

What about my second uncle, Stefan Eisner in Zurich? After having met him once in 1960, I hesitated to call on him again. I did not want to get hurt. I feared another instance of a relative thinking I was approaching him because he was wealthy. In 1986, while we were vacationing in Switzerland, Dobrana persuaded me to call Uncle Eisner's home number in Zurich. His niece answered the phone and informed me that Uncle Eisner's wife had died, that he had remarried and moved with his second wife to Montreal, Canada. She gave me his new phone number. Again, I let time go by without calling him. Ten years later, in the nineties, I called the number in Montreal, and his second wife answered the phone and told me that he had suffered a stroke, was not well, and could not talk. In 2002, I called again, and that time his wife said that he had passed away. When I inquired about the address of his daughter and son in Switzerland, she said she was busy and could not just then look for the addresses and phone numbers. She would look for them some other time. One year later, when I called again, she said she could not find the address or phone number of my uncle's children. Perhaps she had lost touch with her husband's grown children, but did not want to say so. Once again, I felt it was just as well that I never again connected with Uncle Eisner. Families do fall apart. As for the five older brothers and sisters of my mother, the Silbers who emigrated to the U.S. around 1900, I never even tried to find them or their children.

Some families stay close, and some grow apart. My two first cousins, Oliver and Luisa, have become strangers over the many years.

* * *

Back to 1962 in Rome: our parting with family R. was very emotional. We were fond of them, and they liked us. It was hard leaving them alone in Rome, but at least their son Gogo was coming from Germany to stay with them. We promised to write to each other.

Prior to departing from Rome, we spent our last money buying clothing and an extra wristwatch. We preferred to buy clothing in Italy, where it was at that time both cheaper and better tailored than in the U.S. One day before embarcation we traveled by train to Genova to overnight in a small hotel. We explored the city and in the afternoon of the next day, we boarded the ship. Our boat was the *Independence*, a cruise ship beginning the return leg of a Mediterranean cruise. Our two places were vacated by someone who decided to get off and stay a while longer in Italy. Boarding the ship was very confusing. We had to register and "immigrate": the ship was legally considered U.S. territory. In the process, we had to wait in several queues, and everything was in English. The strangest moment after immigration came when we arrived at the head of a queue where a huge man sat behind a counter, and he said in a deep basso voice something that sounded like, "Foist sitt'n er seck'n sitt'n."

Dobrana and I looked at each other. We had been learning English from a British book by Eckersley. "I beg your pardon?" I said, and with my heavy accent I must have sounded equally puzzling to the man behind the counter.

He repeated, only louder, "Foist sitt'n er seck'n sitt'n."

We caught the "seck'n" as probably meaning "second," and so I repeated the word "second."

"Aw rite," the basso thundered with a big grin of satisfaction, and he wrote something on his sheet of paper.

We had no clue what that "second" was all about, but since our answer was obviously satisfactory, we were motioned to move on to the next queue.

A kind lady then approached me and asked in perfect Yiddish, "Zei zent ein griner?" (Are you a greenhorn=immigrant?)

We Are Free

"Yes, we are immigrants, and very green!" I answered, and we started talking in Yiddish.

The lady was from New York and she helped us receive our cabin assignment, which was in the deepest bowels of the ship, not far from the engine room. Too late, I noticed that she even tipped our purser, for we had no idea what the protocol on an American cruise ship was. That "second," our friendly lady explained, meant that we were signed up for the second sitting for dinner. That kind lady remained our mentor throughout the trip.

After an overnight sail and a well-deserved night's rest, we found ourselves the next morning anchored in front of Cannes on the French Riviera. It was a regular stop of the cruise, and we were offered to board a small boat to go ashore and spend the day in town or on the beach. Why not? Were we not on a cruise? We thought we were on a honeymoon while living in Rome, but we never went on a trip, and a cruise was very fitting for another honeymoon. In the small boat harbor, there was a French welcoming party giving out little favors. Dobrana got a tiny bottle of perfume, and I got a carnation in my buttonhole. We went exploring Cannes and spent some time swimming on the beach in front of a hotel. What a good decision it was to go to the U.S. by boat! The next day, it was Gibraltar, then the Azores islands, and then we were off for a non-stop crossing of the Atlantic. Our extended honeymoon would last yet another few days. The sky was blue, we used the pool on the ship to cool off, and in between, we spent time playing table tennis or the newly learned game of shuffleboard, or we tried to read the English books from the ship's library. I remember trying to read *Exodus* by Leon Uris. The title seemed quite appropriate, but my knowledge of English was completely inadequate. One year later in New York, I was finally able to read it, still with frequent use of the dictionary.

Every two days, we moved our watches an hour back. A rabbi from Romania was traveling with us, also as an immigrant. He ate only bananas. Nothing else was kosher enough. He spoke Yiddish and desperately tried to convert me, to make me a religious Jew. It was a shame, he kept saying, that I was lost, for I looked like "en echter Yid" (a genuine Jew). His persistence was annoying, and I felt it bordered on arrogance. I struggled to remain polite. The more he insisted, I told him, the more I was inclined to resist. That stopped him.

In the mid-Atlantic one day, we noticed that the wind had picked up, the ship was rolling and pitching, and the water in the pool was sloshing back and forth so frightfully that nobody dared go in. Despite sunny weather and blue skies, it was too chilly to stand on the deck without a windbreaker. One evening, the ship pitched so that we decided to skip dinner. We were not the only ones who lost their appetite. The ten days passed very fast. On August 22, I woke early and got up on the deck just in time to see the Statue of Liberty as the ship entered New York Harbor. The disembarkation process was slow, but we were in no rush. In fact, we were the last two passengers to disembark. We stepped onto American soil with seventy dollars in our pockets. In front of us stood Michael, to welcome us with a hug and a kiss.

OUR NEW HOME

Prior to our departure from Rome, I received a letter from Uncle Stanislav saying that Michael would be expecting us when we arrived in New York, and he would "take care" of us. I did not really want any aid from Michael, but I had to accept it. Michael was a bit upset that we were the last two passengers to come ashore. Well, somebody had to be last, and perhaps we were a little scared of what we were going into. It was nearly noon. We were at one of the midtown piers, and Michael's car was parked in a lot nearby. The attendant brought out to the street a 1959 Chevrolet, an enormous light blue behemoth with two huge tail fins. We got literally lost in the car, and sitting next to Dobrana, I could barely see over the hood. As we glided along the street, we noticed that most facades had enormous rusty metal steps, balconies, and ladders, and we thought that those were barracks for soldiers, or perhaps firehouses. Michael said they were fire escapes. That part of Westside Manhattan near the piers was not very attractive.

Soon we were passing through central midtown Manhattan with its shiny skyscrapers and beautiful store windows. Michael was taking us to a "very reasonable residential hotel" in the Bronx, and to get there, he said, we had to travel across Manhattan and over the 59th Street Bridge into Queens and from there over the Triborough Bridge to the Bronx. During the long and tortuous ride, Michael told us that he was engaged and would soon be married. We finally arrived at the little residential hotel, which turned out to be a converted apartment building located on the Grand Concourse, the main thoroughfare in the Bronx. Michael treated us to a quick sandwich lunch. He had to leave in a hurry, not to miss a whole day's work. We were happy to be alone. We were tired from the humdrum of disembarking and the long car ride through three boroughs. Our room cost "only" twenty dollars per night, and it shared the bathroom with another room, which was conveniently vacant. It was early afternoon, and full of curiosity, we decided to go for a walk along the Grand Concourse. We were excited: it was our first time walking through New York. It was a nice, warm, and sunny August day, and we wore short sleeves. We walked all the way up to Fordham Road and looked into a large department store, the Alexanders, which is now long gone. Within two hours, a breeze picked up and the temperature dropped about twenty degrees F. Suddenly, we were freezing. We literally ran back to the hotel to warm up, ate something, and then, exhausted from our first day in the U.S., we went to sleep.

As arranged by HIAS, the next day I had to present myself for a ten a.m. interview at Lebanon Hospital, which was in a walking distance from our hotel. I woke up at about eight a.m. and hurried to the bathroom to see if there was any hot water left. There was, and I woke Dobrana to take a shower before the hot water ran out. Yes, we were quite "green," and we would remain greenhorns for quite some time, but we were learning very fast. By the end of our second day, we already discovered that in the U.S. running hot water was available all day and all night, even in the cheapest hotel. This was only one of the many strange new experiences and miraculous discoveries we made in those first weeks and months in our new homeland.

My morning interview with Dr. Morton H., the director of medical education at Lebanon Hospital, went quite smoothly. When I was shown to the door of his office on the second floor, I knocked lightly, and as instructed, I entered. I stood in a large, bright office with a desk in the middle, and at first, I did not see anyone in the room. Then I noticed in front of me two very large shoes with the soles facing me, oddly resting on top of the desk. Right behind the shoes was a pair of legs, and further behind, spread like a wand, an open newspaper with four fingers showing on each side. I stood for a moment in silence and then coughed. The newspaper immediately closed itself, the legs with the shoes moved off and behind the desk, and there appeared a bold head with a friendly, smiling round face. A voluminous red nose was decorated with a pair of thick glasses, behind which looked at me two warm brown eyes. I saw thick smiling lips and a strong chin. The man wore a vest with a gold chain leading into a little pocket, and he leaned back in an oversized office armchair.

"Dr. H.," he introduced himself. He stood up and stretched out his big hand. Hearing my own introduction and poor command of English, Dr. H. spoke to me in a slow and deliberate manner, as one would speak to a small child. I understood almost all he said. He was expecting me; I would start working in pediatrics; I obviously did not speak much English, but babies in pediatrics do not talk much, either, he said.

Dr. H. then took me to the main floor of the hospital and introduced me to Mr. D., the hospital administrator. He was tall and slim, and had a very serious expression with a long, weasel-like poker face, a thin and pointy nose, deep-set blue eyes, thin lips, and neatly divided and oiled gray-black hair. I would start working on Monday, he said, and my salary would be fifty dollars for two weeks of work, minus "deductions," whatever that meant. I would be on call every second night, and my on-call room was in a building across the street. He informed me that the next term for the "ECFMG" (medical equivalence exam) was on October 22, 1962, and he then took me to the medical library and introduced me to Mrs. E., the hospital librarian. In the next few weeks, that kind lady would provide me with all the review books necessary to prepare for the medical equivalence exam.

Within an hour, I was back with Dobrana, who waited for me in the hospital lobby. We ate a quick lunch, and in the afternoon, we went by subway into Manhattan to visit NYANA (New York Association for New Americans) on Union Square, a Jewish-sponsored employment agency whose address was given to us by the HIAS in Rome. Dobrana registered to work as an engineering draftsperson. We walked a little through Manhattan, admired the tall skyscrapers and huge department stores, ate a sandwich from an automated lunch machine at Horn & Hardart, and finally took the subway to Mt. Eden Avenue and our hotel in the Bronx. Our second day in the U.S. was again exhausting. Within two days, Dobrana would receive notice from NYANA that she had a job in an office where she would be drafting electrical lines for a project on a school building; she had to report to the project office for a brief formal interview.

In the early evening of our second day, Michael came to see us in our hotel. Through his fiancée, a Romanian girl who only recently arrived in the U.S. via Israel, Michael found us a furnished apartment that was much cheaper than the residential hotel. It belonged to his fiancée's cousin, who was away on a business trip across the U.S. We would be able to stay in his apartment for three months, paying a modest rent of $60 per month. We happily accepted this opportunity, and Michael immediately moved us to Winthrop Street in Brooklyn. The apartment was on the ground floor, and we had to keep the blinds down all the time to keep out the eyes of the people passing by. The furniture was new, and it was all made of plastic and pressboard. The mattress was covered with plastic, and all the bedding was of nylon or other synthetic fiber that made us sweat at night. We were surprised at the low quality of furnishings, but the rent was low, and this was all we could afford. It was, anyway, only a temporary housing solution.

Dobrana's job was in Manhattan, right on Broadway, on the corner of Central Park South and across from Columbus Circle. Her commute by subway from Brooklyn was about fifty minutes, and my commute to the Bronx took about eighty minutes one way. We were young, and it did not matter. Due to my night-call duty in the hospital, I went home to Brooklyn only every second evening. My work in pediatrics was easy, and I had plenty of time to prepare for the coming exam. The hospital had many foreign physicians, mostly refugees from Cuba who were a little older than I was. Besides several Americans, there were also a few physicians from other countries, like Iran, Thailand, Philippines, Egypt, Romania, UK, and Spain. There was a very friendly American intern from California, Dr. S., who within a few days appeared with a welcome gift for me: a Webster's Collegiate Dictionary. I thanked him very much; it would complement the large Webster's New World Dictionary we kept at home. It was nice to have a dictionary in my room at work. I was getting acquainted with the medical equivalence exam. I found that it was a written test with multiple-choice answers. I never saw this kind of exam before. At first, it seemed very easy; the answers were already given, and one only had to choose the right one. After reading more of the questions in the old exam review book, I realized that in order to properly understand the questions, I needed to improve my English. The trickiest part of the exam would be a patient's history, narrated in English, to be written down as an essay in my own words. I had less than two months to prepare for the exam. In my on-call room, I had the library copy of Harrison's Internal Medicine and decided to read the entire textbook with the aid of the dictionary. At the same time, I diligently reviewed the books with samples of previous exam questions. After five weeks of review and study, I thought my knowledge was adequate to pass the test. I only had to slow down to understand the questions. However, when I heard that most of the Cuban physicians had to repeat the exam, I got a little scared. Being relatively fresh out of medical school, I thought I had an advantage over the Cubans, who were several years older, but even so, this exam gnawed on my mind.

Dobrana earned sixty dollars per week, and her job was not difficult. Her co-workers were friendly and helpful. At work, we experienced quite a few funny misunderstandings because of our poor English. One evening, while I was on call, Dobrana called and told me about a strange phone call she received at home. She could not understand too well, but it sounded as though we owed money for the furniture in the rented apartment. Was that possible?

The next day, I was home in the evening, and the same phone call came again. There was no doubt: we rented an apartment from a man who bought the furniture on installment, and for the last two months failed to make a payment. If we did not immediately pay the next installment, the caller threatened to repossess the furniture.

I called Michael and told him that under the circumstances, we would move out of the apartment as soon as we could. He said he did not think we would be able to do it on our own in less than three months. The next day, we looked in the papers for apartments near Lebanon Hospital, in the Bronx, and within two days, we found a rent-controlled studio apartment that would be vacant and ready by October 1. The rent was eighty dollars per month, payable in advance, but an additional month's rent was required as deposit. Even with our first few salaries, we did not have enough cash on hand to pay the deposit.

I went to the hospital administrator to ask for an advance loan against my salary. With a serious expression, Mr. D. told me that the hospital was not a bank, and it did not give out loans. Then he smiled, took me to the cashier's office, and asked her to write me a check for hundred dollars. This advance would be deducted from my salary over next several months.

On October 1, we moved into our apartment in the Bronx. From the Salvation Army we obtained inexpensive furniture that was in very good shape. The previous tenant had moved to a larger apartment in the same building and left us some dinnerware and kitchen utensils. We were grateful. We still have a few of those odd plates as mementos.

For the first time in our lives, we were living in our own apartment, entirely by ourselves, without sharing the bathroom or kitchen with other people, and we were exhilarated by this luxury. Then Michael called. He was very upset, as we were supposed to stay in the Brooklyn apartment and pay rent for three months. I told him that when we agreed to move in and pay rent, we did not expect unpleasant phone calls with threats to repossess the furniture. We felt that under the circumstances, knowing the habits of her cousin, his fiancée should not have recommended that we move into his apartment.

My only real worry at the time was the medical exam on October 22. As the days went by, I became more and more anxious about it. The multiple-choice exam at first looked easy, but the questions were sometimes tricky, and the trick was in the correct understanding of English. Many questions also appeared to have two correct answers, and one had to decide which was "more correct." In the days before the exam, I frequently had bouts of upset stomach with hyperacidity, and it was not caused by the food, but it was from my nerves. At one point, it got so bad that I thought I was developing an ulcer.

Some of the Cuban refugees at the hospital failed the exam more than once. Michael passed it on his first try, but with a score that was too low for a permanent state license. He had to take it over to improve his score. When the day of the exam came, I shared a large, yellow, Checker cab with five Cuban physicians. The exam was given in an armory building somewhere in upper Manhattan, and during the ride the Cubans in the taxi were talking all at once and very loudly, as if they were trying to outshout one another. They spoke Spanish and wildly gesticulated with their hands. The only words I understood from their conversation were God, Virgin Mary, and President Kennedy. I had no clue what they were talking about. I thought they might be praying to God and Virgin Mary to pass the exam, but I could not understand how the President of the U.S. could help them. All I could think of was that I must pass that exam. *I was completely unaware that the Cubans' great excitement in the taxicab was caused by the Cuban missile crisis. On that day, October 22, 1962, a Soviet fleet carrying missiles was sailing toward Cuba, and President Kennedy responded by calling up the US Army Reserves.*

The exam took a whole day, with a break for lunch. During lunch, I ran into an older colleague from Zagreb, Moira N., who had been in New York for at least three years. She said she was taking the exam for the fourth time. That was scary. A painfully anxious week followed the exam. The letter finally arrived in the mail, and it gave me instant relief. I passed the exam with a high score, more than sufficient to get permanent eligibility for a license in every state. All symptoms of my gastric ulcer quickly disappeared.

On November 1, 1962, I began my second internship, this time in the U.S. My salary was raised to sixty dollars per week, and I was assigned an on-call room on the second floor of the main hospital building. I shared the room with an Irishman, Dr. McD., who just arrived fresh from medical school in Northern Ireland. He was born and raised in Palestine, where his father, a British career officer, was the High Commissioner of Police. Another new intern who passed the exam was Dr. O., an Egyptian who went to school at the American University in Beirut, Lebanon. He had a student exchange visa, meaning that after the internship and residency he had to return home. He had other plans: to marry an American girl and stay in the U.S., and soon he did. Dr. O. and Dr. McD. thought that they were coming to a Lebanese hospital, because of the name of the hospital. As it turned out, Lebanon Hospital was one of the last two remaining hospitals in New York City that still served strictly kosher food.

Dr. McD. soon started actively correcting and teaching me English, and he recommended that I read *The Rise and Fall of the Third Reich*, by L. Shirer. Finally free of the conservative Irish school environment, Dr. McD. plastered the entire ceiling of our shared room with multiple alluring centerfolds from

Playboy magazine. This caused a tense moment when the hospital had a sudden inspection. On short notice, inspectors checked the interns' training program, including our quarters. Our room was found sufficiently clean and tidy, and the two inspectors, escorted by the hospital administrator, did not seem to notice our ceiling decoration. Dr. McD. was a meticulous and diligent physician and very pleasant to have around. Occasionally, though, he got so drunk and sick that I had to carry him on my back into the shower to clean him up, but I liked him all the same. He soon started to practice a new sport. Every lunch hour, I found our room locked with an inside latch. Dr. McD. was making up for all those years spent in a strict, conservative college and medical school. Every day, he spent his lunch with a young, hot, and pretty office secretary from the Department of Surgery. The two took real long lunches. Before our internship was over, the secretary started gaining weight, and Dr. McD. felt obliged to marry her. His family was not at all thrilled with his marriage announcement, and all relations with him were abruptly broken. As he bitterly explained, his parents were aghast that he would marry a woman of Puerto Rican origin, and that he would adopt her five-year-old child from a previous relationship. Soon after his completion of the internship, Dr. McD. moved with his wife and children to New Jersey, where he opened an office for family practice.

Through a connection at work, Dobrana got a significant discount, and we could afford a black and white Zenith television set. When it arrived, we were off to learn "everyday English" by watching all the evening shows. It was the beginning of a new chapter in our lives. We were impressed with all the novelties that we encountered and absorbed on a daily basis. The little shocks in our lives were sometimes overwhelming. Those first colorful years in our new homeland deserve a separate story, the highlights of which I have already sketched. There are just two more memories from that period that belong here.

I eventually became friendly with Dr. H., the medical education director at the hospital, and he became my mentor. One of the first things Dr. H. taught me was that if I ever saw an accident anywhere in public or on the street, I should look straight ahead and walk away as fast as I could. This was against the Hippocratic Oath, which I learned in medical school: a physician should immediately attend to and help any person in need of medical care. Yes, Dr. H. told me, but in the U.S., I could be sued, and my career and my life could be ruined. I felt that there was something strange and wrong with such a system, but it occurred to me that Hippocrates could not have anticipated the U.S. legal system, and I promised Dr. H. that I would follow his advice. Luckily, there never was a chance, and a few years later the U.S. Congress passed the Good Samaritan Law, which protected physicians from lawsuits if they helped someone in an emergency.

About five years after I finished my internship at Lebanon Hospital, I met Dr. H. at a wedding in Westchester County. We brought each other up to date on some personal news, and Dr. H., who was by then fully retired, had confided to me something that dated back to the time when he was my mentor in the

Bronx. All the senior attending physicians at the hospital used to regularly run bets on foreign physicians, betting on who would successfully pass the ECFMG exam. Since I arrived with only rudimentary skills in English and had barely two months to prepare for the exam, the odds of my passing it on the first try were ten to one against me. Dr. H. was the only one who bet on such a "dark horse." With ten to one odds and my passing the exam on the first try, Dr. H. made a few thousand dollars in a time when a first-class stamp still cost only four cents. We both enjoyed a good laugh.

March 19, 1963 was the first anniversary of our exodus from communist Yugoslavia and Croatia, and August 22, 1963 was the first anniversary of our arrival into the U.S. Dobrana and I celebrated those two days as our personal holidays, and every year since, we continued to celebrate those two most important days in our lives, either with a festive dinner with our family, or a feast with our friends, and sometimes quietly, just by ourselves.

CONCLUSION

It is now the end of 2009, seven years after I started to write this memoir, and the time has come to end it. In the middle of 2003, when we received the happy news that we would have a second grandchild, I felt it was time for me to retire. Dobrana had retired already a year earlier. We also wanted to move to be closer to our children and their families. Consequently, my writing had frequent interruptions that often lasted for many months. We frequently traveled and had many good times with our grandchildren, of which there are now nine. I also took a lot of time going through all my files and collections from forty years of professional activity to cull the stuff I no longer needed.

We did go to Zagreb for the fiftieth anniversary of my high school graduation. As we approached by airplane, I recognized in the hazy distance under the mountain Sljeme, the city and its two-spire cathedral, protruding from the edge of the old upper town. Our friends awaited us at the airport and took us home as their guests. Our first impression on the way from the airport was that there had been enormous changes: new roads, many new homes, and apartments in areas far from the city center, numerous cars, and traffic lights. This was no longer Yugoslavia; it was the Republic of Croatia. The nicest part of our visit was the time spent with my oldest and best friend Ivica and his wife Marica. Ivica and I talked for many hours. We went on long walks over the cobblestone streets of the upper town, where traffic was still sparse.

Overall, our visit felt bittersweet. It was filled with moments of pleasure and with other instances that are hard to describe in one word. Dobrana and I visited her father's grave and my grandfather Adam Meier's grave. His remains, we found, were transferred to a new grave owned by David and Luisa Weiner. Grandpa's remains were thus joined with the ashes of his son, Luisa's father, Ernest. We also visited Luisa and David Weiner, who lived in a nice villa in the quiet upper town. Our visit was brief. We had grown apart and knew it already from our last meeting fourteen years earlier with Uncle Felix in Italy. After all these years, we had little to say to each other. We were strangers. Luisa was somewhat distraught, but David, well over eighty years old and completely blind, still smoked cigarettes and had all his wits intact.

Dobrana located and reconnected with her closest friends from school and university. She met them one by one on the main square in the city, either under the large clock or "under the tail" (of the Jelačić horse). She would stay in touch with her friends, but otherwise, this visit was a closure for her.

My meeting with my high school classmates was exciting. Our fiftieth anniversary reunion was well organized. We first made a joint bus excursion into the nearby countryside. The next day, we all met at our old high school, which gave us a small formal reception, and finally one evening, we all had supper at a restaurant. Most of my old classmates I recognized and remembered by name, and most of them recognized me. During and after our dinner, I made sure to exchange at least a few words with everyone. It was touching to find out how they were, how many children they had had, and what they had done. Several of my classmates, I heard, had become very accomplished in their professions, and that was nice to know. The next several evenings, we met with our narrow group of classmates in their homes. With those I was the closest to in high school, I shared reminiscences and we updated each other on our progress. My close friends all looked well, and I was happy to hear that they all lived quite well. Most of them either spent some time abroad or at least visited the West on a few occasions. They all came one evening for dinner at Ivica and Marica's house. Ivan U. also came, and for the first time since I left Zagreb, we had a chance to talk for a little while. He told me he was a widower and lived with his son. He brought with him a large envelope containing some of my photographs from our student days and a few old letters from my uncles in Italy, all of which I left in his apartment long ago, when we abruptly stopped studying together.

I looked around the city to see how much it had changed. The central square of Zagreb and a few adjoining streets were improved, with nicely renovated and well-kept facades. The statue of the historic Croat leader Jelačić on horseback, dismantled by the communists in 1945, was brought back into the center of the square. His saber no longer pointed towards Hungary, but instead was turned in another direction. The rest of the city showed the usual effect of time. It has grown and spread past the previous suburbs. Many new residential areas were built in the former farmlands on the outskirts, especially across the River Sava. A small, modern mall had been built near the central market. The older central part of the city, built during Austrian rule, appeared worn and tired, more so than when I left. Beautiful, old, turn-of-the-century buildings with ornate facades had large gaps with bare bricks where the stucco had fallen off. The great number of cars caused traffic congestion, and parked cars blocked some of the sidewalks. The air, thick with smog and noise, smelled just like in any Eastern European city of similar size. The old central market was lively and delightfully colorful. The butter and cheese, no longer displayed on a vine leaf, still tasted very good. People's voices on the street and in the outdoor coffee houses sounded oddly different: there was a sharp new accent; the cozy old local dialect was no longer heard. Many young and modishly dressed people sat in outdoor coffee houses and whiled away the middle of a workday. Some chattered on their cell phones, exuding an air of feigned importance.

The bookshops were interesting. They prominently displayed new books, some celebrating the now-historic leader Pavelić, and the past heroic deeds of the Ustaše in the time of the Independent State of Croatia. I heard that each year for Pavelić's birthday, one may find tacked to the doors of a Catholic church an announcement for the special mass dedicated to his revered memory. The country's currency, "kuna," was familiar; it was the same as during 1941-45. Some street names have been changed to better reflect the new Croat history.

Conclusion 239

The language has been expanded: I heard some newly coined words that I could understand only in context. One of the more striking words was the "zrakomlat" (air-beater=helicopter). There has been much progress and change, and much has returned to evoke 1941. It all reminded me of the maxim that "history repeats itself." Along with progress, much of the past has marched into the present.

Out of curiosity, I wanted to see, have just a quick look at the bishopry in Križevci. Ivica drove me there. The car ride on paved roads and a highway did not take half a day, as I remembered it from my long return trip to Zagreb in 1945. The bishopry compound facing the main street appeared the same as it was more than sixty years ago, only now it wore scaffolding for renovation. However, only the church and the massive main building still stood. Gone was the tall barn with the hayloft and farm animals, gone was the well with the pump and stone trough in the back courtyard. The muddy duck pond was filled in and covered by a lawn, and the little farm house with the carpentry workshop, smith's forge, and surrounding vegetable gardens have all disappeared without a trace. In place of the barn and the pigpen were some new ground-floor buildings that housed a club with meeting rooms. Gone was the boys' school, too. Most of the main building was rented out to a volunteer society. The third-floor dorm rooms and classrooms were built over, and the huge old heating stoves were replaced by central heating. The bishop's offices became a small museum with a big hall lined with life-sized portraits of previous bishops. A single old nun and one helper were the only permanent residents, and they showed us around. I introduced myself as Petar Bastašić, my name when I was at the boys' school. I asked about some of the priests I used to know, mentioning their names. They were all deceased. After the war, the "American" went back to the U.S. One of the senior priests, Msgr. Bukatko, served for several years as bishop. In the museum, the nun pointed at the large portrait of a bishop whose name was Bastašić. He passed away about hundred and fifty years before, and the nun said, he must have been my relative and ancestor. I took a deep breath. With a chuckle, Ivica helped me out. Looking at me, he said, "He came from another branch of the Bastašić clan." I agreed.

After that visit, I no longer desired to see the village of Dragoševci or the monastery Lepavina, or any other old site I used to know so well during the war. For sure, the hills, the fields, and the sky were still there, but the people were all gone, and the memories that I kept buried in my mind for sixty-odd years would be teased in vain. Anyway, I had my closure with that whole part of the Old World a long time ago, and this visit to Croatia only confirmed it.

After spending a week in Zagreb, our friends saw us off to the airport. For the next two weeks, Dobrana and I traveled through Western Europe, and during that time, we often went hiking in the mountains. The weather was good, and in the tranquility of nature, we could reminisce about all we have seen and experienced in Croatia. Dobrana and I still occasionally speak Serbo-Croatian, the language we grew up with, and we both noticed how much the language and even the accent in Croatia has changed. Languages are "alive," and it is normal that they change. I noticed recently that three new dictionaries appeared in our bookstores: Bosnian, Croatian, and Serbian, though each contains at least ninety-five percent of identical words.

On several occasions during our visit to Zagreb, I noticed with sadness that hate and intolerance towards others was still evident. Even though Croatia won its final war of independence almost ten years before, and even though most of the Serbs have moved out of the country so that Croatia is nearly devoid of minorities, the people's enmity towards their neighbors lingers, and every now and then, it sticks out. I no longer dwell on the past, but find it disturbing when people express the same blind hatred towards others as their elders did in 1941.

As I found out subsequently, the Croat textbooks, just like in 1941, again teach the children the theory that they are not of Slavic but are of Iranian (Persian) descent.

On a better and more hopeful note, we did encounter in Zagreb a few people who expressed openness, understanding, and tolerance for others. I hope that someday, such positive sentiments will become prevalent, even if it takes considerable time. There have been good signs. During the last several years, books have been published in Croatia describing the history and contributions of a thriving local Jewish community before the Second World War and its annihilation by the Independent State of Croatia. [13, 14, 25] The title of one of the books offers a good indication that Croatia now has a free press: *1941, the Returning Year*. I have heard that there have been occasional interactions and sport events between teams from Croatia and Serbia. Thus, there is a ray of light: perhaps in another century, the Balkan people might forget their enmities and gain a more amicable disposition towards one another and for all others.

As a friend of mine said, "Croatia is the right place to have left from".

* * *

In the early nineties, I was invited by a group of U.S. philanthropists to become a charter member of the Museum of the Holocaust in Washington, DC. I accepted the invitation and was happy to contribute toward its construction. For the opening ceremony of the museum, the organizers invited heads of every country to Washington. Even those who were known to have written and openly spoken denials of the Holocaust were invited. When I inquired about the curious choice of invitees, the museum management took a long time to reply to my letters. Finally, I received an answer explaining that the Museum management was hoping that some of the Holocaust deniers might be re-educated by the exhibits.

Eventually, I summoned the courage to go to Washington and visit the Museum. I looked at every exhibit, thoroughly read every inscription, looked at every photograph and every caption. After a full day's visit, I felt numb. The gory images of the exhibits haunted me for several weeks. It was worse than the goriest of horror movies, because the exhibits represented a historic reality. About a year later, I went for a second visit and again I looked at the details in the exhibits: pictures showing piles of children's shoes, gas chambers, crematoriums, copies of documents of the secret plan for the "final solution," the murder of all Jews. Having seen the records of the torture and killing of millions of innocent people, I began to reflect on the individuals who actually ordered and organized or directly participated in the torture and mass murder. What causes such enormous magnitude of criminality in a person? What makes an individual capable of ordering or executing a murder? Or mass murder? Is there a mental disorder? Is there a faulty gene, a fractured chromosome? There used to be a belief that Satan possessed people who committed evil acts. That conveniently put criminality into the realm of mystery. A mystery has to be believed in; it has no substance, needs no proof, and it ignores the science. Today, we seek the answers from science. Some mass murderers, especially some leaders, were undoubtedly psychopaths, and some may have been fanatics with delusions of performing a sacred duty, or had illusions of partaking in a heroic mission that would save their nation, but medical science would consider most war criminals perfectly sane. As it is, most Holocaust executioners are condemned to live for the rest of their lives with full cognizance of their horrible crimes, and even if they showed no remorse, the gory details of their actions were burnt into their memories.

I began to reflect on my feelings about those long-past events in my life and the reason for my long silence. In surviving the Holocaust, one remains wounded and feels victimized, while carrying the burden of sad, painful memories. Those feelings need a closure. Survivors of the Holocaust are left to deal with their burden as they best can. A rare few have found closure in exacting some sort of revenge, but that path is not a solution thirty years after the deed. Many survivors compensate their feelings of loss by a permanent hatred for the whole nation of the perpetrators, as if the Germans or Poles or Lithuanians or any other people living today, could be blamed for the wrongs done by their ancestors. Other survivors, me included, realize that blind hate directed at one or another group of people is pointless. Hate is a self-destructive feeling, and it has to be rationalized away. More than sixty years have passed, and the vast majority of the individual criminals are long gone. The few still alive are now old and decrepit, mere ghosts of their evil past. One does not need to think about those ghosts, nor does one need to dwell any longer on the awful deeds they perpetrated. The mind of a Holocaust survivor needs relief from the feeling of victimization. There is a way out, and it is to look forward, to the future. One needs to open a new page. After having seen the Holocaust Museum twice, I was able to reflect more calmly on my own past. I did survive. I remembered everything with clarity, and I began to feel that I needed to get it out of my system. I needed to write it down, beginning with every memory of my dear parents and the happiness of my early childhood. It took some time before I was ready to sit down and write. Somewhere between thinking about the earliest events of my life and the act of writing them down, I felt a catharsis. Once I began to write down some of my memories, there was relief. Whatever I had bottled up for many years was slowly coming out. The more I thought and wrote about my past, the more I felt at ease about it. It took me over fifty years to achieve the peace in my mind over what happened. It was good to be rid of the burden and realize that the bitter taste was gone, settled, evaporated. I no longer had any grudges, not even against the nameless perpetrators of the crime; they were merely ghosts and shadows. Instead, I had the satisfaction of being able to ignore and thus cast to irrelevance the demons that destroyed my parents and my family and millions of others. I no longer need to think about the evils of a time bygone. I have achieved peace of mind, a state that felt as good as if it were the imaginary nirvana. No longer do I feel like a victim. I am able to think of the past with calm and equanimity. I have turned the page. I am free to move on, enjoy the present, and look forward to what is ahead.

My dream of settling down and raising a family in the U.S. has been accomplished, and I am grateful to those who helped me along the way. At home in the U.S. over the last forty-seven years, we found many friends, people who are good and decent and human, people who do not first question one's ethnicity or religion or color. I am aware that in the twenty-first century, this promised land of my dreams is encumbered by some mighty problems: the U.S. faces many critics, some well meaning, and some not so. From personal experience and from reading and learning about other lands and people and cultures, I believe that despite some failings, our system and way of life in the U.S. is the best. This belief holds true for the vast majority of Americans and for many people outside the U.S. While elsewhere in the world certain powers use nationalism and/or religion to spread hatred and intolerance, the U.S. is still a bastion of relative freedom and a proponent of tolerance. As for the future, I feel that this land, this New World, has the will, the vitality, and the wherewithal to solve any problem. Good old American ingenuity will find a way to overcome all present difficulties.

EPILOGUE

Here are the few remaining threads of my family.

Shortly after we arrived in the U.S., Michael married his fiancée. They had two children, and a few years later, Michael invited his parents, Uncle Stanislav and Aunt Ester, to live with his new family in the U.S. He also invited his first daughter Vesna from Yugoslavia, but after a few years in the U.S., Vesna decided to return and live with her mother in Belgrade, Serbia, where she could afford to go to medical school and become a physician. Uncle Stanislav and Aunt Ester lived for many years in Michael's house and enjoyed their grandchildren. They both passed away in their eighties. Michael, too, has passed away.

Oliver still lives in Zagreb. After many decades of silence, he recently surprised me with a phone call. He wanted the two of us to give a testimony to declare the Professor a righteous person, one who saved lives during the Holocaust. Unfortunately, such testimony is acceptable only from individuals who were at least twelve years old when the action occurred. I was at the time only nine. Let this memoir serve as my monument to the Professor.

Only Oliver managed to obtain from the Croat government his share of the real estate property that three of us inherited in 1945 from Uncle Isac and my mother.

Bluma had Aunt Ester's share of property, and when she heard from a friend that the Croat government had returned some of the nationalized real estate to its rightful heirs, she applied for return of her share. After several years of inquiries and appeals through three different lawyers in Croatia, she was finally informed that her application had "missed the deadline." I never tried to request the return of my property share. When I left Croatia and Yugoslavia, I wanted to look ahead and did not wish to look back. Perhaps my misappropriated property should be considered an extremely high tuition for my university education. *Long books have been written about the robbery of Jews during and after the Second World War in all countries of Europe that were either occupied by Nazis or that had collaborated with them, including "neutral" Switzerland.* [20, 23]

Left alone in Zagreb with a little son, Bluma, after ten years of marriage divorced her estranged husband Karel, who had gone to "seek a better job" in Germany. Karel stayed in Germany and married the owner of the factory where he worked. Bluma re-married and went to live with her second husband in London, UK. After several years, Bluma and her new husband and son Mirko came to live in the U.S. to be near her parents and her brother Michael. Bluma now lives in Florida.

Ernest and Ursel I., who showed me that not all Germans were Nazis, remained our steadfast friends, and over many years, they have become a part of our family. We have regularly stayed in touch and visited each other on many occasions. Ernest passed away, but Ursel, now in her mid-nineties, remains as sharp as ever.

The "Professor" was Dr. Stjepan Zimmermann, a Catholic priest with a PhD degree in philosophy. He was active as a writer and professor of philosophy and theology at the University of Zagreb. He retired just before the beginning of the Second World War. The Professor was a magnificent person, a true Human. He saved my life when he freed me from the local prison just before I was to be sent to death in a concentration camp; his interventions also saved the lives of Oliver and Uncle Stanislav and his family. His attempt to save my parents was thwarted. After arriving in the U.S., I regularly corresponded with the Professor. In 1963, I received his last letter, letting me know that he was "slowly drifting into a long sleep," and that he was happy knowing that Dobrana and I would have a good future. He passed away shortly thereafter. Uncle Stanislav provided me with a large framed picture of the Professor sitting at his writing desk and looking up and ahead.

BIBLIOGRAPHY

1) Weber, L. ed. *The Holocaust Chronicles.* Lincolnwood, IL: Publications International, Ltd.,1999.

2) Yahil, Leni. *The Holocaust—The Fate of European Jewry.* New York: Oxford University Press, 1990.

3) Kertzer, David I. *The Popes Against the Jews, the Vatican's Role in the Rise of Modern Antisemitism.* New York: Alfred A. Knopf, 2001

4) Hellman, P. *The Auschwitz Album.* NY: Random House, 1981.

5) Dedijer, Vladimir. *The War Diaries of Vladimir Dedijer.* 5th ed. Ann Arbor, MI: The University of Michigan, 1990.

6) Lanzmann, Claude. *Shoah, an Oral History of the Holocaust—Complete Subtitles of the Film Shoah.* NY: Pantheon House (Random House), Inc., 1985.

7) Levi, Primo. *The Drowned and the Saved.* NY: Vintage Books (Random House), Inc., 1989.

8) Müller, Filip. *Eyewitness Auschwitz—Three Years in the Gas Chambers.* Routledge & Kegan Paul, Ltd., 1979.

9) Hitler, Adolf. *Mein Kampf.* NY: The Haughton Mifflin Company, 1971.

10) Djilas, Milovan. *Wartime.* NY: Harcourt Brace Jovanovich Inc., 1977.

11) Rivelli, Marco Aurelio. *L'Arcivescovo del Genocidio—Monsignor Stepinac, il Vaticano, e la Dittatura Ustascia in Croazia, 1941-1945.* Milan: Kaos Edizioni, 1999.

12) Marsden, Victor E., trans. *Protocols of the Learned Elders of Zion.* Boring, OR: CPA Book Publisher, 1934.

13) Goldstein, Ivo and Slavko Goldstein. *Holokaust u Zagrebu.* Zagreb: Novi Liber, 2001.

14) Goldstein, Ivo. *Židovi u Zagrebu 1918-1941.* Zagreb: Novi Liber, 2004.

15) Park, Jacqueline. *The Secret Book of Grazia dei Rossi.* NY: Simon & Schuster, 1997.

16) Dedijer, Vladimir. *The Yugoslav Auschwitz (Jasenovac) and the Vatican—the Croatian Massacre of the Serbs during World War II.* Buffalo, NY: Prometheus Books, 1992.

17) Distel, Barbara, Ruth Jakusch, eds. *Concentration Camp Dachau 1933-1945.* Brussels: Comité International de Dachau, 1978.

18) Benz, Wolfgang and Barbara Distel, eds. *Dachau Review 1—History of Nazi Concentration Camps: Studies, Reports, Documents.* Volume 1. Brussels: Comité International de Dachau, 1988.

19) Lindsay, Franklin. *Beacons in the Night—With the OSS and Tito's Partisans in Wartime Yugoslavia.* Stanford, CA: Stanford University Press, 1993.

20) Bower, Tom. *Nazi Gold—The Full Story of the Fifty-Year Swiss-Nazi Conspiracy to Steal Billions from Europe's Jews and Holocaust Survivors.* Harper Collins Publishers, Inc., 1997.

21) Klemperer, Victor. *I Will Bear Witness: 1933-1941. A Diary of the Nazi Years.* NY: Random House, 1998.

22) Cain, Kenneth, Heidi Postlewait, and Andrew Thomson. *Emergency Sex and Other Desperate Measures. A True Story from Hell on Earth.* New York: Hyperion, 2004.

23) Chesnoff, Richard Z.. *Pack of Thieves—How Hitler and Europe Plundered the Jews and Committed the Greatest Theft in History.* New York: Phoenix, Doubleday (Random House), 1999.

24) Djilas, Milovan. *The New Class.* Henry Holt & Company, Inc. 1974.

25) Goldstein, Slavko. *1941. Godina Koja se Vraća.* Zagreb: Novi Liber, 2007

INDEX

"Amerika" -- USA in German language: ix, 20
Aryan race: 17, 117
Auschwitz: 33
Austrian-Hungarian Empire: 1
Balkan -- geographic region in south-eastern Europe: i (title page)
carabinieri: 31
commissar: 61
communism, communists: 55
Communist Party (of Yugoslavia): 55, 79, 92
Cyclone, cyclonization: 108
Četniks -- ultra-nationalist Serb fighters during WWII (see Wikipedia): 116
DDT -- common pesticide (banned in 1972): 79, 108
Domobrani: 41, 86
Eastern Orthodox (religion): 38
ECFMG -- Educational Commission for Foreign Medical Graduates: 230
Eparchy of Križevci -- the district of Greek-Catholics in Yugoslavia: 38
Fascism, Fascists: 31, 107
Glagolica -- ancient Slavic alphabet: 38
Greek-Catholic (religion): 38
HIAS -- agency helping resettlement of refugees: 220, 222
Iron Curtain: 151
Jasenovac: 25
Kike -- derogatory term for a Jew: ix, 126
Kristallnacht -- Nazi rampage against Jews: 17
kulak -- wealthy farmer: 120
kuna -- currency of "Independent State of Croatia" and Republic of Croatia: 238
Lepavina -- monastery in Croatia: 83
Mihajlović, Draža, general, leader of ultra-nationalist Serbs: 116
"Muslim Division" -- Army of Muslim volunteers in Bosnia during WWII: 115
Nazism, Nazis: 31, 98, 117, 124, 149, 205
Nuremberg Laws: 22
Palestina -- Palestine: 20
Partisans -- communist resistance fighters during WWII in Yugoslavia: 55, 116
Pavelić, Ante, leader of Ustaše: 2, 22
politkom (political commissar): 60
Roma -- a nation scattered throughout Europe, originating in India: 115
Serbo-Croatian -- language spoken in Bosnia, Croatia, Montenegro, and Serbia: 7, 37

Slavic languages: 2
Slavonic, Old -- ancient language of Slavs: 38
Slavs -- tribes originating in the area of today's Ukraine: 2
sulfonamide -- synthetic bactericidal agent: 24
Šimrak, Janko, Greek-Catholic bishop: 82
Tito, Marshall, Josip Broz -- leader of Yugoslav communists: 116
Turkish (Ottoman) Empire: 2, 38
Uskoci -- Slavic refugees from Turkish Empire: 38
Ustaše -- Croat volunteer army in WWII (see Wikipedia): ix, 2, 115
Vojna Krajina: 83
Yiddish -- language of Ashkenazy Jews, based on fifteenth century German: 94
Žumberak -- region of Croatia at the border of Slovenia: 30, 37

www.ingramcontent.com/pod-product-compliance
Lightning Source LLC
Chambersburg PA
CBHW051750040426
42446CB00007B/302